OPPOSITE RELIGIONS STILL?

For my parents, D.F.L. and J.M.L.

Opposite Religions Still?

Interpreting Northern Ireland After the Conflict

B.K. LAMBKIN
Principal
Lagan College, Belfast

Avebury

Aldershot • Brookfield USA • Hong Kong • Singapore • Sydney

Published by
Avebury
Ashgate Publishing Limited
Gower House
Croft Road
Aldershot
Hants GU11 3HR
England

Ashgate Publishing Company
Old Post Road
Brookfield
Vermont 05036
USA

British Library Cataloguing in Publication Data

Lambkin, Brian
    Opposite religions still?: interpreting Northern Ireland
    after the conflict
    1. Irish Question 2. Christianity - Northern Ireland - 20th
    century 3. Northern Ireland - History - 1969- 4. Northern
    Ireland - Religion
    I. Title
    261.7'09416

    ISBN 1 85972 163 X

Library of Congress Catalog Card Number: 96-83266

Printed and bound by Athenaeum Press, Ltd.,
Gateshead, Tyne & Wear.

Contents

Tables

Acknowledgements

In the first place I would like to thank the Governors of Lagan College, my colleagues and the principals, trial teachers and trial pupils of the nineteen schools associated with the *Opposite Religions?* project. Without their generous support and co-operation, together with that of many local clergy, this book would not have been possible.

I owe an especial debt of gratitude to Dr J. E. Greer and Dr S. J. Connolly at the University of Ulster, Coleraine for their advice, support and encouragement. My thanks are also due to the All Saints Educational Trust; the Department of Education of Northern Ireland; the Northern Ireland Centre for Learning Resources; the Institute of Irish Studies, Queen's University, Belfast; the Ulster Folk and Transport Museum, Cultra; the Farmington Institute for Christian Studies and Manchester College, Oxford for their support and use of their facilities. I am grateful to Dr E.P.McElhinney, Dr J.F. Long, and Mr N.L. Richardson for opportunity to consult their unpublished theses and to Rev Dr I.M. Ellis for access to his book prior to publication. For information, advice and assistance I am grateful to Mr A. Anderson, Mr K. Anderson, Mr and Mrs J. Boner, Mrs D. Brown, Dr A.D. Buckley, Professor R. Buchanan, Mr A. Campbell, Dr. M. Crozier, Dr R. Davison, Professor S. Dunn, Dr B. Fitzpatrick, Dr R.A. Gailey, Dr M. Hill, Mr D. Kinnen, Ms L. Lyndsey, Mr B. McAleese, Mr V. McIver, Mr D. Mitchell, Mr R. Marshall, Mr R. Mullan, Mr M. O'Neill, Dr A. Robinson, Mrs J. Smith and Mr G. Woodman. For their help with the processing and presentation of data I am indebted to Mr C. Todd and Mr B. Meegan. I also have to thank Dr J. Meegan and Dr M.K. Muhr who were kind enough to read all of the draft for me. The text has benefited greatly from their comments but the responsibility for the shortcomings which remain is mine alone.

Finally, a special word of thanks to my wife, Kay, and to Bréanainn, Angus and Magdalen for their patience and understanding while this project was being brought to completion.

Preface

Ireland has two religions and the majority cannot talk about their religion above their breath, for fear of appearing bigoted, intolerant and offending our patronizers.

The Leader, 5 January, 1901.

I would like to solemnly protest in the name of the Lord, Jesus Christ, the great King and Head of the Church. You can't reverse 400 years of history. The Mass is a blasphemous fable and a dangerous deceit.

Rev I. Paisley, *remarks addressed to Cardinal Hume in Westminster Hall crypt where Mass was being celebrated for the first time in four centuries.*
Irish Times, 2 August, 1978.

The idea of 'opposite' is a comparatively late human invention.
Empson 1930, 225

Introduction

The conflict in Northern Ireland faces educators with a formidable and forbidding task of interpretation. Schoolchildren need to know why Northern Ireland over the last twenty-five years, compared with England, Scotland, Wales and the Republic of Ireland, has been so violent.

The children of Northern Ireland transferring from primary to secondary school in September 1996 were born in 1985. That was the year of the Anglo-Irish Agreement and the sixteenth of the conflict. In October 1993, at the time of the bomb on the Shankill Road and the shooting in Greysteel, they were eight. In 1994, the year of the para-military cease-fires, they were nine. The ceasefires were holding in 1995-96 as they did their 11+ exams, but there was still no political settlement. It is natural that they, like the children before them, and the children for many years to come, should want to know what the fighting was about. What are we to tell them?

Interpreting Northern Ireland is a forbidding task because there is still no commonly agreed explanation amongst the experts (the academics, political leaders, religious leaders and media commentators) for educators to rely on. The latest book to survey the wide range of competing interpretations speaks of 'a meta-conflict, a conflict about what the conflict is about' (McGarry and O'Leary 1995, 1).

To complicate matters further, many parents and teachers are uncomfortably aware that their personal interpretations may not be objective since, to a greater or lesser extent, they themselves have been actors in the conflict. Small wonder if many prefer to say nothing, or as little as possible about it.

Avoiding the issue, however, is unlikely to be either satisfying or prudent in the long run. In the absence of a satisfactory explanation from their teachers, children will draw their own conclusions. Research reported on in this book

1

indicates that most schoolchildren in Northern Ireland think that the fighting has been about religion. So deep is the divide between Catholics and Protestants that they refer to each other as if they belong to 'opposite religions'. The following statements, collected in 1990 from eleven to fifteen year olds, give some impression of the variation in their perceptions of the divide (author's italics):

- I think it is awful the bitterness between *the religions*. We treat each other like aliens.
- *The Catholics' way of religion* may be right but I agree more with *the Protestant religion*.
- It is hard to pray and be in *the Catholic religion* and other people in *some other religion*. It would be easier if we were all in *the same religion*.
- Some Catholics think they are better than Protestants and the other way round. Children now don't know *which religion* to choose.
- People consider Catholics and Protestants as being *separate religions*, so how can *both religions* be Christians?
- There are only a few elements in society who hate members *of the other religion*.
- *Both religions* worship God even if they worship in different ways.
- God said that he wanted us all to become one family in his home. This is not what we are doing. In fact it is totally *opposite*.
- If everyone who went to church were Christians, then they should hold no grudges against *the opposite religion*.

Hence the title, *Opposite Religions Still?*. After the fighting, is the fundamental opposition of Catholicism and Protestantism resolved, or does it persist?

This book is concerned with how Protestant and Catholic schoolchildren in Northern Ireland perceive their own and each other's religious traditions and how they perceive the conflict and the inter-connection of religion and politics. It is also concerned with the question of what teachers should tell them about these things and how. In short, it is about how to interpret the story of community relations in Northern Ireland in a way that will help to make things better rather than worse.

This, of course, assumes that the conflict is capable of interpretation at a time when it is not clear to all that it is. As respected a commentator as Maurice Hayes has reached the profoundly gloomy conclusion that it may not be:

There is a fond and commonly held belief to which people cling in modern society that every problem must have a solution ... a belief that failure to resolve a problem reflects badly on the participants, who must be stupid or irrational or just bloody-minded, or on the government who should be able to manage things better, or on the politicians who could do it if only they had the will, or on the churches or on the media or on outside agitators or whatever. There are, however, problems that are not amenable to solution (Hayes 1995, 320).

If some people cling fondly to the belief that all problems are soluble, others cling just as fondly to the belief that the Northern Ireland conflict is not amenable to solution - that it 'passes all understanding', and that 'anyone who thinks he understands what is going on in Northern Ireland is obviously confused'.

The purpose of this book is to assert, with McGarry and O'Leary, that 'Northern Ireland is complex, but its conflicts, and theories about its conflicts, are structured and explicable' (1995, 3). It argues that a consensus about the interpretation of the conflict, or conflicts, is in the process of emerging. This emerging consensus centres on resolving the problem of the role (still deeply controversial) which religion has played in the overall conflict.

Further, the book argues that an important part of the peace building process after the conflict will be the mediating of a broadly agreed interpretation to as wide an audience as possible. Finally, it addresses the question of how this may best be done.

Chapter 1 presents the evidence for the emerging consensus on the interpretation of the conflict, particularly the work of Whyte, Darby, Dunn, Hickey and Bruce. Chapter 2 argues that the work of Boyle and Hadden on *The Choice* (between separation and sharing) opens up the way for a theory of the conflict's intractability. Chapter 3 develops such an intractability theory, based on the concept of 'choice modulation' and on the 'opposite religions still?' question. Chapter 4 addresses the problem of deep-seated ambiguity about 'culture', 'tradition', 'community' and 'religion'. It traces the development of 'cultural traditions' within the work of the Community Relations Council and also the development since 1970 of a series of school curriculum development projects concerned with 'cultural traditions'. Chapter 5 describes a further project in this series, the *Opposite Religions? Project 1988-92*. Chapter 6 discusses the results of *Opposite Religions?* and addresses the question 'opposite religions still?' Chapter 7 considers the practical implications of a programme of education for *The Choice* between a one-community, one-religion view of the future and an opposite-communities, opposite-religions view. Chapter 8 argues the specific need for a larger-scale educational programme and investment in a major institution to support the making of *The Choice*; for national and local government to co-operate with the Churches and the education service, including schools, universities and museums, in establishing a Centre for Religion in Ireland.

1 Interpreting 'the conflict about the conflict'

Northern Ireland is famous for the intractability of its conflict. For educators concerned with how to explain the fighting to schoolchildren their task is formidable and forbidding because they face a problem of 'double intractability': the interpreting of the conflict has become as intractable as the fighting itself.

An intractable conflict is one which has resisted repeated attempts at its resolution, peaceful or otherwise. The most intractable violent conflicts of all are those where neither the interested parties nor disinterested observers can agree as to the nature of the conflict. The Northern Ireland conflict is of this type. Rival, opposing interpretations continue to vie with each other for supremacy of explanatory power.

As long as this remains the case, the challenge to the educator is unenviable: how to interpret to schoolchildren the range of competing interpretations? With adults so at odds with each other, the teacher risks compounding the problem by introducing students to the intricacies of the conflict's intractability. However, the task of interpreting Northern Ireland is showing signs of becoming more manageable. The 'meta-conflict about the conflict' may be resolving itself. There is growing evidence that competing interpretations may be converging gradually on new paradigm or type of explanation. About this type of explanation there is good prospect of consensus forming.

Out of the conflict has grown what has been called the 'community relations industry'. Since one of its main functions has been to interpret the conflict, we begin with it.

The growth of the 'community relations industry'

The 'community relations industry', which has grown substantially since 1969, is a form of employment, related to the 'heritage industry' (Hewison 1987). It capitalises on the negative circumstances of civil conflict with the aim of rectifying them. Conflict research and interpretation is a considerable part of this industry. The protracted and intractable nature of the conflict has resulted in Northern Ireland becoming proportionately one of the most heavily researched areas on earth. The Centre for the Study of Conflict at the University of Ulster, for example, is devoted to research of this kind and to informing and supporting the development of community relations policy. It is the intractability of the conflict, with its relatively restrained nature, which has generated and sustained the community relations industry.

In itself, the term 'community relations' is a strong symptom of the conflict about interpreting the conflict. It is ambiguous. Does it signify relations between two opposing sides of the one community or relations between two opposite communities. Is the ambiguity deliberate or not? Either way, it is a symptom of the complex nature of the conflict and the so far intractable difficulty of coming to an agreed interpretation of it.

A brief survey of the development of community relations policy will set the context for considering how interpretation of the conflict has developed.

The Community Relations Commission, 1969-74

Community relations policy in Northern Ireland is about activities designed to promote better contact, and so better mutual understanding, between the Catholic and Protestant communities. As part of its package of reform measures in 1969, the Northern Ireland Government established a Community Relations Board (later called Commission) with half its members drawn from each community in Northern Ireland. A Minister of Community Relations was also appointed. The Community Relations Commission (CRC) adopted a community development strategy designed to raise the self-confidence of local communities through voluntary organisations. The hope was that, eventually, these local groups would feel sufficiently secure to begin dealing with their neighbours across the sectarian divide (Gallagher 1995).

This official community relations infrastructure did not last long. The Minister of Community Relations of the Power Sharing Executive of 1974 abolished the Commission on the grounds that the political settlement of power-sharing had obviated the need for such a body (Hayes 1995, 180-181).

There was a fallow period from the Executive's abolition of the Community Relations Commission and the still-birth of its 'shared-schools scheme' in 1974 until the late 1980s when the government developed a new community relations policy. This led eventually to the setting up in 1990 of the Northern Ireland Community Relations Council (NICRC). Such a Council had been one of the main recommendations of a paper prepared for the Standing Advisory Commission on Human Rights (Frazer and Fitzduff, 1991). Not surprisingly for a body charged with carrying out government policy for Northern Ireland as a whole, the new Council preferred not to see Catholics and Protestants as separate, opposite communities. It explained unambiguously what it was about: 'Community relations, simply defined, endeavours to bring *the two sides of our community* towards greater understanding.' (NICRC, 1992)

Since 1993, NICRC has been responsible for the disbursement of grants to groups which wish to engage in single identity or cross-community contact work. The Council divides its activities between eight different types of such work: anti-sectarian; anti-intimidation; justice and rights; political options; inter-church (religious options); conflict resolution; mutual understanding; and cultural traditions.

Community relations in schools

The NICRC has no remit for work in schools. However, the Department of Education of Northern Ireland (DENI) has responsibility for community relations work in schools and it has acted to ensure that the last two types of community relations work listed above become part of the life of all schools. Through the *Education Reform (Northern Ireland) Order (1989)* the government committed itself to support initiatives towards the development of planned integrated schools and provided that Education for Mutual Understanding (EMU) and Cultural Heritage (CH) would become compulsory cross-curricular themes in the new common curriculum for all schools.

Schemes involving contact between pupils in Protestant and Catholic schools, although not compulsory, are now strongly encouraged. Financial support is available from DENI through the Cross Community Contact Scheme, introduced in 1987, for schools which wish to incorporate contact activities as part of EMU and CH.). The effectiveness of cross-community contact schemes has been discussed by Trew (1989). In 1995 'over a third' of schools in Northern Ireland were taking part in the Cross Community Contact Scheme (DENI 1995, 2).

7

Broadly speaking, the wide range of activities promoted under the heading of community relations have been well received by schools and by the community at large (Robinson and Smith 1992Cumulatively, they probably helped to create conditions which were favourable to the announcement of the ceasefires in 1994. However, the improvement of contact between Protestants and Catholics has not so far resulted in a shared understanding of the nature of the conflict. Gallagher (1995) has noted a general confusion about current community relations policy:

> Is it seeking to identify the factors which we hold in common in Northern Ireland, or is it attempting to acknowledge, legitimate and, in the best of all possible worlds, celebrate the things we hold differently? Is it part of a process which seeks to isolate extremists, however they are defined, or is it seeking inclusive strategies to create ways in which as many people as possible can be included in a peaceful settlement? (1995, 40).

The confusion at the heart of community relations policy may be traced back to the failure to agree about the nature of the conflict. The ceasefires have not changed this aspect of the conflict fundamentally. The need to agree is as great as ever. Not long before the announcement of the ceasefires a leading commentator could write: 'the conflict is now so deeply embedded that few people can imagine it not being there' (Bruce 1994, 112). Part of adjusting to the cessation of violence, and ensuring that it persists, is the struggle to understand what the so deeply embedded conflict was about. Ironically, the main obstacle to understanding is the bewildering range of conflicting interpretations which are on offer: the 'meta-conflict about the conflict'.

Interpreting conflicting interpretations

Arguably the most convincing view of the range of conflicting interpretations of the conflict is that put forward by Darby and Dunn:

> There is not so much a single Northern Ireland problem, easily characterised and classified, as a set of interlocked and confused problems. ... So the sort of arcane debates that try to establish, for example, whether it is a religious problem, or an economic problem, or a political problem are thought to be pointless, since it is all of these and others as well (Dunn 1995, 7-8 and cf Darby 1995, 21).

This view has much to recommend it. It avoids the simplistic analysis of previous interpretations and recognises complexity. It urges that all the different forms of separation in Northern Ireland (political, economic, social, religious) need to be analysed and worked at. Ultimately, however, this view is unconvincing because it implies that the conflict has been no more than the sum of the problems which constitute it. What is still missing is an explanation of how these disparate problems have come to be held together as a 'set' which is greater and more terrible than the sum of its parts. This is the kind of explanation or interpretation which adults need to be able to agree upon before they can begin to answer their children's questions about the fighting.

The story of how interpretation of the conflict has reached its current state of bewildering complexity is instructive. It points out the direction in which consensus about interpretation may lie. If agreement can be reached on why interpretation of the conflict has proved so intractable, there may be a basis for proceeding to agreement about the nature of the conflict.

John Whyte in *Interpreting Northern Ireland* (1991), his magisterial guide to the range of opposing interpretations, concluded that ambiguity about the nature of community relations in Northern Ireland is deep-seated: 'there are almost as many interpretations of the community divide as authors' (103). Nevertheless, Whyte did succeed in finding an organising principle or theme which enabled him to classify such a daunting range of explanations of the conflict. That theme was religion:

> A thread through the maze of differing interpretations can be found. It is to be seen in the varying answers to the question 'how far is the Northern Ireland conflict religious?' This question seems to fascinate writers on Northern Ireland. In most parts of Europe religious wars went out in the seventeenth century, yet here we find Protestants and Catholics fighting each other in the late twentieth. The question of whether the conflict if really religious, or whether the labels simply mask a conflict over economic issues, has aroused endless discussion (1991, 103).

Large-scale projects aimed at establishing common ground on the nature of the conflict have not been lacking. Perhaps the most high-powered was the *New Ireland Forum*,1983-4, which set out to 'initiate a process which will permit the establishment and development of common ground between both sections of the community in Northern Ireland and among all the people of the island' (1984, 7). More recently, *Initiative '92*, which resulted in the *Opsahl Report*, (Pollack 1993) sought to 'inquire into possible ways forward' and give the people of Northern Ireland 'an opportunity to express themselves, to overcome their sense of impotence and helplessness after nearly a quarter of a century of political violence and deadlock' (1993, 3). *Opsahl* concluded that 'religion may or may not be the prime cause of the conflict: it is certainly a potent component of it' (101). The conclusion of Beeman and Mahony was slightly different: 'there are inescapably religious dimensions to the conflict, but religion is a misleading metaphor if used to characterize it as a whole, however intertwined religious identification has become with the historical, political, economic, and cultural issues also involved' (1993, 158).

The fundamental controversy, however, continues. For example, as recently as November 1994, the *Belfast Telegraph* felt it necessary to editorialise thus:

> Northern Ireland's problem - and the violence that stems from it - is essentially *political*. It is based on the conflicting aspirations of *two politically-divided communities'* (my italics, 19/11/94).

This contrasts with the following analysis in a letter to another newspaper:

> 'Andersonstown Republican' (*Irish News* 8/1/94) states that the presentation of the conflict here in Ulster as *religious* by the British enables them to blame the victim. The victims *are* to blame because the conflict *is* religious and unless that is understood we will never achieve a solution (*Irish News* 8/2/94).

Another manifestation of the controversy is in adult education courses with titles such as the following (which lists the dimensions of the conflict competing for dominance):

> WHAT IS ... A WAY OUT OF THE CONFLICT IN NORTHERN IRELAND?
> An attempt will be made to look briefly at the conflict in Northern Ireland (Political, Religious, Cultural, Socio-Economic and Psychological) ...
> (University of Ulster DACE, 7/10/94)

A range of conflicting explanations are to be found in recent submissions to the Forum for Peace and Reconciliation on 'The Nature of the Problem and the Principles Underlying Its Resolution' (McGuiness 1995, 5-91). So the 'arcane debates' about the nature of the conflict continue. The attempt by Darby and Dunn to cut through them by denying dominance to any one of the consitutent problems (political, social, economic, religious etc) is helpful (Darby 1995, 21). It dispenses with the need to achieve agreement on 'the main problem' before a 'solution' can begin to be implemented. Work on solutions can go forward on a large number of fronts without having to wait for the breaking of the interpretive logjam. In fairness, however, it should be acknowledged that this relatively sophisticated analysis owes its existence to the logjam of 'arcane debates' to which it is a response.

The arcane debates began with the outbreak of civil conflict in 1968. One early work in particular was influential in setting the context for controversy about the nature of the conflict and in particular about the role of religion.

Holy War in Belfast was first published in August 1969 and it is highly significant that this was the work of a journalist and trade unionist, Andrew Boyd, not of a professional historian or political scientist.

In 1968 very little literature was available on the community divide in Northern Ireland. There was, therefore, a ready market for Boyd's book. What he offered was a narrative account of the origins and development of 'religious bigotry' in Belfast. His description of the violence as 'religious' found favour with the many journalists given the task of explaining the outburst of violence to a puzzled world. Boyd's title, 'Holy War', has stuck in the mind.

In this way a simplistic explanation of the conflict as being one based on religious intolerance between Protestants and Catholics gained a hold at the beginning of the troubles. This may account, in part at least, for the role of religion becoming so controversial. Subsequent commentators have been at pains to point out the inadequacy of the simplistic religious explanation and to counter-stress the importance of other factors such as the economic, political and psychological, sometimes to the exclusion of the religious dimension altogether.

The first statement this century ever to be made jointly by the leaders of the four largest Churches in Northern Ireland (Roman Catholic, Presbyterian, Church of Ireland, and Methodist) was issued in 1970. Its main concern was to deny that the conflict was a religious war. Divisions, the church leaders said, 'arise from deep and complex causes - historical, political and social - but the religious differences between professing Christians are not the primary cause' (*Belfast News Letter*, 30 May, 1970). Nevertheless, this did not prevent journalists and politicians from viewing the conflict as religious and seeking statements, appeals and documents from the church leaders to help end it:

> They seemed to think that the Churches could work miracles of which the secular world was incapable. In this expectation they were exaggerating the religious element in the conflict; they thought that, if Roman Catholic and Protestant churchmen said the same thing, there would be nothing left to fight about (Gallagher and Worrall 1982, 203).

Politicians and churchmen alike gradually developed more nuanced interpretations of the conflict and its intractability. A report commissioned by the four main churches in 1976, *Violence in Ireland*, did acknowledge that there was a religious dimension to the conflict but could arrive at no consensus about it:

> There exists a religious dimension to the quarrel. Members of the Working Party are not agreed as to the strength of this dimension, the

11

extent to which it is found in individual Churches, or the relative importance to be attached to it as compared to social and political factors (Worrall 1976, 20).

The writings of Cardinal Cahal Daly, Roman Catholic Archbishop of Armagh, illustrate well how thinking on the role of religion in the nature of the conflict has undergone development. In contrast to the initial joint statement of church leaders in 1970, he acknowledged in 1975 that he was 'deeply convinced that the Churches have a certain blame for the genesis of the situation and a real responsibility in regard to it'. But he also made plain just how limited he considered that blame to be: 'it is clear to me that the situation is not one of religious war, nor one of rival denominational theologies or spiritual allegiances. It is rather one of competing cultures, rival nationalisms conflicting social classes and economic interest groups'. He suggested that a 'colonialist model' of the conflict was more relevant than a 'religious model' (Daly 1979, 14-15).

In 1979 Daly reiterated his view that 'the relevance of the strictly religious factor is marginal, rather than central' and argued that 'the use of the terms "Protestant" and "Catholic" to describe the parties in the conflict has become so unhelpful as to be positively an obstacle to objective analysis and the search for a solution' (Daly 1979, 144). During the 1980s, however, he modified his thinking about the role of religion to the point where he could offer a more objective overview of how there had come to be competing interpretations of the conflict:

> Neither the religious nor the political analysis of the Northern Ireland problem should be developed to the exclusion of the other. Both aspects must be included in any adequate definition of our problem. Each explanation has been unilaterally developed by interested groups as part of a hand-washing exercise. I suggest that governments and politicians have sometimes developed the religious war model as an excuse for opting out of their political and governmental responsibilities. Equally, Churchmen have appealed to the political model as a means of opting out of their religious responsibilities as Churchmen. Politicians should be the last people to deny or to minimise the political elements in the conflict. Churchmen should be the last to deny its religious aspects (Daly 1991, 190).

This careful balancing of political and religious models comes close to the desciption of the conflict by Darby and Dunn as a 'set of problems' which includes, *inter alia*, a religious problem and a political problem. It is possible to see now that interpretation of the protracted conflict has been going through a series of stages and has become progressively more sophisticated.

In the opening stage of conflict, the various groupings of actors were preoccupied with attaching blame to others, thereby exculpating themselves. In the second stage, a willingness to acknowledge partial responsibility emerged. In the third stage, a recognition of the baffling complexity of the conflict and its multi-dimensional and intractable nature has emerged.

Darby and Dunn's 'set of problems' analysis belongs to this stage. Their argument is that, since the conflict is not reducible to a single or dominant problem, the search for 'a solution' must necessarily be futile. The most practical way forward is to identify and analyse all the relevant problems, tackle them separately, and hope that the cumulative effect will be conflict management which will result, eventually, in conflict reduction.

However, there is a weakness in this approach. It does not take account of Whyte's central insight that it is religion, not politics or economics or 'culture', which provides the key theme to interpretations of the conflict. Nor does it rise to what might be called 'Whyte's challenge'.

Whyte's challenge

Whyte described how, in the earliest phase of the Troubles, the dominant interpretation was what he called the 'external conflict paradigm'. According to this paradigm (model or picture of interpretation) the most important question to ask about the conflict was: 'which external actor is mainly responsible for the problem in Nothern Ireland - is it Britain or the Republic?' Although they disagreed in their answers to this question, both unionists and nationalists emphasized in their analysis the external relations of Northern Ireland (1991, 258).

Whyte then traced how this external conflict interpretation declined in popularity and gave way to an 'internal-conflict paradigm' [author's italics]:

> According to this interpretation, the crucial conflict is between *the communities* in Northern Ireland. Though this conflict is influenced by the relations which Northern Ireland has with Britain on the one hand and the Republic on the other, those relations are not the heart of it. There would still be tensions between *the two communities* no matter what wider framework was adopted for the region. This interpretation can be considered the dominant paradigm over the last twenty years (1991, 258).

Whyte considered that the shift to the internal-conflict paradigm was an improvement because it led researchers to look into aspects of the conflict which had been often neglected. However, the fact that disagreement about the nature of the conflict continues shows that the paradigm has not solved all the difficulties. He concluded: 'Perhaps the time has come when we should start looking for a new paradigm' . This is Whyte's challenge: to find a new paradigm, model or picture of the conflict which will interpret satisfactorily both its complexity and its intractability.

Whyte admitted that he did not know what shape a new paradigm would be likely to take but he suspected that 'even now researchers are articulating the theories which will lead to the new paradigm' (1991, 259). His suspicion has proved to be correct.

The response to Whyte's challenge

Whyte described the evolution of conflict interpretation as far as he was able. He showed how the initially-dominant external conflict paradigm came to be displaced by the now dominant internal conflict paradigm. On the basis of continuing dissatisfaction with it, he predicted that the internal conflict paradigm would in turn be displaced. He might have added that the new paradigm would be unlikely to arise from a completely new perspective; most likely it would emerge from a synthesis of the two opposing paradigms, integrating the most valuable features of each. Further, the new paradigm synthesis would probably build on the (admittedly few) substantial points of agreement already established between researchers. Whyte found these to be six:

1. The conflict is to be seen primarily as one between the communities in Northern Ireland ...

2. The two communities are deeply but not totally divided. Though the factors which divide them are more important than the factors which unite them, the latter do exist.

3. Catholics are at a substantial disadvantage, economically and socially, as compared with Protestants.

4. The division beween the communities comprises a mixture of religious, economic, political, and psychological elements.

5. Protestants on average are more concerened to maintain the border than Catholics are to do away with it; although a substantial number of Catholics feel as strongly opposed to the border as most Protestants feel in favour of it.

6. In contrast Protestants are more uncertain about their national identity than are Catholics. Most Catholics describe themselves as 'Irish', while

14

Protestants have been more inclined to tack between the labels 'British', 'Ulster', and even 'Irish' (1991, 244-245).

Given these points of agreement, the daunting programme for the new paradigm would be to account for and resolve what Whyte discovered to be the major points of disagreement between researchers:

1. While the majority of authors agree that the primary conflict is between two communities in Northern Ireland, even those who agree on this point vary among themselves about how much subsidiary responsibility should be attributed to British and/or Irish policy.

2. While most authors agree that the division between the communities is substantial but not total, they disagree among themselves on where to put the emphasis as between factors making for division and factors making for integration.

3. There is no consensus on the most appropriate labels to use for the two communities. 'Protestant' and 'Catholic' is one possible pair; 'unionist' and 'nationalist', or even 'Ulster British' and 'Ulster Irish' are other possibles. The religious labels are the most commonly used, but they are not universal.

4. While there is agreement that Catholics are at a disadvantage as compared with Protestants, there is less agreement on how extensive that disadvantage is, or the reasons for it. In particular, there is disagreement on how far the disadvantage is due to discrimination.

5. While there is agreement that the conflict results from a mixture of religious, economic, political, and psychological factors, there is no agreement on their relative importance. *In particular, there is a divergence of view on how much stress to put on religion* [author's italics].

There is widespread *disagreement* on some issues. The most important of these is the most practical - namely, what should be done? Even those who substantially agree in their diagnosis of the problem reach no consensus on how to resolve it.

Thus, after twenty years of study by hundreds of researchers, there is still only partial agreement on the nature of the problem, and none at all on the nature of the solution. (1991, 245-246)

Whyte's central insight was that religion provides the key theme to the range of interpretations of the conflict. As it turns out, this is what unifies the body of work building towards the new paradigm: each author is concerned with

15

resolving the role of religion in the conflict in a way which gives it central importance.

John Hickey's *Religion and the Northern Ireland Problem* (1984) was the first detailed work of academic analysis to argue for the paramount importance of religion in the conflict. Hickey suggested that the religious dimension had been ignored or dismissed by researchers because of the reduced role which religion now plays in the new pluralistic societies of western Europe. He criticised those who treat the terms 'Protestant' and 'Roman Catholic' as simply labels for ignoring that they do in fact differentiate between two sets of religious beliefs. His book analyses the content of those religious beliefs, demonstrates the social consequences which flow from them, and indicates how they contribute to the conflcit.

Most importantly, Hickey asked why the different religious traditions in Northern Ireland have persisted and still exert considerable force when, in the rest of the United Kingdom, they have long since lost most of their force (1984, 63-4). His answer, in short, was that 'the religious divide in Northern Ireland is not based purely on the symbolic membership of a group with different political ideologies, but is rooted in different interpretations of the Christian faith, which, in turn, help to form attitudes as to what 'society' and its institutions should be about' (87).

In support of his thesis, Hickey offered a detailed historical explanation of how the 'politico-religious tradition' of Northern Ireland has survived uniquely as a 'living fossil' from the time of the sixteenth and seventeenth centuries, when it was possible, throughout Protestant Europe, to identify allegiance to Rome with disloyalty to the State. In Northern Ireland, Protestantism 'has remained the religion it was in early post-Reformation England - a bulwark against the imperialism of Rome on the one hand, and a defence of the purity of the Christian faith against the errors of Popery on the other' (66-7).

Steve Bruce's *God Save Ulster: the religion and politics of Paisleyism* (1986), pushed further the case that the conflict is 'rooted in different interpretations of the Christian faith'. Like Hickey, Bruce stressed the uniqueness of the politico-religious tradition in Northern Ireland: 'That Paisley so stands out from other religious and political leaders in Europe in his synthesis of religion and politics suggests what is well known from other sources: that Northern Ireland is an exception among modern democracies' (1986, 2).

Bruce also traced the roots of this uniqueness back to the seventeenth century Plantation of Ulster when 'the interaction of religious ideology and social conflict established the foundations of the later development of political ideologies' (13). But Bruce paid closer attention in his analysis than Hickey to the complexity of religious history, particularly to the divisions within Protestantism, mainly Church of Ireland and Presbyterian, and to internal divisions between liberals and fundamentalists.

The major contribution of Bruce was to highlight the orthodoxy of the fundamentalist position and to argue persuasively against the view that Irish evangelical Protestants such as Ian Paisley have 'somehow invented a new set of religious beliefs to legitimate their political struggles' (14). Modern historians seeking to transcend the present-day divisions of Orange and Green have, according to Bruce, 'exaggerated the popularity of the liberal position':

> The liberals are innovating. They are giving up beliefs and practices that previous generations held dear. It is not my intention to offer any judgement on the morality or theological validity of such movements. The job of the social scientist is to describe and explain; the reader may make his or her own judgements. All that needs to be established is that the Scots settlers belonged to an earlier Presbyterian culture which held distinctive beliefs which were crucially opposed to many of the cardinal beliefs of the Roman Catholic Church (1986, 6-7).

What were the distinctive beliefs so crucially opposed? Like Hickey, Bruce identified doctrines relating to mediation between God and Man, disagreement on Eucharistic doctrine, and objection to the accretion of various 'non-Scriptural' beliefs and practices such as the sacraments of confirmation, penance and extreme unction. There was also fundamental disagreement about organisation and authority based on conflicting 'descending' and 'ascending' theories of church government and about the idea that religious merit was transferable (indulgences) and the idea of predestination.

In arguing to establish the importance of religion in the face of its neglect by other commentators, Hickey had committed the cardinal sin of conflict interpretation: he had exaggerated his case. The specialist who exalts his aspect of the conflict above the rest invites being humbled at the hands of other specialists. By calling the conflict 'religious' Hickey had elevated the narrow sense of the term (commitment to doctrinal belief and practice) and so invited the counter-argument that he was as guilty of neglecting political and other elements as others had been of neglecting religion.

Bruce, however, has been more successful than Hickey in winning support for the view that the conflict should be called 'religious'. He widened the argument by emphasising the broad, rather than the narrow, meaning of religious. He pointed out that Protestants willingly accept a religious label even when their personal commitment may be weak or even non-existent. This is negative self-identification based on the argument 'I am not a Catholic, therefore I am a Protestant' (which, vice versa, can apply equally to Catholics).

Most Protestants, Bruce argued, are concerned with identity rather than supremacy and the only secure identity which they have derives from evangelical Protestantism. The alternatives - socialism, liberal unionism, ecumenism - are unsatisfactory because they erode the difference between themselves and Catholics. While it is true that the antagonists are not contending about religious doctrines or interests, the conflict should still be called 'religious' because those on the Protestant side need and use religion as a badge of identity.

Whyte's judgement was that, although Hickey and Bruce had argued a powerful case, it was still not possible to speak of a consensus in their favour (1991, 104-7). Better, he thought, to follow Jenkins (1986, 18) and describe the situation as 'a conflict with a religious dimension'. Since then, however, new work, notably by McSweeney (1989) and Fulton (1991), has added weight to the Hickey/Bruce analysis of the conflict as being religious.

Before considering Fulton's work in particular, it is worth noting that this 'religious' interpretation was making some headway with church leaders. The development of Cardinal Daly's thinking has already been mentioned. To a certain extent, Hickey and Bruce had been anticipated by Gallagher and Worrall. Writing as committed Protestant churchmen they had asserted that 'it is this coincidence of political and theological factors that renders the issues so intractable' (1982, 191; cf Bruce 1986, 249). They had identified the source of the conflict's intractability.

They also acknowledged 'the sectarian element in the conflict' (210). What they did not do, however, was give religion a central role. They implied that ecumenical development is 'normal' within the world-wide Christian tradition and that it is only 'a conflict of nationalistic and material interests' which has prevented ecumenical development from taking place in Ireland. This was exactly the kind of liberal view which Bruce criticized for underplaying the centrality of the fundamental opposition between Catholicism and Protestantism in western Europe since the Reformation and for obscuring the fact that it is the ecumenists, not the fundamentalists, who have been the 'innovating minority' (1986, 6-7).

Some church leaders have accepted in broad terms the analysis of Hickey and Bruce. In 1989, David Stevens, now General Secretary of the Irish Council of Churches, was prepared to go beyond Gallagher and Worrall and attribute a more central role in the conflict to religion:

> So we have a potent history of antagonism, of fear, of grievance and anxiety. Churches have been assemblies of the Irish, Scots and English

who have helped maintain these memories; indeed have almost given them transcendent meaning. (Stevens 1990, 57)

The way forward, according to Stevens, is ecumenism, which is defined as 'recognising the other side as fellow Christians'. This interpretation of the role of religion places ecumenism in an historical context which does justice to the centrality of the opposition between Catholicism and Protestantism and which explains convincingly why ecumenism is perceived as 'a threat to the boundaries of the community' (Whyte 1991, 65).

Not all commentators from a church background, however, share Stevens' view. For example, a former Director of the Irish School of Ecumenics, Robin Boyd, denies that religion is anything like as deeply implicated in the conflict as Hickey, Bruce, and Stevens suggest:

This does not mean that the Troubles in Ireland are a religious war in the sense that people are fighting about theological questions. It is true, however, that with very few exceptions all the Irish people on one side are Protestants, and all on the other side are Catholics. And the struggle is really about *power*: who in this small island is to control political power? Can the two sides trust each other? (Boyd, 1988, 83).

The weakness of this defence of religion is indicated by the questions which it begs: why should there be a struggle for the control of power? and why are the two sides are unable to trust each other in the first place? It also illustrates the continuing absence of consensus on the role of religion in the conflict. And so the debate continues, but there are further signs of the importance of religion being acknowledged.

Like Stevens and Daly, Archbishop Eames, Church of Ireland Archbishop of Armagh, has come close to adopting the Hickey/Bruce analysis:

To argue that it is a question of a religious conflict alone is to so isolate one aspect as to ignore the vital interplay of others which complicate the general picture and make it virtually imposible to define the precise nature of the religious dimension of the troubles (Eames 1992, 139).

Daly and Eames alike resist going the whole way with Hickey and Bruce in attributing paramount importance to religion because both are committed to a defence of religion from the charge of 'sectarianism', which is based on the idea of 'secularisation'. Daly puts it this way:

I suggest that the religious dimension is very often a religion surrogate, a secularised sediment of a former genuinely religious conviction. Secularised religion often retains the passionate conviction of religious belief long after the original religious belief has been discarded (1991, 190-1).

Eames puts it this way:

> Northern Ireland shows what happens when Protestantism or Catholicism becomes the object of secularisation. It must not be forgotten that there has long been an extremely close identification between a process of secularisation and sectarianism (1992, 139).

This defence or apology for the role of religion in the conflict depends on making a distinction between 'good religion' and 'bad sectarianism', attributing the increase in the latter to decline in the former as a result of the apparently inexorable process of secularisation. It is a defence which has received a powerful challenge recently from Fulton (1991).

Fulton points out that this particular understanding of religion 'hides religion's contribution to Ireland's divisions from many catholic and some protestant minds'. Religion in Ireland has been treated as 'a measureable quantity of an intrinsically good substance, of which there can be more or less' (1991, 9). When negative elements related to religion appear, both religious and secular investigators tend to use the term 'sectarian' to describe such acts and attitudes. Sectarianism is also used to describe what are frequently considered to be non-religious phenomena, such as ethnic and class divisions. The term 'religious' is used only in relation to extremism in the form of militant protestant fundamentalism.

Fulton compares levels of religiosity with levels of support for political violence (publicly and unanimously condemned by church leaders, both Catholic and Protestant) and points to the apparent contradiction: 'levels of support for violence cannot be reconciled with the levels of good religiosity unless they are both attributed to a number of the same people' (1991, 16). Research among children has verified the connection between strong religious feeling and attitudes to violence. Strongly religious Protestant children appeared to be 20% more likely to endorse the use of violence for political purposes than their less religious fellows, while among Roman Catholic children the comparable figure was 30% (McMaster 1993, 11; Rea 1982, 36).

Fulton's argument is that we need to 'overcome the established categories of positive religion and negative sectarianism' in order to clarify the role of religion in Ireland's divisions, both in the past and in the present. He suggests that, in the case of the Roman Catholic Church, 'there is little theory of bad religion except of that religion which other churches and religions might possess'. Eagerness to defend their own church and its social policies, such as the maintenance of separate catholic schools, led Irish bishops in the early stages of the present conflict to deny that religion played any role at all (1991, 16).

To the charge that they have no theory of 'bad religion', the largest Churches in Ireland have reacted recently with a joint response. In 1993, a Working Party of the ecumenical Irish Inter-Church Meeting published *Sectarianism: a Discussion Document.* Its conclusions are a further indication of how the tide has been turning in favour of the Hickey/Bruce analysis (see also Williams and Falconer 1995). The *Violence in Ireland Report,* which was the previous attempt of the Churches to come to grips jointly with the issue, had defined 'sectarianism' as a 'frame of mind' (1976, 71). In contrast, *Sectarianism* defines it as:

> a complex of attitudes, beliefs, behaviours and structures *in which religion is a significant component* [author's italics], and which:
> (i) directly, or indirectly, infringes the rights of individuals or groups, and/or (ii) influences or causes situations of destructive conflict (Irish Inter-Church Meeting, 1993, 8).

As its authors point out, this is a much better way of defining sectarianism than saying that it is a 'frame of mind'. It avoids the difficulty of 'mind-reading' by focusing attention on the measurable consequences of religious attitudes, beliefs, behaviours and structures. Most importantly, it recognises, *contra* Daly and Eames, that what might be called mainstream or normal religion, as distinct from degenerate or secularised religion, *can* have bad consequences. In other words, religion should not be regarded as an 'intrinsically good substance'; there can be bad aspects to it as well as good.

It remains to be seen how much support the *Sectarianism* discussion document definition receives. It moves further in the direction of the Hickey/Bruce analysis but pulls up short of it, describing sectarianism as a complex in which religion is only a 'significant' rather than a 'central' or 'paramount' component. For the time being, it remains the case that the established categories of 'good religion' and 'bad sectarianism' together constitute the main obstacle blocking general acceptance of the Hickey/Bruce analysis. According to these cagtegories, sectarianism is thought of as non-religious because it is the result of secularisation, not of religion *per se.*

A wider acceptance of the *Sectarianism* discussion document's definition would bring agreement on the nature of the conflict closer. The difficulty boils down to deciding whether or not 'sectarianism' is 'religious'. It depends, of course, on one's definition of religion. So long as commentators, including church leaders such as the Archbishops of Armagh, choose to exclude sectarianism from their understanding of religion there is an impasse.

In the meantime, Bruce has tried to find a way out. He reports in *The Edge of the Union: the Ulster Loyalist Political Vision* (1994) how his first book in 1986 ran into difficulty over the ambiguous meaning of 'religious':

> In *God Save Ulster*, I began my explanation of the role of religion with the dramatic assertion that 'the Northern Ireland conflict is a religious conflict'. Though subsequent argument detailed exactly what I meant by that, a number of authors have misunderstood my point. O'Duffy, for example, suggests that I see 'the conflict primarily as a religious war, as a relic of the Reformation/Counter-reformation struggle' (1994, 130.)

In *The Edge of the Union*, Bruce seeks to avoid such a misunderstanding by resolutely calling the conflict 'ethnic' rather than religious and by explaining carefully how 'ethnic' means 'religious':

> The key point is the centrality of evangelicalism for the Ulster loyalist's sense of ethnic identity. It defines the group to which he belongs, it figures large in the history of that group, it legitimates the group's advantages (such as they are), and it radically distinguishes the group from its traditional enemy. ... I am arguing that the Northern Ireland conflict is an ethnic conflict and that religion plays an important part in the identity of the Protestant people. ... Many middle-class Protestants and Catholics manage to remain relatively uninvolved, but even they cannot entirely escape being judged and reacted to on the basis of their perceived ethnic identification (1994, 25, 30, 145)

'Ethnic' as the preferred epithet for describing the conflict has also come strongly to the fore with the establishment of the prestigious INCORE (Joint International Programme on Conflict Resolution and *Ethnicity*) at the University of Ulster, but it is doubtful whether the elusive consensus on the nature of the conflict can be achieved simply by agreeing to call it 'ethnic'. As Fulton has pointed out, ethnic divisions, like class divisions, are frequently considered to be 'non-religious' phenomena. Calling the conflict 'ethnic' will suggest to many, therefore, that religion is not important and so undermine Bruce's purpose.

Conversely, the same problem faces the *Sectarianism* discussion document if it succeeds in commanding support for its definition of sectarianism as 'a complex ... in which religion is a significant component'. The logical next step would be to make 'sectarian' the preferred epithet for describing the conflict. But since 'sectarianism' is frequently considered to be a religious phenomenon, calling the conflict 'sectarian' will suggest to many that only religion is important, so also undermining Bruce's purpose. To qualify 'sectarian' by saying that it also includes non-religious components would be to empty the word of useful meaning. If 'sectarian' were to be the all-embracing term for describing the nature of the conflict, it would likely be interpreted by many as meaning little more than that there are two sides to the conflict.

A more satisfactory way out of the terminological morass is needed. The Hickey/Bruce analysis appears sound. Support for it is growing, as the *Sectarianism* discussion document shows. However, substantial objections to it remain and not all of these can be dismissed simply as deriving from vested interests (parties to the conflict defending themselves from blame, or experts defending the importance of their area of expertise) or from misunderstanding of terminology. McGarry and O'Leary put the case against the Hickey/Bruce analysis most trenchantly:

> Explanations which accord primacy to religion create blind-alleys for policy-makers and inhibit understanding. They absolve important political agents of responsibility. If the antagonisms are religious, then they cannot have been caused by the historic legacies of colonial conquest, plantation and oppression, by the Stormont regime's practice of political and economic discrimination against nationalists, by successive British governments' mismanagement in Ireland before and after 1972, or by British political institutions. If the conflict is religious then the historic nature of the Republic's nationalism, as opposed to its Catholicism, receives less attention than it should. Explanations which emphasize the primacy of religion therefore need to be exposed to strong light. When that happens, they evaporate, leaving little residue (1995, 213).

Here is a measure of the gulf separating rival interpretations of the conflict. What is required for the merit of the Hickey/Bruce analysis to become generally convincing is an acceptable way of saying that religion is central to the conflict without implying that the conflict is only about religion (and not about all the other things which McGarry and O'Leary list as being important). Of course, a new epithet or form of words will not in itself be persuasive. It needs to be supported by an explanation of why it has taken so long for a generally acceptable description of the conflict to emerge. Consensus on how to describe the conflict is only likely to be achieved if a convincing argument can be brought forward to explain why consensus has been so elusive hitherto and how this new description is one to which all can subscribe because it denotes an acceptable synthesis of the rival interpretations. Consensus on description of the conflict needs to be underpinned by a theory of the intractability of conflict interpretation, which itself is a symptom of the intractable nature of the conflict.

At this stage it can be asserted that Whyte's challenge is on the verge of being met. A new paradigm of explanation of the conflict is emerging (synthesising the merits of the older external conflict paradigm and those of the newer internal conflict paradigm). It is likely to give central importance to the Hickey/Bruce analysis of the importance of religion because of the growing support for it.

However, the Hickey/Bruce analysis in its present state is not sufficient on its own to be accepted generally as the new paradigm. It is too easily criticized as merely a variant of the internal conflict paradigm.What is still lacking is a theory of intractability to justify giving central importance to the Hickey/Bruce analysis.

Recent work by Boyle and Hadden (1994) has opened the way for such a theory of intractability by focusing attention on what they call *The Choice* which faces people in Northern Ireland. The next chapter turns to look at the concept of this 'core choice' in some detail and attempts to develop the kind of theory of intractability required.

2 Interpreting *The Choice*

Boyle and Hadden in *Northern Ireland: The Choice* (1994) ask if the twenty-five years of 'relatively restrained' communal conflict to date has been merely a prelude to a full-scale civil war and a thoroughgoing ethnic separation. Like Darby and Dunn, they seek to cut through the 'arcane debates' about the interpretation of the conflict. The rights and wrongs of the conflict's origins and long development are seen as being beside the point. They argue that the nature of the conflict can be formulated quite simply for present practical purposes:

> Every ethnic or communal conflict is unique. But what has happened in Kosava, Croatia and Bosnia may help to remind us of the terrifying force which sentiments of national or communal identity may generate, and that one of the fundamental choices that arises out of most conflicts of this kind is between separation and sharing: whether the different communities can go on living together and sharing their facilities and their structures for government or whether their differences can be accommodated only by living apart. Living together does not, of course, rule out all forms of separate provision. Distinctive communities, like those of Belgium, may agree to maintain separate educational systems and separate social facilities without conflict. And separation may take many forms - from residential and social segregation to the development of separate systems of local self-government and ultimately complete territorial and constitutional separation. *But there is a clear choice to be made between policies based on the acceptance of separation and policies based on the objective of sharing* (author's italics, 1994, 2-3).

This is *The Choice*, or 'core choice', facing people in Northern Ireland. Lennon describes the same choice in religious terms:

25

... We come back to our basic question: what is the priority for *the Christian community* in Northern Ireland: is it reconciliation with justice, or is it the maintenance of *separate communities*? (author's italics, Lennon 1995, 124).

Boyle and Hadden are ruthless in their analysis. They assess the current balance between structures for sharing and separation and calculate the likely outcomes of policies which develop one or the other. By eschewing any historical explanation, their approach concentrates the mind starkly on the practical decisions which need to be taken and which policies stand the best chance of working. But the formulation of a core choice between separation and sharing begs an important historical question: how have Catholics and Protestants come to be faced with such a choice in the first place? Further, it begs the moral question: what criteria should Catholics and Protestants apply in making The Choice?

This is how the concept of The Choice opens up the way to a theory of the conflict's intractability. Firstly, it raises the historical issue of how it has become possible for Catholics and Protestants to picture each other as belonging to 'opposite communities' or 'opposite religions'. And secondly, it raises the moral or religious issue of whether they should continue picturing each other in this way.

The origins and development of the opposite-religions picture

Before the Reformation in the sixteenth century, the peoples of western Europe all regarded each other as belonging to the same religion, Christianity. They saw a one-religion picture. At the same time, they were aware of Judaism and Islam as other religions in the sense of aberrations or perversions of 'true' religion, rather than as alternative religious systems in the modern pluralist sense (Bossy 1982). The breaches between Rome and various Protestant groups brought about a paradigm shift to a two-religions, or opposite-religions, view of Christianity. (The concept of paradigm shift is borrowed by Küng (1991) from the work of Kuhn (1970) on the history of science.) The shift meant that Catholics and Protestants began to regard each other as belonging to different religions, as separate from each other as Judaism and Islam from Christianity. Modern historians writing about the period still follow the contemporary usage when they distinguish between 'the old religion' and 'the new religion' (Dudley Edwards and O'Dowd 1985, 65, 76).

Of course, the shift to the new way of seeing religion was gradual: 'the Ireland of later Tudor times was a very complex, not to say confused society, where people were only slowly and often painfully working out that they were Catholics, not Protestants (Corish 1981, 17). The detail of how this original Catholic / Protestant divide developed to the point where it became complete is not of concern here (see Robinson-Hammerstein 1994). What is important is that, by about 1600, a point had been reached where Catholicism and Protestantism were mutually understood to be separate heretical and schismatic religious systems in violent opposition to each other. In short, they had become opposite religions.

The *Thirty-Nine Articles of Religion* agreed by the Anglican bishops in London in 1562 stated simply that 'the Bishop of Rome hath no jurisdiction in this Realm of England' (Article XXXVI). In response, the Bishop of Rome excommunicated and deposed Queen Elizabeth I of England. The papal bull *Regnans in excelsis* (1570) stated that Christ 'has entrusted His holy Catholic and Apostolic Church, outside which there is no salvation, to one person alone on earth, namely to Peter the Prince of the Apostles, and to Peter's successor, the Roman Pontiff ...'. It went on to condemn Elizabeth for 'having by force prohibited the practice of *the true religion'*. The opposition of the two religions, - one 'true', the other 'false' - was now complete.

The development of Presbyterianism and Independency in the British Isles complicated the picture but did not alter the fundamental opposition between Catholicism and Protestantism. Rather, it intensified it. Whereas Anglicans had simply rejected the papacy, Presbyterians went further and formally identified the Pope with the Antichrist:

> There is no other head of the Church but the Lord Jesus Christ. Nor can the Pope of Rome, in any sense, be head thereof: but is that Antichrist, that man of sin, and son of perdition, that exalteth himself, in the Church, against Christ and all that is called God (*Westminster Confession of Faith* 1646, Chapter XXV.VI).

The extent to which the Catholic / Protestant divide continued to be regarded as complete may be judged from Pope Pius IX's condemnation of the following propositions:

> XVIII. Protestantism is nothing more than another form of the same true Christian religion, in which form it is given to please God equally as in the Catholic Church.
> XXI. The Church has not the power of defining dogmatically that the religion of the Catholic Church is the only true religion (*Syllabus of Errors*, 1864).

Clearly, the opposite-religions paradigm two hundred years later was still orthodox. However, the very fact that solemn condemnation was thought necessary for such propositions is indication that a new 'ecumenical' one-religion picture was emerging to challenge the opposite-religions picture.

Divisions within Protestantism went almost as deep as those between Protestantism and Catholicism. The *Westminster Confession of Faith* defined the Christian church as consisting of 'all those throughout the world that profess *the true religion* ... out of which there is no ordinary possibility of salvation'. It went on to warn that some individual Churches (including Protestant ones) 'have so degenerated, as to become no Churches of Christ, but synagogues of Satan' (Chapter XXV.II,V). Some Protestants could regard their own denomination as being the only 'true' religion and all the other denominations, Protestant as well as Catholic, as opposite 'false' religions.

There were further divisions. Fundamentalists within each of the Protestant Churches distinguished between those who were 'saved' (those who had 'true' religion) and those who were not. Thus, at the beginning of the twentieth century, the Anglican bishop, J. C. Ryle, warned: 'take notice, you may be a staunch Episcopalian, or Presbyterian, or Congregationalist, or Baptist, or Methodist, or Plymouth Brother - and yet not belong to the true Church. And if you do not, it will be better at the last if you had never been born'.

A further paradigm shift within Christianity, which has been under way since the beginning of the twentieth century, is towards a new one-religion paradigm, that is seeing Catholics and Protestants as belonging to the one religion, rather than to opposite religions. The initiative for this 'ecumenical movement' in western Europe came first from within Protestantism. It is usually dated from the Edinburgh Conference of 1910, although much was owed to earlier developments (Ellis 1992, 5). As a response to the problems of Protestant disunity, this movement led eventually to the formation of the World Council of Churches in 1948.

So far as the Protestant Churches are concerned, their paradigm shift in an ecumenical direction has not been uncontested and is by no means complete. In the 1970s a campaign for withdrawal from the World Council of Churches gained momentum in the Presbyterian Church in Ireland and led to formal withdrawal in 1980 (Holmes 1985, 173-174).

The same paradigm shift has been taking place in Protestant / Catholic relations. The Roman Catholic Church has moved to a position where, through the declaration of the Second Vatican Council, *Unitatis redintegratio* (1964), the one-religion model or picture of Christianity is now clearly the foundation of official church policy:

No more is there talk of 'schismatics and heretics' but rather of 'separated brethren'. No more is there an imperial demand that the dissident return in penitence to the Church who has no need of penitence;

instead there is recognition that both sides are guilty of the sins of division and must reach out penitently toward one another (Brown 1969, 67).

This position, orthodox since the 1960s, is in sharp contrast to that of 1928 when Pius XI, in his encyclical *Mortalium Annos*, described Protestantism as 'a false Christianity quite alien to the one Church of Christ'. However, the paradigm shift was under way then, even if not obviously so in Catholic-Protestant relations. The same Pope, the previous year, had referred to the Eastern Orthodox Churches as 'separated brethren':

> For a reunion it is above all necessary to know and to love one another. To know one another, because if the efforts of reunion have failed so many times, this is in large measure due to mutual ignorance. If there are prejudices on both sides, these prejudices must fall. Incredible are the errors and equivocations which persist and are handed down among the separated brethren against the Catholic Church; on the other hand, Catholics have also sometimes failed in justly evaluating the truth, or on account of insufficient knowledge, in showing a fraternal spirit (see Brown 1969, 50).

Remarkably, the same rationale underpins the Cultural Heritage and Education for Mutual Understanding (EMU) initiative which is current education policy in Northern Ireland schools. The basic argument for this initiative is that it is important to overcome mutual ignorance in order to improve relations; mutual knowledge and understanding can overcome the bad effects of division.

How complete, then, is the shift from the fundamentalist to the ecumenical paradigm in the Catholic and Protestant Churches? The key question is whether or not they regard each other as Christians. In Ireland, education and marriage provide the classic test cases. The sharpening of confessional differences on both issues is well documented (for education see Akenson 1970; Farren 1985, 1986, 1989; for marriage see Cosgrove 1985, and for mixed-marriage see Lee, R. 1979 and Robinson, G. 1992).

The 'core choice' made by the Roman Catholic Church and the Protestant Churches was clearly in favour of separation rather than sharing. The Roman Catholic line on mixed marriage, for example, which had been more or less tolerant before the Famine, gradually became less so during the latter part of the nineteenth century and resulted in the *Ne Temere* decree of 1908. In his response to *Ne Temere*, the Church of Ireland Archbishop of Armagh, J.A.F. Gregg, illustrated how the issues of education and mixed-marriage were inter-linked and how they were seen generally from the opposite-communities, opposite-religions perspective:

It is a crying shame that men with Protestant names should let their children who ought to be strengthening *our community* grow up as Romanists, giving their blood and brain and energy to *a community which would drive us out of the land if it could* ... Mixed marriages tend to rob us of the next generation, and we need to bond ourselves together to stop the leakage. Parents need not throw their children into unnecessary association with Roman Catholics, either in school or in society. If *the barrier* is broken down or even weakened, those who played together as children will naturally say when they grow up, 'If you let us play together then, why should we not marry now?' Keep up *the distinction*, I would entreat you. Make the idea of marriage with a Roman Catholic as much out of the question as a marriage within the prohibited degrees. Make it the first idea with your children that marriage with a Roman Catholic is not for them; that such a marriage cannot be entered into on fair and equal terms, but only on terms of shame and dishonour (author's italics, Gregg 1943, 9).

Here Gregg was articulating the fundamental objection to integrated education: that it may lead to mixed-marriage and so to a breaking down of the boundary between the Catholic and Protestant communities. In response to the freezing in Catholic / Protestant relations, conversely those between Anglicans, Presbyterians and Methodists became warmer in solidarity against a common enemy.

It was not the case that no attempts were made to establish ecumenical contact between Catholics and Protestants before the 1960s. In Ireland, the *Mercier Society* (1941-44) held meetings in Dublin to discuss matters of faith with non-Catholics, but with a view to bringing them into the Church. It was eventually closed by Archbishop McQuaid (Ellis 1992, 52-53). The *Clonard Mission to non-Catholics* in Belfast fared rather better, from 1947 to 1968. Its changing emphasis reflected the changing relationship between Catholics and Protestants during the period.

Initially, the *Clonard Mission* preachers emphasised that its purpose was information-giving. Catholic teaching on a chosen topic was explained, then questions submitted by listeners were answered. After the service, the congregation was invited to inspect the church and the sacristy with the sacred vessels, vestments and liturgical books. In the wake of Vatican II, the Mission changed its name first to *The Mission for our Separated Brethren*; in 1966 to *Talks for all religious communions on Vatican II*; and finally in 1967 to *Lectures for all communions*. These name changes parallel the Vatican's change of emphasis by renaming in 1961 the Church's votive mass for unity from the more negative *Ad Tollendum Schisma* to the more positive *Pro Unitate Ecclesiae*.

Such efforts as these made little impact on the Catholic / Protestant divide in Ireland. Fionnuala O'Connor reports of Catholics that 'many have clear memories of being taught that all those "outside the faith" were lesser Christians, lacking the fullness of truth' (1993, 172). Commenting in 1949 on the prospect of round-table conferences with Protestants, Cardinal Conway said: 'there is the danger that Catholics, in accepting merely equal rights of speaking at the meeting, may give the impression that they accept in principle that the Catholic Church is on an equal footing with other religious bodies' (Conway 1950, 360-365). Similarly, the Church of Ireland bishops were still using the language of sectarianism and heresy in responding in 1950 to the dogma of the Assumption of the Blessed Virgin:

> By its various enlargements of the ancient Catholic creed to contain the twelve new articles of Pope Pius IV's creed, the two new articles of Pius IX in 1854 [Immaculate Conception] and 1870 [Papal Infallibility], and this new dogma of 1950, the Roman Catholic Church is shutting itself further and further away from *the rest of Catholic Christendom* into being a self-enclosed corporation - a sectarian organisation, governed by its own private and self-determined Rule of Faith, which those who are content with the ancient Rule of Faith and the Primitive Church Order, can only reject as heretical (Gregg 1950).

It will be noted that the Church of Ireland bishops were seeing a one-religion picture, but only just. The Catholic Church, they believed, was in serious danger of splitting itself off completely from 'the rest of Catholic Christendom' to form a 'sectarian organisation' which is 'heretical'; in other words, an opposite religion. This is the continuous line of tradition running back to the Reformation which ecumenists claim: however deep the Catholic / Protestant divide has become, their separation has never been complete or final; the two sides have remained, however tenuously, connected as parts of the one religion. The laity, however, could be forgiven for thinking that the breakdown between Catholicism and Protestantism was complete and irretrievable.

Presbyterians, for example, remained mindful of the injunction of the *Westminster Confession of Faith* regarding mixed marriage: 'those who profess *the reformed religion* [author's italics] should not marry with infidels, Roman Catholics or other idolaters'. Roman Catholics, especially in the nineteenth century when fear of proselytising was strongest, were forbidden even to be present at an act of worship in a Protestant church. When changes to the *Code of Canon Law* in 1917 allowed for passive attendance at services such as weddings and funerals, the older attitude persisted in Ireland. So, the funeral of Douglas Hyde, the first President of Ireland, in St Patrick's Church of Ireland cathedral, Dublin, in 1949, was not attended by the Taoiseach or the Catholic members of the Cabinet.

On the eve of the Second Vatican Council (1962-65), then, the Irish Roman Catholic and Protestant Churches lived in almost total isolation from each other. There is no evidence to suggest that - apart from a very few - Protestants and Roman Catholics thought they belonged to the same religion as the one 'people of God' (Ellis 1992, 97). This needs to be remembered when considering the achievement of the first joint statement by the Church leaders in Northern Ireland in 1970.

In 1970, in the first phase of the Troubles, the Irish Catholic bishops were responding with a new sense of urgency to the *boulversement* of Vatican II. The *Decree on Ecumenism* explained how the Roman Catholic Church had come to shift, officially at least, from the opposite-religions paradigm to the one-religion paradigm, which includes, rather than excludes, Protestantism:

> In this one and only Church of God from its very beginning there arose certain rifts, which the Apostle strongly censures as damnable. But in subsequent centuries much more serious dissensions appeared and large communities became separated from full communion with the Catholic Church - for which, often enough, men of both sides were to blame. However, one cannot charge with the sin of the separation those who at present are born into these communities and in them are brought up in the faith of Christ, and the Catholic church accepts them with respect and affection as brothers ... it remains true that all who have been justified by faith in baptism are incorporated into Christ; they therefore have a right to be called Christians, and with good reason are accepted as brothers by the children of the Catholic Church (Flannery 1975, 455).

Like the Church of Ireland bishops in 1950, the Vatican took the view that the Catholic / Protestant divide had never been complete or final: they became 'separated from full communion', but there was always 'partial', albeit extremely attenuated, communion. There was a retreat from the position which regards the Roman Catholic Church as co-extensive with the Christian religion. It was made clear that Protestants are included in statements such as: 'the brethren divided from us also carry out many liturgical actions of *the Christian religion*' (author's italics, Flannery 1975, 455).

At present, the Roman Catholic Church and the Churches of the Anglican Communion, including the Church of Ireland, are quite clear that they recognise each other as Christians. Evidence of this is a continuing series of Agreed Statements on *Eucharistic Doctrine* (1971); *Ministry and Ordination* (1973); and *Authority in the Church* (1976). The official position of the Presbyterian Church in Ireland with regard to the Roman Catholic Church,

32

however, remains somewhat ambivalent. A report of the Doctrine Committee to the General Assembly in 1988, which was charged with answering the question 'do we regard each other as Christians?', admitted: 'some Presbyterians ... are reluctant to use the term Christian about the Roman Catholic Church' (Presbyterian Church 1988, 9-10). This report illustrates that while many Presbyterians see the ecumenical one-religion picture, many others still see the older opposite-religions picture.

Describing the 'ways of seeing' Catholic / Protestant relations as shifting paradigms (models or pictures) should not be misunderstood. The Roman Catholic Church and the Protestant Churches all believe in 'the one catholic church'. Therefore they are committed theologically to a one-religion paradigm of Christianity. This is an ideal which has remained unchanged since the time of Christ. In practice, however, and often very nearly in theory, both Catholics and Protestants since the Reformation have behaved as if they saw each other as belonging to opposite religions. Fundamentalists on both sides continue to aim mainly at safeguarding the Reformation (or Counter-Reformation) achievement. Ecumenical Protestants and Catholics aim to put the ideal of unity more closely into practice by behaving in their dealings with each other as if both belong to the same religion.

If the shift at the time of the Reformation to the opposite-religions paradigm was slow and painful, so has been the subsequent shift to the new one-religion paradigm. Murphy (1988) has identified shifts in self-perception by the Catholic community in Ireland every fifty years or so over the last two hundred and fifty years. For example, in the 1830s being a Catholic meant 'to regard Protestantism with the fundamentalist anti-heretical antipathy of two centuries earlier'; whereas in the 1880s 'it no longer necessarily included a virulent anti-Protestant element. In purely religious or evangelical terms, that particular battle was over and done with and, theologically speaking, Irish Catholicism now viewed its erstwhile adversary rather with condescending contempt than rancorous hostility' (Murphy 1988, 455).

Nevertheless, the sense of having ancestors who were persecuted for their faith remained an important part of the historical sense of identity of Irish Catholics. This is evident in de Valera's confessional constitution of 1937, which entrenched rather than weakened the opposite-religions paradigm. The central problem in drafting its religious clauses was how to strike a balance between the rights due to what de Valera believed to be the One True Church and the civil liberties which should be extended to other churches. Article 44 tried to have it both ways by recognising 'the special position of the Holy Catholic Apostolic and Roman Church as the guardian of faith professed by the great majority of the citizens' while the Church of Ireland, the Presbyterian Church in Ireland, the Methodist Church in Ireland, the Religious

Society of Friends in Ireland as well as the Jewish Congregations and other religious denominations existing in Ireland were simply 'recognised'. The balance of emphasis was still in favour of the opposite-religions paradigm.

In 1972, the balance tipped the other way when that clause of the Constitution was deleted. The ecumenical movement had made sufficient headway for the Roman Catholic Church in Ireland to be positively embarrassed by its 'special position'. This embarrassment was compounded by the reporting of the conflict in Northern Ireland in the media which was constantly emphasising the religious divide. The result was a critical reaction to traditional, dogmatic stances which were now seen as, partly at least, to blame for the conflict.

The Second Vatican Council had promoted three influential ideas: the primacy of conscience; the Church as 'the people of God'; and the need for a more 'Protestant' emphasis on Christ-centred and Scripture-based theology. These had combined to produce a climate in which the opposite-religions paradigm was no longer acceptable to many. By 1972, government ministers in Ireland were no longer proclaiming their willingness to submit to the ruling of the Catholic bishops (Whyte 1980, 232) but rather asserting that they would 'legislate for all the citizens in the whole public interest and that their religion is their own affair' (Murphy 1988, 138). The phrase 'the whole public interest' indicates a clear, secular (pluralist) commitment to the one-community paradigm.

Shifts in self-perception in the Protestant community in Ireland were not so regular but took place nevertheless. In the eighteenth century, Protestants had regarded themselves as constituting the Irish nation in much the same way as South African whites formerly perceived themselves to be the people of South Africa. The notion of a Protestant (Church of Ireland) nation died with the Act of Union in 1801 as did the notion of Presbyterian republicanism: 'the awareness of being Protestant had far less to do with religious belief and practice (apart from evangelical spurts and some spiritual renewal after disestablishment) than with a consciousness of being a loyal garrison under ever more pressing siege' (Murphy 1988, 136). Ever since, an important element of Protestant religious consciousness has been fear and distrust of Catholicism (rather than condescension), which tends to anchor it still within the opposite-religions paradigm.

Estimates of the progress made by the ecumenical movement vary. However, it is clear at least that the shift to the new one-religion paradigm is far from complete anywhere in the world. In 1992, the outgoing general secretary of the World Council of Churches, Dr Emilio Castro, deplored a Vatican statement on 'certain aspects of the Church as understood as Communion' which, he said, 'cast a chill over ecumenical efforts towards reconciliation'; presenting 'a vision of conversion interpreted as a simple return to Catholicism' (*The Tablet,* 5 September, 1112). Since then there has been little to report of warming in the 'ecumenical winter'. So far as the two test cases of ecumenical intent in Ireland are concerned, despite some progress, the issue of mixed-marriage is still contentious (Robinson, 1992). According to O'Connor, 'Church attitudes have become more politic on mixed marriage, maybe, but it's still dislike at the bottom, a reflection of what people want, as segregated housing is' (1993, 321). There is still no official co-operation between the Churches in the running of religiously integrated schools in Northern Ireland:

> It was clear that the main established Churches were not prepared to support the development of integrated education. The Committee regrets this. In the attitudes of the Churches we detected a feeling that separate systems of education gave a sense of security to *both main denominations*. Having some control over a system meant that *each community* need not fear encroachment by *the other side*. Indeed the view was expressed to us by some churchmen that education should develop within *the two communities* before one 'opened up' to the other (author's italics, British-Irish Inter-Parliamentary Body 1994, 5) .

Catholics and Protestants in Ireland, therefore, have been participating in the world-wide shift within Christianity from the Reformation / Counter-Reformation paradigm of opposite religions to the new ecumenical one-religion paradigm. In Ireland as a whole, the balance appears to have tipped in favour of inclusiveness, or sharing. In Northern Ireland, however, things seem much more evenly balanced. The paradigm shift seems poised at a critical point of transition, someway short of its critical mass. At present there is no strong sense of the inevitability of pluralist or ecumenical progress. The protracted conflict in Northern Ireland has probably sustained as much as it has challenged the opposite-communities, opposite-religions paradigm.

That is how people in Northern Ireland have come to be facing *The Choice* of Boyle and Hadden in religious terms: should Catholics and Protestants be one religion or opposite religions? The inter-connected story of how they have come to be facing the same choice in secular terms (should Catholics/Nationalists and Protestants/Unionists be one community or opposite communities?) has been well documented by experts on the political, economic and social (non-religious) aspects of both the external and internal conflict paradigms. What is of key importance is how the various opposite-communities stories (political, economic and social) and the opposite-religions stories (the Catholic / Protestant story and, to a lesser extent, the

Protestant / Non-Conformist story) are inter-connected as sub-plots of the epic conflict.

Criteria for making *The Choice*

In order to choose rationally rather than instinctively or emotionally, people in Northern Ireland need to understand the historical development of the core choice which faces them. They also need to understand the moral criteria (political and religious) which apply. There is therefore little prospect of people making The Choice rationally until Whyte's challenge has been met satisfactorily.

In order to meet Whyte's challenge, the major task of the new paradigm of conflict interpretation (synthesising the merits of the dominant internal conflict paradigm and the older external conflict paradigm) is twofold: first, to identify the dominant theme; and second, to explain convincingly how the other themes relate to it. Boyle and Hadden have cut through the interminable arguing of the critics and identified separation and sharing as the dominant, all-pervasive theme. This offers a sound basis for an agreed interpretation of the conflict.

However, some like Darby, Dunn and Hayes have argued either that there is no dominant theme to the conflict or, if there is, it is so inextricably woven into the complexity of sub-themes that its nature is indeterminable. If they were correct, depressing consequences would follow. A sound rational or ethical basis for making The Choice would never be attainable. We should be condemned to the intractability of conflict interpretation in perpetuity. If on the other hand (as Boyle and Hadden argue) there is a dominant theme to the conflict, and if the question of its fundamental nature or character (religious, political, economic, psychological etc) can be determined, then a sound rational or ethical or moral basis for making the core choice is attainable.

Leaving further consideration of this question aside for the moment, we may conclude that, as long as the outcome of the Northern Ireland conflict remains in serious doubt, many Catholics and Protestants will prefer to stick with the traditional core choice and go on still seeing themselves as opposite communities and opposite religions. At the same time, many will also be attracted to the picture of one community and one religion. This raises the question of how people in Northern Ireland have managed to stay poised precariously for so long between the alternatives of the core choice. What has inhibited them from making a decisive choice one way or the other? Might there be good reason for not choosing decisively? The next chapter turns to these issues.

3 Interpreting 'choice modulation'

There is a connection between Northern Ireland's state of poise between the alternatives of Boyle and Hadden's *Choice* (separation or sharing) and the intractability of its conflict. It can be found in the phenomenon of 'choice modulation', which is the way people modulate or switch, more or less unselfconsciously, between the alternatives of separation and sharing.

If intractable violent conflicts are those which resist repeated attempts at their resolution, peaceful or otherwise, the most intractable of all are those upon whose nature neither the interested parties nor disinterested observers can agree. Intractability of this kind, however, is not to be confused with inexplicability. The theoretically intractable is the explicable awaiting a breakthrough; insight into what is still being overlooked.

Of course, the act of explaining the intractable in theory does not make it less so in practice, but it may help the actors eventually to make it more tractable. What has been overlooked is the phenomenon of 'choice modulation', about which can be developed a theory of the Northern Ireland conflict's intractability.

Intractability Theory

In the case of Northern Ireland, the most obvious starting point for a theory of the conflict's intractability is the 'meta-conflict about the conflict'. It seems reasonable to suppose that the conflict about the conflict must be derived in some way from the intractable nature of the conflict itself. The first step, therefore, is to account for the meta-conflict about the conflict. It seems probable that a successful theory will be centred on the role of religion since, as Whyte showed, this is the most controversial issue of interpretation.

In order to explain why the issue of the role of religion in particular is still intractable, suppose that something has been overlooked; that there exists some kind of phenomenon, as yet undetected, whose effect is to inhibit researchers and commentators from reaching consensus about the role of religion and also, perhaps, consensus on the nature of the conflict itself. Assuming such a phenomenon or mechanism, what are its distinctive features most likely to be and where is it most likely to be found?

On the principle that it is often the most obvious things which are the hardest to see, suppose that this hypothetical mechanism is obvious but has so far escaped critical identification and analysis because it is so embedded in the way of life of people in Northern Ireland that it is taken for granted.

Further suppose that this mechanism has both positive and negative social functions related to the conflict which balance out each other. It has remained undetected because its overall effect is neutral. On the one hand, it helps people subconsciously (otherwise they would be aware of it) to 'cope' with the conflict. On the other hand, this benefit is offset by a cost: the subconscious coping strategy also has the effect of embedding the conflict more deeply. This hypothetical mechanism, therefore, must be ambiguous in character: while helping to make the conflict tolerable it prolongs it.

Finally, suppose that, in order to have such a massive effect, this coping strategy must be simple, available to all and used to a greater or lesser extent by all, young and old alike. It is under everyone's nose. Therefore, once pointed out, it should seem (infuriatingly) obvious.

If these are sensible criteria to apply in the search for a phenomenon or mechanism which may be responsible for the intractability of the role of religion in the Northern Ireland conflict, can a coping strategy be found which meets them?

A coping strategy: 'choice modulation'

The argument of the previous chapter, based on the work of Boyle and Hadden, suggests that the best place to search for such a coping strategy may be at the point of balance between the alternatives of the core choice. There such a coping strategy can be found at work. The question is how have people in Northern Ireland managed to cope for so long in such a precarious position, as a society which has not opted decisively for either the one-community, one-religion choice, or the opposite-communities, opposite-religions choice? The answer seems to be that they have done so by choosing (subconsciously) both alternatives. This coping strategy can be named as 'paradigm modulation' or 'choice modulation'.

38

Paradigm modulation is a pronounced feature in the critical transition phase of paradigm shift from the old Reformation / Counter-Reformation opposite-religions, opposite-communities paradigm to the new pluralist and ecumenical one-community, one-religion paradigm. As shown in Chapter 2, this paradigm shift is more or less complete in most of western Europe, but Northern Ireland is a place apart because there the shift is still in the critical transition phase. (It may be helpful here to think of the analagous process by which Evolution has come to displace Creationism as the dominant paradigm of human origins.)

During this critical intermediate phase, only a minority remains unequivocally committed to the established opposite-religions, opposite-communities paradigm and only a minority had yet become committed to the emerging one-community, one-religion paradigm. The majority are uncertain, confused, or uncommitted, in the manner of floating voters. They switch or, more accurately, they modulate between the opposite-religions, opposite-communities paradigm and the one-community, one-religion paradigm, according to changing social circumstances.

In certain situations the traditional paradigm (picture or choice) will seem more appropriate; in others the more progressive, emerging paradigm will seem more appropriate. 'Modulating' (hence 'paradigm modulation') is more accurate than 'switching' because it describes a change in mentality (mode of thought or mind-set) which takes place in the individual sub-consciously, enabling the possibility of thinking, as it were, in two different keys without any awareness of discord.

The most striking indication that Northern Ireland is still in the critical phase of transition, where paradigm modulation is the norm, is the peculiar way in which Catholics and Protestants speak of each other as belonging to 'a different religion' or, more remarkably, 'the opposite religion'. This is a usage not still found generally amongst Catholics and Protestants elsewhere in western Europe.

Examples of paradigm ambiguity

A teacher in a letter of application for a post in an integrated school in 1994 wrote: 'I aspire to teach in an environment where I may help to foster good relations between pupils of *our two main religions* in Northern Ireland'. Another applicant the same year wrote: 'I have felt the importance of bringing *the different religions* together ... I train and coach two netball teams. We travel and play *teams of different religions*'. A survey for Ulster Television, called *Whither Northern Ireland?*, asked parents whether the following would be a factor influencing their choice of school: 'an opportunity for your child to mix with children of *the opposite religion*' (author's italics, 1990, 13).

The context in each case made clear that it was Catholicism and Protestantism which were being thought of as different religions, not Christianity and one of the other world religions, as in the following newspaper headline: 'TWO RELIGIONS FORGE ONE PEACE. The Vatican and Israel signed their historic accord last week' (*Catholic Herald* 14/1/94). That headline contrasts with the following one: 'RELIGIONS IN EQUAL NUMBERS IN 50 YEARS. Protestants and Catholics will be equal in number in Northern Ireland in 50 years time according to leading statistician Edgar Jardine ...' (*Belfast Telegraph* 6/5/94, quoting from a paper called significantly *Two Communities: Population Changes*).

The ambiguity of 'religion'

So deeply embedded is the ambiguous use of 'religion' in Northern Ireland that even a researcher as aware of the importance of religion as Hickey has helped perpetuate it. In the questionnaire from which much of the data for his ground-breaking book was taken, he asked for responses to statements such as: 'I would be quite happy if someone of *the other religion* moved in next door' (Hickey 1984, 132). Similarly, the survey *Northern Ireland Social Attitudes* asked questions such as 'How many of your neighbours would you say are *the same religion* as you?' (Stringer and Robinson 1991, 13).

Researchers seem to feel constrained to use 'religion' in this special Northern Ireland sense when investigating inter-community relationships in order to focus their respondents' attention exclusively on the Catholic / Protestant divide. To use the more strictly correct (but equally ambiguous) 'religious denomination' (which also can refer to either a sub-set of Christianity or to a world religion like Islam) would cause an awkward ambiguity. It would bring divisions between different Protestant groups, as well as the Catholic / Protestant divide, within the scope of the question.

Usually, it is clear from the context which of the two meanings of religion is intended. Sometimes, however, it is not. Take, for example, the following:

> There are players of *different religions* who play for Northern Ireland (*Belfast News Letter*, 4/4/90).
>
> Employers must ensure people of *different religions* are treated with parity when employment-related decisions are taken, the Fair Employment Commission said today (*Belfast Telegraph* 6/12/94)
>
> I valued the stress laid on reaching out to people of *other religions*. It wasn't known as ecumenism in those days ... (David Bleakley, *Belfast Telegraph* 17/4/95).

In these examples it is not unequivocally clear that the intention is to distinguish only between Catholicism and Protestantism. The next pair of examples are certainly ambiguous:

> You will be more than welcome to attend any of the events in a chaplaincy which is not *your own religion* (*Queen's University Student Handbook*, 1989-90, 52).
>
> A copy of St Patrick's Parochial Hall from Portaferry is to be built at the other end of [the Ulster Folk and Transport Museum, Cultra]. It will house an exhibition on *the religions* of Ireland (*Irish News*, 4/4/90).

These examples are ambiguous because the reader may well know that Queen's University does have a Jewish chaplaincy and the Ulster Folk Museum does intend to include non-Christian religions in its exhibition, so the distinction between Christianity and other world religions could also be intended as well as the Catholic / Protestant distinction.

In the next group of examples, it is not clear whether religion means: (a) one of the main world religions; (b) either Catholicism or Protestantism as a whole; (c) one of the various denominations within Protestantism; or (d) some combination of these.

> More than 80 per cent of those aged under 30 share *the same religion* as most of all their friends (*Irish News* 13/6/92, reporting on the publication of Mapstone, R., *Attitudes of Police in a Divided Society*).
>
> Lots of studies have shown that students, especially those who remain at home, continue to socialise and mix with people of *the same religion* (Peter O'Neill, NUS/USI spokesperson, *Belfast Telegraph* 16/3/92).
>
> On some of the videos, the young people are filmed attending Church and meeting people of *a different religion or denomination* (*Belfast Telegraph* 16/10/89, reporting on the publication of a video for schools by *Veritas*).

Sometimes it is quite clear from the context that religion does mean one of the Protestant denominations. In the following case it means Presbyterian:

> An outing to Rosemary Presbyterian Church introduced 130 Catholic and Protestant GCSE pupils to the traditions of *Ulster's major religion* (*Times Educational Supplement* 25/11/88).

However, forms such as 'the Presbyterian religion', 'the Church of Ireland religion' or 'the Methodist religion' are rare in Northern Ireland because they are inhibited by the more common form, 'the Protestant religion'. A speaker would not feel comfortable saying a sentence such as 'The Presbyterian religion is different from the Church of Ireland religion but both belong to the Protestant religion'. It sounds absurd because the first part seems to contradict the second.

In the next pair of examples, the context makes plain that the 'religions' in question are Catholicism and Protestantism:

> Cardinal Daly said visits by church leaders to *communities of different religions* would 'depend on the willingness of the local clergy and local communities to receive us' (*Irish News* 31/10/91).
>
> John Bruton, leader of Fine Gael, said 'However it's not the same as actually sharing the same classroom with somebody of *a different religion*' (*Belfast Telegraph* 10/6/92, commenting on the Education for Mutual Understanding programme in Northern Ireland).

In the next group 'both religions' means unambiguously either Catholicism or Protestantism as a whole:

> Neighbours of *both religions* today said 'Good Samaritan' Mr Murray, who had all his belongings packed, reluctantly postponed the move for several weeks (*Belfast Telegraph* 8/7/92, reporting on Mr Murray's murder).
>
> The lawyer argued that the school's submission that its reservation of places for top quality students was vital to its ability to attract a broad academic mix of *both religions* was incorrect (*Belfast Telegraph* 2/4/92, reporting on a judicial review sought by an integrated school).
>
> Residents from *both religions* organised a swift campaign against the proposal, claiming the centre would merely become a flashpoint for sectarian violence (*Belfast Telegraph* 18/4/95).

In all the examples above, 'religion' is used in a neutral sense. No value judgement of superiority or inferiority is implied. On occasions, however, the context can make clear that higher status is being ascribed to one 'religion', so implying the lower status of 'anti-religion' or 'false religion' to the other(s):

> The Orangeman must ... love, uphold and defend *the Protestant religion* (*Junior Orangeman's Catechism*, quoted in Hickey 1984, 78).
>
> As *the Catholic religion* is *the only true religion*, it is an insult to put it on the same level as *other religions* (letter to the *Irish News* 2/5/90).
>
> I long that God will send a mighty revival of *true religion* to these shores once again (Hazlett-Lynch 1990, 55).

This usage, which implies that Catholics and Protestants belong to opposite religions, is an indication of the continuing strength of the opposite-religions paradigm. Only within that paradigm or framework of thought can headlines such as the following be properly understood:

HOLY 'SNUB' TO MAYOR DEFENDED.
The Catholic Bishop of Limerick, Jeremiah Newman, has defended his decision not to allow the City's Mayor, a member of the Church of Ireland, to read the lesson at Mass' (*Belfast Telegraph*, 16/3/94).

Conversely, the context may make it clear that 'religion' means 'the Christian religion' (Christianity) and that Christianity includes within it both Protestantism and Catholicism. In other words, the meaning is to be understood within the framework of the one-religion paradigm. In such cases, the context may imply no more than the dispassionate, scientific view of the student of world religions; or it may also imply commitment to the ecumenical ideal of Christian unity. Both senses, perhaps, are intended by the following editorial reference to: 'the rights and wrongs of *different brands of the Christian religion*' (*Belfast Telegraph* 21/9/87).

The ambiguity of 'community'

The phrase 'communities of different religions' (cited above) suggests that the concepts of religion and community are connected in an important way in Northern Ireland. So also does the review headline 'RELIGIONS IN EQUAL NUMBERS IN 50 YEARS' for the book by Jardine called *Two Communities: population changes*. The connection between religion and community is evident in the similarly ambiguous ways in which they are commonly used.

The ambiguity of community in 'community relations' has already been referred to in Chapter 1. The Northern Ireland Community Relations Council intends the meaning to be relations within one community but others may read relations between 'opposite communities', as in this headline:

DIVIDED COMMUNITY - MURDERS ARE A SYMPTOM OF
POLARISED POLITICS.
The killing of a mother of two in the Ormeau district and the wounding of a father and his handicapped son in North Belfast are equally barbarous acts which leave *both communities* appalled ... Like it or not, the effect of the prolonged debate ... has been to divide Northern Ireland more decisively into *two opposing camps* (*Belfast Telegraph*, 15/4/94).

The description is of one 'divided community' community but the divide is now seen as complete. Effectively, the picture is of one community no longer; it has become two communities in 'opposing camps'. The correspondence with the opposite-religions picture is almost exact: 'both religions' could be substituted comfortably for 'both communities' in this context. At times of maximum 'community tension' such as this, the fear is that 'the community divide', which for years has been threatening to split apart completely, may at last have done so.

The Northern Ireland conflict may be 'relatively restrained' compared with others in the world but the possibility of complete community breakdown remains immanent and has periodically been perceived as imminent. Another point of maximum tension was reached as recently as July 1995 when a Belfast City councillor called on the RUC to 'swamp the streets' in order to stem 'spiralling sectarian violence in North Belfast'. He claimed that Protestants were 'facing a vicious campaign of ethnic cleansing' (*Belfast Telegraph* 17/7/95). In August, Orange Order Assistant Grand Master, Jeffrey Donaldson, claimed that the recent attacks on Orange halls were 'part of an ethnic cleansing campaign against Protestants' (*Belfast Telegraph* 17/8/95).

To counter this abiding fear of community disintegration, community leaders frequently stress the oneness of the community. In the North Belfast case just cited, for example, an RUC Chief Inspector called for co-operation from 'people on both sides of the community'.

More pointedly, John Robb, leader of the *New Ireland Group*, wrote to the newspapers in 1994 to urge the congratulation of 'Bishop Samuel Poyntz, who stated on Radio on April 28 that we are indeed *one community* even though it is composed of *different people* embracing a number of *overlapping traditions*' (*Belfast Telegraph* 6/5/94).

However, in spite of the bishop's insistence on the oneness of the community, shortly afterwards he spoke more from the perspective of the opposite-communities, or opposite-religions paradigm when he called on the Government to provide 'a body or bodies which would protect the ethos of those controlled schools which on the whole serve the educational needs of the Protestant (transferor) Church members' (*News Letter* 19/5/94). In urging the cause of segregated schools, Bishop Poyntz was echoing a recent statement by Archbishop Eames reported under the headline:

DON'T INTERFERE WITH OUR SCHOOLS MINISTERS WARNED
The future of our schools, as Church of Ireland schools [in the Republic of Ireland], must be guaranteed so as to preserve the choice that Church of Ireland parents currently have to send their children to schools which reflect *their tradition and outlook*' (author's italics, *Belfast Telegraph*, 17/5/94).

In response, Ian Paisley jun. accused the churches of an 'apartheid mentality' over education (*Belfast Telegraph* 20/5/95).

This is a good illustration of paradigm modulation, which amounts to having it both ways without being aware of the contradiction. On the one hand we can insist on the oneness of our religion and our community and on the other insist on segregated education for our opposite religions and communities.

Paradigm modulation is not restricted to community leaders. It is a part of everyday discourse. Normally it is unobtrusive and passes unremarked. Occasionally, as the following anecdote illustrates, a discord is heard:

> Two friends in conversation agreed that 'integrated education is the way forward for this place'. Later, they overheard a parish priest asking a boy which secondary school he would be going to. The boy named an integrated school. 'Well I hope you don't stop serving on the altar and you don't lose your religion', the priest replied. 'My sentiments exactly, Father', said one of the friends. 'You two-faced so and so', said the other.

This is not to say that paradigm modulation necessarily impugns the integrity of any individual. Usually it takes place effortlessly, without self-awareness, and probably all are subject to it to some degree. It may take a strong effort of introspection, but even those most committed to seeing Catholics and Protestants as one community and one religion may recognise in themselves the atavistic attraction of the opposite-communities, opposite-religions picture, especially at times of heightened community tension. This has been called 'church hall syndrome'. Most adults in Northern Ireland have probably had thoughts, spoken or unspoken, about what they would do if the conflict got too bad. If the worst came to the worst, most would know instinctively in which sort of church hall in what sort of area they would feel safer. In the event, everyone would know which of the opposite communities they would be perceived as belonging to.

Conversely, although those most committed to seeing Catholics and Protestants as opposite religions may not be attracted at all by the one-religion paradigm, they are more likely than not to be attracted to the one-community paradigm. Few, if any, find difficulty with talk of 'the wider community' or 'the whole community' or 'the entire community'. This idea of one community transcends the divide between the Catholic/Nationalist community and the Protestant/Unionist community. Symptomatically, however, agreeing on a name for it (Northern Ireland, the North of Ireland, Ulster, the Province, the Six Counties) is a difficulty.

Modulation between paradigms seems to be a necessary part of discourse in Northern Ireland. For example, the editorial line of the *Belfast Telegraph* has been to emphasise the oneness of the community. This is indicated by the paper's preference for expressions such as 'the two sides (or sections/ghettoes/traditions/cultures) of the community', rather than 'the two communities'. But 'the two communities' form is not always avoidable. The editorial 'Portadown Showdown' (10/7/95) illustrates [author's italics] how a person may modulate imperceptibly from 'one community' to 'two communities':

> Ten months after the terrorist ceasefires which brought high hopes of a permanent end to violence, Northern Ireland's peace process is firmly logjammed. Rather than providing a springboard for future reconciliation and mutual acceptance, peace has laid bare the fundamental fractures in *this community*.
>
> Even in the darkest days of the Troubles, there was a common interest which spanned *the two traditions in the province*. Terrorism was the common enemy causing equal anguish to *all sides*. Although the paramilitaries drove people into *ghettoes*, there was a mutual desire on the part of *the majority of Ulster people* to see the violence ended.
>
> The ceasefires did not bring peace ... It needs people to find a formula for living together, for respecting *each other's traditions and cultures ...*
>
> Northern Ireland's marching season is the time when the raw nerves of *the community* are exposed most blatantly ...
>
> The stand-off between Orange Order members and police in Portadown is not just about a march route. It is about *one community* saying that compromise has gone far enough ...
>
> The peace process is at a very fragile juncture. It is easy to exhort *the two communities* towards compromise, but it is difficult to put those words into practice. A fearful *unionist community* faced with a determined and a demanding *nationalist community* is in no mood to make political concessions.

It is worth noting that in this context the communities are called Unionist and Nationalist, rather than Protestant and Catholic. This is because the political labels are usually preferred when the context is one which emphasises the political process, as in this case. The religious labels tend to be preferred (in contexts not obviously religious) when the emphasis is on social or economic behaviour, as distinct from the political behaviour, as, for example, in the context of anonymous sectarian violence or discrimination in employment.

Whyte's summative interpretation of the conflict placed segregated education and segregated marriage centre stage as the two factors which do most to divide Protestants as a whole from Catholics as a whole (1991, 48). It is not accidental, therefore, that in everyday life paradigm tension is likely to be strongest (and paradigm modulation most evident) whenever it comes to choice of school or choice of marriage partner. While many prefer the one-community, one-religion paradigm when they tell opinion pollsters that they are in favour of integrated education and have no objections to mixed marriage or to having neighbours of 'the opposite religion', it may be a different story when it comes to selecting a school for their own children or approving their choice of marriage partner, or when the religious balance of the street becomes unfavourable. Then they may modulate to the opposite-communities, opposite-religions paradigm.

Segregated education and segregated marriage are the institutions through which the opposite-religions paradigm is most fundamentally realised in society. When it is recalled that the role of the churches is central in regulating the mechanisms of both segregated education and segregated marriage, the view is inescapable that religion must have a central role in the conflict, notwithstanding other factors which limit the power and influence of the Churches (such as the uneven outreach of the Churches, their weakness in working class areas, the commitment of some Church leaders to ecumenism, and the subdivision of Churches into smaller groupings).

The extent to which the Northern Ireland conflict is religious can be judged by asking on what grounds endogamy (segregated marriage) and segregated education are primarily justified - political, economic, cultural, social or religious grounds? The answer must be religious because the language used to justify them is fundamentally religious in character and the institutions which regulate them are religious.

However, to say that the conflict is religious without careful qualification is to invite misunderstanding, as the reception of the Hickey/Bruce analysis (discussed in Chapter 1) illustrates. The conflict may be said to be fundamentally religious in the sense that segregated marriage and segregated education, which are religious rather than political or economic or ethnic imperatives, embody the deep structure of the conflict. They ensure that the conflict is protracted by maintaining mutual ignorance and fostering the growth of malignant stereotypes in a situation where other reasons for conflict exist (cf Whyte 1990, 27-28). This is how religion and community are inter-related. The opposition of religions (Catholicism and Protestantism) constitutes the core or deep structure of the opposite-communities paradigm.

The deep structure of core choice modulation

The concept of 'deep structure' is borrowed from Chomsky (1980). The essential feature of a deep structure is that, although simple in itself, it is capable of generating complexity. The intractability of the conflict about what the conflict is about now becomes explicable. It is the sheer complexity of the conflict's surface structures (in all their political, economic, social, psychological, artistic, linguistic and religious aspects), which continues to frustrate consensus about the nature of the Northern Ireland conflict. Resolution of the controversy about the complexity into a consensus explanation or interpretation lies not in demonstrating the importance of one dimension of the conflict over the rest. Neither does it lie in ever more detailed studies of regional variation in all possible dimensions of the conflict, or futher study of comparable conflicts, valuable though these may be. Rather, it lies in understanding how the deep structure which generates the complexity of the conflict works.

The Northern Ireland conflict is 'religious' in the heavily qualified sense that religious is probably the word which best describes the origin and character of its core mechanism or deep structure. Circumstances require each individual either to actively make or passively accept a core choice about the nature of the divide between Protestants and Catholics. Collectively and cumulatively, these active and passive choices have had, and continue to have, far-reaching political, economic and social consequences, regardless of whether or not individuals are religious believers.

Most people in Northern Ireland in their social life (even atheists as the well-known and symptomatic joke has it) are perceived to be either Catholic or Protestant. Individually, their core choice is between preferring to believe that Catholics and Protestants are fundamentally similar to each other or that they are fundamentally different from each other. Choosing the first way helps to consolidate the one-community, one-religion paradigm. Choosing the second way helps to consolidate the opposite-communities, opposite-religions paradigm. To a greater or lesser extent, because of the particular circumstances of Northern Ireland (arising from its particular historical development), the choice is intolerably stark for virtually everyone. Paradigm modulation is the coping strategy for making the choice tolerable by hiding it.

At the same time, however, paradigm modulation compounds the intractability of the conflict. It can only work if it is so deeply embedded in social discourse as to be hidden from view. At present it functions as a subconscious process, an instinctively learned, unquestioned survival mechanism. Were people to become aware of it, some would insist on articulating it as a moral issue. Some would name it as 'doublethink' or hypocrisy and begin resisting its temptation. In this way it would start to lose its effectiveness. The longer paradigm modulation stays hidden, the longer it retains its effectiveness. But the conflict becomes correspondingly more protracted and intractable.

48

Staying hidden

How has paradigm modulation contrived to remain hidden? Why are those who are committed to seeing Catholics and Protestants as one religion normally prepared to accept, without demur, the assertion that they belong to different or opposite religions? Why has there been no campaign against this 'political incorrectness'? The answer must be that the Catholic / Protestant divide in reality is so great that different or opposite religions has to be tolerated as a description of it. It cannot easily be gainsaid. Objection would only be taken if it was clear from the context that a theological point was being made with the intention to deny that Protestants, or Catholics, are 'true' Christians. Such cases in social discourse are comparatively rare.

Conversely, why do those who are committed to seeing Catholics and Protestants as belonging to opposite religions not object when it is asserted that they are both Christian? Provided that the assertion is made from a neutral or secular perspective (as most frequently it tends to be), there is no difficulty. Because of some fundamental similarities (belief in Jesus Christ, use of the Bible etc), it is understandable and acceptable that outside observers should regard Catholics and Protestants as members of the same religion. Objection, however, would be taken if it was clear that a theological point was being made and that the exclusive truth claims of Protestantism or Catholicism (less likely since Vatican II) were being challenged. Again, such cases are comparatively rare.

The same holds good for the use of community, and even more so because there is no case for theological objection to talk of 'the Protestant community' or 'the Catholic community'. The semantic range of community is somewhat wider than that of religion. It is possible to talk about members of 'the Catholic community' and 'the Protestant community' belonging to 'the one community' of Northern Ireland. However, it is not so possible to be logically consistent and speak meaningfully of people who belong to different or opposite religions as simultaneously belonging to the same religion. The idea of a community consisting of two opposing communities is comprehensible. The idea of a religion consisting of two opposing religions is not. This becomes evident when the idea is put this way: 'he belongs to the opposite religion but he belongs to the same religion as I do'. Such a sentence occurs rarely, if ever, because it sounds absurd or wantonly paradoxical. Yet it is common for both parts of the sentence to be stated separately. This is the crux. The two parts signify the mutually exclusive paradigms of religion between which most people in Northern Ireland are able to switch or modulate, apparently unselfconsciously.

Modulating like this is tolerated unquestioningly because the issue rarely, if ever, arises. A vicious circle operates to prevent it from being articulated. Northern Ireland is still balanced precariously in the critical transition phase of a world-wide paradigm shift in Christianity. There is no clear consensus yet (no definitive core choice) in favour of the one-community, one-religion paradigm. Accordingly, the words community and religion in common usage are deeply ambiguous. This suits all concerned, especially those (possibly the majority) who are undecided, the modulators or 'floating voters'. Continuing lack of consensus, or avoidance of making the choice, entrenches the ambiguous use of community and religion. The more deeply it becomes entrenched, the less people are aware of it. The less aware of it they become, the less likely it is that the ambiguity will be noticed, let alone articulated. One effect of the hidden ambiguity is to facilitate good community relations. The other is to inhibit discourse on the nature of the conflict, as this pairing of exactly contemporaneous extracts illustrates:

> *The two communities* have drifted apart. They have *different religions*, go to different schools, play different games and are exposed to completely different influences. They do not understand each other because they seldom come into contact with each other (editorial, *Irish News* 7/11/90).

> The Institution said the proposals, currently under consideration, 'may exemplify *a common religion* but it will most certainly not be Christian' (report of an attack on plans for a core syllabus in Religious Education for both Protestant and Roman Catholic pupils by the Independent Orange Order, *Belfast Telegraph* 7/11/90).

On the face of it, the comments of both the *Irish News* and the *Independent Orange Order* are set in the framework of the opposite-religions paradigm. The context makes quite plain that the *Independent Orange Order* is fully committed to seeing opposite religions. The immediate context of the *Irish News* comment is ambiguous. The wider context, however, reveals that the paper is in fact fully committed to the one-community, one-religion way of seeing things. It expresses support for the then newly appointed Archbishop Daly in his 'work for reconciliation to build bridges and to champion the cause of church unity'.

The unexamined ambiguity of community and religion inhibits discourse also at the academic level. For example, at a conference in 1991, the President of the Conference of Major Religious Superiors, Sister Helena Donoghue, in drawing attention to the difficulty of defining 'religion', demonstrated unwittingly the baneful effect of its ambiguity:

A 'religion' as it is commonly understood, relates very often to a specific church or denomination, a gathering of people with common values and common patterns of worship, common scriptures and who give expression to these both externally and publicly i.e. *the Catholic, the Anglican, the Methodist, the Jewish, the Islamic **religions*** (Longley 1991, 148).

If this is indeed how religion is commonly understood, then the impression must be widespread that the divisions between Christians (Catholics, Anglicans, and Methodists) are as deep and as theologically significant as those between Christians, Jews, and Muslims. This is not so much a case of paradigm modulation as paradigm confusion. The way in which another speaker at the same conference, Thomas Kilroy, used religion illustrates the effect of the confusion:

> What gives all these conflicts their dark potency is the claim of the Elect, the Chosen People, the One, True Faith, in other words the claim of unique access to divine truth. This claim on one side is intolerable to the other since if it were true it would immediately undermine the other faith. One cannot exaggerate the rage and terror which such absolutism inspires, nor the barbarity which it is capable of causing (Longley 1991, 137).

Kilroy then proceeded to talk about *'the Christian religions'* (138). This has to be considered as an abuse of language. Implying, even if not deliberately, that the various Christian denominations are equivalent to other world religions makes difficult, if not impossible, proportionate comparison of Christianity with other world religions (which have similar internal divisions of their own).

The ambiguity of religion has remained hidden. I am aware of no specific call in the literature for clarification of the meaning of religion. Given its unexamined ambiguity and the consequent scope for misunderstanding and suspicion in discourse, it should not be surprising that the role of religion in the conflict has proved so controversial.

The closest approach to a call for clarification of the meaning of religion was made by Professor Ron McAllister at a conference open forum in 1990:

> I also wonder about the distinction between word 'the Church' and 'the Churches'. I wonder what is in people's heads when they use a word like 'the Church'. Then we say the Church is the people of God but exactly who make up the Church and what is the distinction between the Church and the Churches? I am listening very much as an outsider trying to understand what people in Northern Ireland are thinking about when they

are using *very common, very everyday terms that one wouldn't ordinarily ask about* (Lee 1990, 74).

It is probably indicative of the entrenched nature of the ambiguity of religion and community that McAllister's question received no recorded answer. What he had identified as important was the ambiguity of 'church' in common discourse. This ambiguity is connected with those of 'religion' and 'community'. 'The Church' (the people of God) is another way of signifying the one-community, one-religion paradigm; 'the Churches' (Catholic and Protestant) can be another way of signifying the opposite-communities, opposite-religions paradigm. Church, community, religion; these are 'the very common, very everyday terms that one doesn't ordinarily ask about'. They are so basic that people are generally predisposed to leave them unexamined.

Some readers may recognise that they get annoyed, infuriated even, at the 'careless' way in which religion (or community or church) is used in Northern Ireland. It is a fair bet, nevertheless, that any who have tried to protest will usually have been met with indifference from their interlocutor or an accusation of hairsplitting. In this way the key ambiguities remain undisturbed and for good reason. To disturb them would be to disturb so much else, not least the delicate balance which sustains the integrity of society or 'the wider community' in Northern Ireland. Paradoxically, the balance is achieved by virtually everyone modulating gracefully (and so unobtrusively) between the one-community or one-church, one-religion vision and the opposite-communities or opposite-churches, opposite-religions vision of how things are or should be.

Having it both ways

One may recognise within oneself the desire to choose both sides of the ambiguity simultaneously. I, a Catholic Nationalist (or Protestant Unionist), wish to regard you, a Protestant Unionist (Catholic Nationalist), as my fellow citizen, or as my fellow Christian. At the same time, however, I must believe that my political or religious group is better than yours (for if it were not, I would neither wish to belong to it nor would I tolerate our separation). How can I have it both ways?

As happens normally in western Europe, both preferences may be accommodated within limits. Provided that two groups perceive their similarities to be fundamentally greater than their differences, there can be polite agreement between them to differ whenever necessary. There is tension but it is tolerable and it may even be creative. The tension only becomes destructive when distinct groups perceive the differences between them to be fundamentally greater than the similarities between them, so that, to a greater or lesser extent, each feels obliged to deny validity to the other in order to protect its own identity. Normally in Northern Ireland, this denial of validity goes to the extent of preferring segregated education and segregated marriage. But, from time to time, it may go further. Certainly, before 1969 it went further in education and marriage and also in politics, housing, employment and sport.

The need to confer validity on each other's group (in order to maintain 'the one/wider/whole/entire community' with all its social and economic benefits) is counter-balanced. There is also the need to deny validity (in order to maintain the political, economic or religious integrity of 'the different/other/separate/opposite communities'). The tension between the two needs accounts for the dynamic of paradigm modulation. Both needs must be held in balance. The consequences of failing to do so (breakdown of civil order or loss of political or religious identity) are unacceptable to most. Paradigm modulation is the coping strategy evolved for keeping a more or less even balance between the two. Making the core choice definitively, therefore, is avoided purposefully. The reward is a 'relatively restrained' conflict through which most manage to lead what they perceive to be 'normal' lives. The cost, however, is a conflict which is both protracted and intractable.

Ambiguity of the seventh type

Empson (1930) classified seven types of ambiguity. The ambiguities of 'community' and 'religion', between which people in Northern Ireland modulate, conform to the seventh type of 'full contradiction' or 'opposites'. As Empson pointed out, 'the contradiction must somehow form a larger unity if the final effect is to be satisfying' (1995, 226). The alternatives of the core choice in Northern Ireland are opposites: one community or opposite communities, one religion or opposite religions? The unity of these ambiguities is maintained by modulation. The final effect is satisfying to the extent that the precarious point of balance between the alternatives of the core choice is preserved.

Learning to modulate instinctively

How, then, is the apparently instinctive skill of paradigm modulation transmitted from one generation to the next? Virtually all schoolchildren in

Northern Ireland are enculturated into 'the Northern Ireland community'. Simultaneously, they are enculturated into either the Protestant community or the Catholic community. They receive influential signals that Catholics and Protestants are fundamentally different from each other (that is to say, their community prefers the opposite-communities, opposite-religions paradigm). They are sent to separate schools and learn that inter-marriage with the 'other side' is not normally acceptable. This is religious belief at its most primitive level.

In order to avoid the kind of misunderstanding which bedevils discussion of the role of religion in Northern Ireland, it might be better to call it 'proto-religious', meaning a fundamental belief which is a necessary condition for the subsequent development of religious (and political) identity within either the Protestant or the Catholic community. It is 'proto-religous' in that, going back to this embryonic stage, the religious and political aspects of identity are not yet differentiated from each other. Proto-religious identity is prior to both religious identity and political identity proper. Proper religious identity is prior to political identity because children are normally initiated into the churches of their parents before they are initiated into their poltical parties.

By the time they begin to assert their religious and political identities, virtually all schoolchildren will have been through the stage of acquiring a proto-religious, and hence a proto-political, identity. Some will be in the process of acquiring proper religious identities (becoming full (adult) members of their religious community). Some of these, but not all, will also be acquiring proper political identities (which may or may not involve joining a political party). Others will be acquiring proper political identities but without becoming full church members. Others again will not be developing either proper religious or political identities. The development of their identity will remain arrested at the proto-religious stage but at least they will know what they are not and hence what they are, either Protestant or Catholic.

In short, religious labels are prior to political labels. The catch-all question of the gang of youths in the town park to the strange child is normally 'What religion are you?' - an inquiry that cannot be considered properly religious or political.

In a sense it is irrelevant whether or not individuals proceed beyond this embryonic or 'proto-religious' stage and go on to develop a properly religious (or political) personal commitment - with the vital proviso that they have assented (passive assent by silence is good enough) to their group's core choice and do not mix unnecessarily with or marry into the other side. Even if individuals lapse from their religious commitment, the process of secularisation *per se* does not necessarily undermine their sense of belonging to the group which gave them their social, if not political or religious, identity through family and school. As O'Connor describes it in the Catholic community:

> 'Lapsing' has become common enough for community censure to have lost much of its force. What counts is that you are still willing to be identified in terms of your origins, especially if you stand vigilant against open or covert incitement of anti-Catholicism. 'Falling away from the faith' is one thing. Denying your religious origins and therefore your own identity is another (1993, 332).

To put it another way, it is less often a case of religious people becoming secularised, and more often one of ordinary people never becoming fully politicised or religionised. They are not developing beyond the basic stage of proto-religious and proto-political (Catholic/Nationalist / Protestant/Unionist) identity. As long as this basic Catholic or Protestant identity is not threatened by the adoption of an alternative religious or political identity in its place, the religiously-based status quo is sustained. The 'active' memberships of the Catholic and Protestant Churches may not be as large as formerly, but the fundamental binding force which they have had on their respective communities since the Reformation is still effective.

Extending the argument, we can say that even if a majority of Catholics and Protestants were to cease practising their religion, religion would nevertheless continue to legitimise power relations between them (as it has since the original Reformation split) until such time as the religious taboos on inter-marriage and joint schooling ceased to be respected by majorities on each side. This observation counters substantially the objection of McGarry and O'Leary to the centrality of religion in the conflict on the grounds that 'no social scientist has satisfactorily demonstrated that theological beliefs are particularly important either individually or in aggregate in explaining political violence in the region' (1995, 212). Basic religious (or proto-religious) beliefs, both Catholic and Protestant, are expressed in social forms of separation (marriage and schools). Because these basic beliefs have not been rejected by a majority in either community, they continue to have their foundational binding force.

Children, therefore, are in a potentially confusing situation. While receiving signals from their local community that they should see the opposite-communities, opposite-religions picture, they are also receiving counter-signals (from two different directions) to the opposite effect. From one direction, the leaderships of the four main Churches signal more or less strongly their preference for ecumenical co-operation between Christians and for the one-religion picture. From another direction, the government (through its community relations policy in general) and schools (through their policies on EMU and Cultural Heritage in particular) signal their preference, again more or less strongly, for cross-community contact and the one-community picture. Schoolchildren are caught in the tension between the two sets of signals.

This is the kind of situation which might be expected at the critical stage of transition between the older opposite-religions picture and the new one-community picture. The next chapter considers the limited extent to which educationalists have tried to help pupils resolve the tension by addressing the moral issue of which is the better way of seeing things. As it turns out, the issue has not often come close to being articulated as such. Neither has confusion amongst schoolchildren been observed to any great extent. Despite being caught in this tension, schoolchildren, like their parents and teachers, do not normally experience confusion because they also have learned the skill of modulating between the two sets of signals.

Gradually, they become aware of ambiguity about 'religion' in the world of adults. They may think it odd, especially in their adolescent years as they begin to assert their social identities both inside and outside the classroom. For the most part, however, they are given no clear lead by adults in resolving the ambiguity. Adults rarely even hint at there being an issue. So schoolchildren are rarely presented with a situation in which they are required to consider making a conscious choice to prefer one way of seeing Catholics and Protestants rather than the other.

If they make no conscious individual choice, then they will tend towards one picture or the other according to their particular circumstances but they will probably continue to be uncertain or vague (perhaps confused) as to which is more correct. A consequence of being uncertain or vague about this issue is an inability to understand and articulate the nature and extent of the religious divide in Northern Ireland - does it divide one imperfectly united religion (Christianity), or does it separate completely two opposite religions (Catholicism and Protestantism)? In turn, this inability places a severe limitation on the ability to understand and articulate the nature of the Northern Ireland conflict. So, by default, schoolchildren develop the adult skill of modulating between paradigms, without being aware of doing so. In this way lack of consensus among adults about the role of religion in the conflict is perpetuated in the succeeding generation.

What the 'modulator' sees

To a greater or lesser extent, everyone in Northern Ireland modulates in the way they talk about or picture the Catholic / Protestant divide. For those who are anchored firmly in the perception of one community, one religion, or opposite communities, opposite religions, modulation is relatively slight; as when an ecumenist tolerates being spoken to about 'the opposite religion' or a fundamentalist tolerates Catholics (or Protestants) being referred to as if they were Christians. The true modulators are those who, like floating voters, are not committed to either perception. They are capable of interpreting the same picture either way. What, then, does this shifting picture look like?

The outlines of it can be picked out from the way in which writers on the religious divide, such as Gallagher and Worrall (1982), use certain key terms. The key, foundational terms of the shifting picture are 'community', 'religion', and 'divide' itself. A constellation of other terms cluster around these.

Community

Take the term community first. Gallagher and Worrall modulate between the older Reformation and the new ecumenical paradigms. On the one hand, they see the one-community picture and refer to 'the community' (79, 94, 116) and to 'our divided community of Northern Ireland' (88, 93). On the other hand, they refer to 'the two communities' (105, 171), 'the Catholic and Protestant communities' (147), 'relations between the communities' (201), 'increasing polarization between the communities' (211), and 'politicians of both communities' (66). It is indicative of their modulation that 'communal conflict' (194) is ambiguous.

They use 'side' as a synonym for 'community', as in: 'the other side' (64, 72, 192); 'on either side' (72); 'neither side' (97); 'their own side' (211). They also use 'tribe' (201) as a synomym for community. 'Factions' and 'mobs' are sub-groups within both communities or tribes, as in: 'warring factions' (56) and 'mobs of both factions' (55).

The two communities are differentiated in terms of size and territory. Their relative sizes are indicated by phrases like 'one community-of-identity and a smaller community-of-identity' (201) and by 'the minority' (68) or 'the minority community' (65, 75).

'Section' and 'area' are used to describe the territory belonging to each community, as in: 'sections of the community' (47); 'one section of the community' (73); 'different sections of the community' (93); 'Catholic no-go areas (72); 'barricaded Protestant areas' (72). 'Quarters' (111) and 'circles' (169, 118) describe terrritory also.

Religion

As with 'community', Gallagher and Worrall modulate in their use of 'religion'. On the one hand they see the one-religion picture, as in: 'Christian Ireland' (72); 'Christians on both sides' (117); 'Christians of different denominations' (132). On the other hand, they see two religions, quoting (without comment) references by others to 'the Catholic religion' (141) and to 'the Protestant religion' (195), and themselves using 'children of different religions' (156). The two religions are referred to as 'Catholicism' (146) and 'Protestantism' (47, 55, 151). Catholicism is qualified as 'Roman Catholicism' (47, 194) and Protestantism as 'Irish Protestantism' (197); 'Evangelical Protestantism' (36); 'outspoken Protestantism' (61); 'rabid political Protestantism' (194); and 'Paisleyism' (36). Other related terms are: 'Protestant opinion' (97); 'Protestant belief' (120); and the Protestant mind' (185). 'Protestant mobs' (190) is paralleled by '"Catholic" paramilitaries' (71).

Church

Gallagher and Worrall also modulate in their use of 'church'. They see the one-religion picture when they refer to 'the Churches' (111) and the opposite-religions picture when they refer to 'the two groups of Churches' (161). Synonyms for 'religion' are 'denomination' (132); 'affiliation' (2); 'faith' (196); and 'persuasion' (49, 50, 52).

Heritage

Further, they modulate in their use of 'heritage'. On the one hand, they refer to 'a shared heritage' (168). On the other hand, they refer to 'different cultural heritages' (168); 'our [RC] spiritual heritage' (108); and 'the Protestant heritage' (191). How do they picture the distinctive features of 'the Catholic heritage' and 'the Protestant heritage'? Quoting from the Irish Catholic bishops *Directory on Ecumenism*, they highlight: the Sacrifice of the Mass; the adoration of Christ in the Eucharist; devotion to our Blessed Lady and the Saints; reverence and loyalty towards the Vicar of Christ on Earth; prayer for the faithful departed; and esteem for the religious life and priestly celibacy. They also acknowledge 'fundamental and Christian values' in the Catholic heritage which are not necessarily distinctively Catholic: the sacredness of unborn life; the indissolubility of marriage; the essential unity of the interpersonal and procreative ends of married love.

How do they picture 'the Protestant heritage'? Quoting from a publication of the Orange Order (Dewar 1959, 23) they highlight: opposition to 'the fatal errors and doctrines of the Church of Rome'; avoidance of 'any act or ceremony of Popish worship'; resistance of 'the ascendancy of that church'; abstinence from 'all uncharitable words, actions, or sentiments' towards Roman Catholics. Other important features, which may not necessarily be distinctively Protestant are: veneration of the Heavenly Father; faith in Jesus Christ, the Saviour of mankind; cultivation of 'truth and justice, brotherly kindness and charity, devotion and piety, concord and unity'; obedience to the laws; study of the Holy Scriptures.

The religious divide

'Divide' is the term which Gallagher and Worrall employ most frequently (reflecting common usage) to describe the boundary between Catholics and Protestants, as in: 'the religious divide' (141, 183, 192, 211). The divide is pictured as consisting of several 'divisions', as in: 'the maintenance of divisions based on fear and suspicion' (139).

Perception of the depth or breadth of the 'religious divide' varies. It is measured according to a scale of synonyms. The most gentle is 'communal separation' (198). More severe is is 'chasm', as in: 'the chasm between Christian communities' (151). Most severe of all is 'religious apartheid' (195).

Chasm

'Chasm' is Gallagher and Worrall's most vivid image for the religious divide. They develop it by refering to solutions to the conflict which 'founder on the rocks of religious emotion' (191). These rocks, presumably, are located in the chasm between the opposing religions. They propose 'building bridges' across the chasm. They make it clear they are committed to the vision of one community and one religion: it is 'the will of God that all Christians should come together' (136). The aim in Northern Ireland is to achieve 'reconciliation between the communities' (200) and 'to build a united community' (184). Although they do not use the language of paradigm shift, they do distinguish in effect between the supporters of the opposing paradigms of religion as 'those passionately seeking unity as an aid to the healing of society, and those deeply suspicious of it as some kind of surrender to the interests of others' (194).

Part of the mental picture of the religious divide as a chasm is the broken bridge which used to span it (or precariously does still, just). 'Bridge-building' is Gallagher and Worrall's metaphor for the 'new way' (186) and for the 'substantial change of aspirations by one community or other or both' (190), which is needed for the project of reconciliation and unity to succeed. Bridge-building, they say, is the activity about which 'the battle for or against ecumenism' is being fought (143).

'Battle' does not seem to be putting it too strongly. They quote the Reverend Ian Paisley's attack on the Archbishop of Canterbury, Michael Ramsey:

> The Archbishop is like Terence O'Neill - he is a modern bridge builder. A bridge and a traitor are alike in one thing - they both take you to the other side. In this day of crisis both O'Neill and Ramsey would like to take us to the other side (*The Revivalist*, April 1966).

For 'the other side', of course, read 'opposite community', 'opposite religion'.

Given that Gallagher and Worrall are representative in their terminology of most writers on the community divide in Northern Ireland, these are the broad outlines of the shifting picture through which all parties to the conflict visualise the religious divide. Central to the action of the picture is the 'battle' for the bridge. This is both a religious and a secular battle. It is a religious battle about re-building 'the old bridge' (as ecumenists and fundamentalists see it) and it is a secular battle about building 'new bridges' (as pluralists and separatists see it).

The unfortunate effect of this shifting or ambiguous picture of the Catholic / Protestant divide is that it helps to lock all parties into the conflict because the central action is perceived as a battle and battles are settled normally by the surrender or retreat of one side or the other. In this case the sides are the unholy alliances of, on the one hand, the (religious) ecumenists and the (secuclar) pluralists and, on the other, that of the (religious) fundamentalists or separatists and the (political) hardliners or separatists. (The political separatists are those who wish to separate Northern Ireland from the United Kindgdom or keep it separate from the Republic of Ireland.) In other words, the intractability of a fight to the last ditch is built into the way most people visualise the conflict.

And there is a further complication. Although people generally see the two sides of the battle as fixed, the theory of paradigm modulation suggests that they are not. Certainly, there are constant cores to the two sides but the rest are in flux. A substantial proportion (perhaps a majority) is continually shifting (modulating) sides, coming and going both ways. Even if shifts are only marginal or momentary, the effects of their size or timing on the conflict can be considerable, particularly in logjamming or sinking peace initiatives. So the two sides continue eluding attempts to pin them down and the intractability of their opposition is compounded.

Intractability explained

Paradigm or choice modulation meets the criteria set for the hypothetical phenomenon or mechanism which it was supposed above might be responsible for the conflict's intractability. It is so deeply embedded in everyday conversation and in academic discourse that it passes unnoticed. It does have a positive social benefit: it is an instinctively learned strategy that helps people, to a greater or lesser extent across the whole range of political and religious opinion, to live together as 'one community', thereby helping them to cope with the simultaneous conflict between them. At the same time, paradigm modulation has the negative effect of prolonging the conflict. Because it is so deeply embedded in discourse, it passes largely unnoticed and unquestioned. Its hidden action promotes ambiguity in all discussion of the role of religion in the conflict. This has resulted in so much misunderstanding and suspicion that no consensus about the role of religion has been achieved and hence no consensus about the nature of the conflict.

Finally, once pointed out, paradigm modulation meets the criterion of seeming infuriatingly obvious.

Making the choice decisively

This is not to say that paradigm or choice modulation only takes place in Northern Ireland. It is basic human behaviour to modulate between two (or more) points of view on any issue on which one has not made up one's mind. For most people in western Europe, however, Boyle and Hadden's core choice between separation and sharing is not an issue. The choice has been made decisively in favour of sharing. What is distinctive about Northern Ireland is that there it has not.

Without denying the continuing importance of the 'external' actors in the conflict, we may ask: now that the need for a definitive core choice has been identified, will the 'internal' actors end the conflict by making it decisively? Probably not, if the choice is only presented in the frighteningly stark, take it or leave it terms of Boyle and Hadden's proposed structures for sharing or separation. The old habit of paradigm modulation is strong and with good purpose. Why forsake the status quo, which is in effect a finely attuned mixture of sharing and separation, for the uncertainties of any radical change?

There may be a better chance if it can be explained to people why it is that they still avoid making the core choice decisively. The chance may be better still if they see that there need be no *trahison des ancêtres*; no surrender (all things considered) of their ancestors' not inconsiderable achievement in living together without unrestrained conflict. Fear of betraying the sacrifices of one's ancestors is possibly the most powerful factor which inhibits decisive choice in favour of sharing. For example, a recent defence of separate Catholic schools by Monsignor Denis Faul, a committed campaigner for community reconciliation, appeared under the headline 'Integration would betray sacrifices' (*Belfast Telegraph*, October 30, 1995).

In other words, people may need to understand how things have come to be the way they are and appreciate what a sophisticated coping strategy it is they have been using before they can be challenged successfully to move on. They may even find they can use their instinctive skill at modulating more effectively if they start to use it consciously.

A consensus needs to form about the interpretation of the conflict before a consensus can form about the core choice itself. And the consensus interpretation must account for two things: first, the origins and long historical development of the core choice; and second, the continuing maintenance of the (precarious) point of balance between the alternatives of the core choice, upon which Northern Ireland is still poised.

Therefore, there is a need for an educational programme which will challenge individuals to question the way they see the Catholic / Protestant divide. This is not to say that they have not already been challenged to do so. That has been a major preoccupation of the community relations industry. Rather, what was lacking before was a productive conceptual framework within which to put the question.

Perceptions, probably of every conceivable aspect of each dimension of the conflict, have certainly been challenged already. No doubt, perceptions of how the divide should manifest itself in the complexity of the conflict's 'surface structures' have changed in many cases, and often for the better (in fair employment, for example). The overall effect, however, has not been coherent. The deep structure (core choice modulation) of the conflict is still largely unchanged.

An indication of this and of the continuing importance of the concepts of 'bridging the divide', 'the two communities' and 'the two religions' is the appearance of all of these together in the same newspaper as recently as the summer of 1995. They were expressed in the following items: a letter to the editor headed 'Build *bridges*, don't block them'; a claim that attacks on Protestant churches and halls are 'symptomatic of the republican agenda which is to ethnically cleanse Ulster of *the Protestant community*'; and a public apology for a press statement about an incident involving the RUC which 'should not have included the reference to *the religion* of the officer, a Catholic' (*Belfast Telegraph* 2 August).

With agreement on interpretation of the conflict's intractability, the core question for an educational programme can now be framed: how have I come to be committed (strongly or weakly) either to the sharing vision of one community, one religion, or to the separation vision of opposite communities, opposite religions? Most may find, through the educational process of considering this question, that they have been like floating voters, maintaining a finely balanced coalition of the two visions by modulating discreetly between them.

After reflecting on this, they may see three possible options. The least attractive is likely to be decisive choice in favour of the opposite-religions, opposite-communities picture and commitment to a thoroughgoing separation, segregation or *apartheid* (keeping Catholics and Protestants and the United Kingdom and the Republic of Ireland apart).

It is less easy to predict preference for the other two options. On the one hand, the modulators or 'floating voters' may decide to anchor with those already committed to the vision of one community, one religion. In doing so they would take leave for the last time of the minority still sticking with the older vision of opposite religions and opposite communities. The core choice would then have been made decisively in favour of sharing. On the other hand, however, the modulators may decide that refining the balance of the status quo between structures for separation and for sharing by consciously sophisticated modulation offers the best way forward. The core choice then would still be open.

Putting the core question (how have I come to be committed, strongly or weakly, either to the sharing vision or to the separation vision?) and inviting consideration of the three main options would be good education. It would not be 'social engineering' of the sinister type which aims at a predetermined outcome. Any educational programme which was 'closed' would be bound to provoke a hostile reaction on all sides and fail. The core choice is genuinely open-ended. The most that an educational programme can hope to do is to raise the historical and moral awareness of those choosing freely to as high a level as possible.

Leaving further consideration of such a large-scale educational programme to Chapter 7, the next chapter examines the experience to date of curriculum development in Northern Ireland which is relevant to schoolchildren's understanding of the conflict and their education for *The Choice*, the core choice between separation and sharing.

4 Education for *The Choice*

How have educators helped schoolchildren in Northern Ireland to understand the conflict in which they participate? This chapter reviews the series of curriculum development projects which have addressed the issue of 'cultural traditions' in schools over the last twenty-five years with the aim of improving community relations.

The effectiveness of these projects has been limited by a general difficulty of interpreting 'cultural traditions'. There is a climate of ambiguity or vagueness about 'community', 'church' and 'religion'. The same climate surrounds 'culture' and 'tradition'. At present, there is no commonly agreed framework for the analysis of 'cultural traditions'. The deep-seated ambiguities about culture and tradition, which flourish in the absence of one, need to be understood in order for such a framework to be established. Education for *The Choice* - through curriculum development projects concerned with 'cultural traditions' in particular - is likely to be more effective once there is such a commonly agreed framework.

The difficulty about interpreting 'cultural traditions' is related to the problem of the conflict's double intractability and paradigm or choice modulation. This chapter traces the origin and development of 'cultural traditions' and discusses the difficulty of their interpretation in relation to Education Reform (Cultural Heritage and Education for Mutual Understanding) and the writing of Irish history.

Education for bridge-building

Central to the thinking of educators in teaching about the conflict in Northern Ireland has been the idea of 'bridge-building' across the 'chasm' of the religious divide. The following newspaper editorial, commenting on a community development project in Belfast, illustrates the point by commending:

> the vital business of persuading young Catholics and young Protestants that they all belong to the same human race. They have to *bridge* prejudice, fear, hatred, ignorance and all the other emotional attitudes fostered by ghetto living in the Belfast conurbation for more than a century (*Irish News* 20/1//89).

Greer sees the classic picture of the religious divide when he describes educational strategies for contributing to a resolution of the conflict as 'bridge-building':

> The *chasm* between *the two communities* can be *bridged*, but it is deep and dangerous and it runs through almost every facet of life ... So the complex reasons underlying the Northern Ireland conflict have to be recognized and the nature of the *chasm* appreciated by those who wish to make a contribution to *bridge-building* (1987, 443).

He goes on to suggest that building bridges in Northern Ireland is 'a slow and difficult business' and that 'many small bridges will probably have greater success than a few large ones' (448).

Related to the idea of bridge-building is that of 'cultural traditions' or 'cultural heritage'. On either side of the chasm are two communities or cultures, each with its own set of traditions (heritage). The educational projects which are reviewed briefly here may be considered as attempts to build small bridges. Each of them challenged schoolchildren to examine their cultural traditions, in particular their religious traditions. Most of them challenged schoolchildren from the communities or cultures on either side of the chasm to make contact with each other. Their cumulative effect was to help prepare the way for the kind of educational programme, identified in the previous chapter, which is needed to focus powerfully on the core choice between separation and sharing.

If paradigm or choice modulation is a hidden but observable phenomenon with important effects as is claimed, it should be evident in projects of this kind. It is. What becomes apparent is how the inter-related ambiguities of 'community', and 'religion' (to which may also be added those of 'culture', 'tradition' and 'cultural traditions') have inhibited the emergence of a coherent intellectual framework for such projects.

Curriculum development: improving community relations

Several writers, notably Dunn (1986), Greer (1987), Farren (1991), Richardson (1992), and Burgess (1993) have studied a series of curriculum development projects carried out in Northern Ireland since the early 1970s which have sought to address the problem of how schools might contribute to an improvement in community relations. Prior to the outbreak of civil disturbances in 1968 there had been virtually no recognition of the need for schools to play a role in improving community relations. A lone voice, crying in the wilderness since the 1940s, had been that of Malone (1940).

The Schools Project in Community Relations, 1970-72

In 1970 the then Ministry of Education appointed the headmaster of a large Belfast secondary school, John Malone, as Director of the *Schools Project in Community Relations*. Its main aim was to establish contact between Catholic and Protestant pupils through residential meetings at the 'neutral' venue of the Ulster Folk and Transport Museum, Cultra. This initiated a tradition of such work which continues today under the title of Education for Mutual Understanding, although it is indicative of its slow rate of development that a teacher was not appointed to the full-time staff at Cultra for the specific purpose of co-ordinating such visits until 1990. Malone and his colleagues developed teaching materials which were influenced by the *Oxford Moral Education Project* (McPhail 1972). The publication of these materials, however, was prevented by the Ministry of Education - despite a meeting between Malone and the then Minister, Paul Channon - on the grounds that they were 'too politically sensitive'.

In calling for 'the creation of an extra dimension of awareness within every teacher's work', Malone's team were years ahead of their time. They anticipated what eventually became the cross-curricular themes of EMU and Cultural Heritage. Malone cautioned against expecting too much of projects like the *Schools Project in Community Relations*. He argued that educational initiatives on their own would never be sufficient to bring about the required improvement in community relations and, in any case, ones like this were too short-lived to be successful.

The Schools' Curriculum Project, 1973-78

The subsequent *Schools' Curriculum Project*, also under Malone's direction, was the first longer-term project of this kind. Its main aim was to strengthen the moral purpose of education by focusing on the first years of post-primary education mainly through local studies. Local studies were not new in schools at the time but this was the first time they had been used deliberately as a means of promoting understanding and tolerance among pupils of the lifestyles and traditions of others.

Although the project aimed to both challenge pupils' attitudes and to change educational structures, it was probably more influential in doing the latter. Malone took the view that the main need in education was not centrally related to the religious divide. More fundamental was the need to address, as he saw it, the structural injustice of segregation by ability at the age of eleven and to provide more support for the less able pupil. His argument was that, if schools could interest and motivate them, pupils would be less likely to turn to violence as a solution to problems. This view was influential in the eventual development of the *Schools' Support Service* 1978-82 and of the current curriculum support services of the Education Boards. It was also influential in the introduction of a comprehensive curriculum for all schools in Northern Ireland from 1989 onwards.

However, Malone's team did also work towards a curriculum which would emphasise what the two communities have in common rather than what divides them. Their positive achievements in developing successful teaching strategies and suitable teaching materials did influence the eventual introduction of EMU and Cultural Heritage.

The Schools' Cultural Studies Project, 1974-80 and 1982-84

Running in parallel with the *Schools' Curriculum Project* at Queen's University, Belfast, was another project with a similar focus at the New University of Ulster, Coleraine. The *Schools' Cultural Studies Project* was concerned with 'increasing levels of tolerance, personal awareness and mutual understanding' among Catholic and Protestant schoolchildren, mainly in post-primary schools (Robinson 1981). It differed from Malone's projects, however, in two important respects.

Firstly, it was heavily influenced by the analysis of the conflict by Skilbeck (1976). Skilbeck described the 'divided culture' of Northern Ireland as 'highly ideological'; 'militant and aggressive'; 'encapsulated and fixed'; 'lacking in complexity and diversity'; and 'highly reproductive'. He viewed teachers as 'naive bearers of the culture'. In order to escape from inter-communal conflict, he argued, Northern Ireland required a more open and tolerant society. Rather than simply helping to reproduce the culture, schools should actively participate in its reconstruction. They could assist in effecting the necessary changes by seeing themselves as agencies 'for social amelioration, for cultural development, and for the support and strengthening of democratic processes in our beleaguered society' (1976, 4).

Secondly, rather than innovate through existing curriculum subjects such as English, Geography and History as was Malone's method, this project team sought to establish a new school subject, called Cultural Studies, which eventually had its own Certificate of Secondary Education (CSE) examination syllabus. They developed teaching materials which invited pupils to acquire an understanding not just of their own and other communities but of the whole process of the evolution of cultural identity and of the way in which people from different traditions perceive and relate to each other. They adopted the 'secular' approach of social studies, relying in particular on the procedure of 'values clarification', whereby the pupils choose freely from alternatives after consideration of their consequences, affirm publicly that they are happy with their choice, and act upon the choices which they have evaluated positively.

There were, however, difficulties. Although the project was concerned with a comprehensive analysis of Northern Ireland culture (way of life), the structure of the teaching materials did not differentiate clearly between the different dimensions of culture (political, economic, social, artistic, religious etc). No coherent attempt was made to examine the inter-relationship between religion and politics. In this respect, the project was influenced by the prevailing school of sociological thought (referred to in Chapter 1) which neglects, marginalises or denies the importance of religion *per se* in the conflict.

The project had a somewhat chequered history. The directorship changed hands several times before Robinson took over in 1976. The Department of Education refused to receive the evaluator's report and the University of Ulster refused to publish it (Richardson 1992, 77). Nevertheless, it did achieve an 'unfreezing' of attitudes in pupils and 'increased awareness' (Jenkins, 1980, 77). Like the *Schools' Curriculum Project*, it generated a considerable literature about itself and further research arising from it (Lambkin 1993, 85).

Between them, the *Schools' Curriculum Project* and the *Schools' Cultural Studies Project* achieved major breakthroughs. They demonstrated that curriculum development could bring about a significant improvement in community relations in Northern Ireland, even in an educational climate which could scarcely have been less favourable. They developed teaching materials which incorporated the main objectives of what would later become the compulsory cross-curricular themes EMU and Cultural Heritage. And they both established substantial networks of schools which became models for the current DENI *Cross-Community Contact Scheme*.

However, the projects were restricted in their effectiveness. For the most part their teaching materials were not attractively produced. Funds were not available for publishing them to commercial standard and outside the project schools their circulation was very limited. More importantly, they were open to fundamental criticism for their neglect of some important dimensions of culture.

Neglect of the inter-connection of religion and politics has already been mentioned. Farren (1991) has pointed to the neglect also of language and the creative arts. Given the demonstrable neglect of the religio-political dimension, it is both ironic and indicative of the controversial role of religion in the conflict that Farren should complain that these projects had the effect of 'exaggerating and misinterpreting the role of religion' because 'the cultural traditions in Northern Ireland are more frequently referred to as either Catholic or Protestant than in any other terms' (1991, 51).

In fairness, the neglect of the religious dimension by these two projects cannot be attributed entirely to their 'secular' social studies orientation. They were clearly committed to the one-community paradigm and, for them, that was sufficient. Running contemporaneously (although with virtually no collaboration between them) were two other projects with similar aims but with a specifically religious focus. Rather than using a 'secular' approach with Social Studies (English, Geography, History) teachers, these were inter-church projects, using a 'religious' approach with Religious Education (RE) teachers, committed to the one-religion paradigm as well as to the one-community paradigm.

The Looking at Churches and Worship Project, 1978-86

This project, reported on by Richardson (1992), was the joint initiative of the Irish Council of Churches and the Roman Catholic Irish Commission for Justice and Peace as part of its joint Peace Education Programme. It was aimed at pupils aged 10-12 and grew out of a previous project, *Free to Be*, for the 8-12 age group. This, in turn, had grown out of a project, directed by J.R.B. McDonald, at Stranmillis College in the mid 1970s, which was the first of its kind in Northern Ireland to make use of church buildings as an educational resource.

Looking at Churches and Worship shared the aim of the *Schools' Curriculum* and *Schools' Cultural Studies* projects of promoting 'tolerance and understanding for practices which are different'. Unlike them, however, it was explicitly committed to 'exemplify the common heritage shared by all Christians by emphasising those things which they commonly share though may differently express'. In other words, it was committed religiously to the one-religion paradigm. It was 'ecumenical' but only in the weak sense of 'improving inter-church relations', not the strong sense of 'promoting organic church unity'. This enabled those churches and individuals opposed to ecumenism in the strong sense to participate.

The analysis of culture which *Looking at Churches and Worship* developed was more sophisticated in that it clearly differentiated the religious dimension as one aspect of culture. Not only did it differentiate (through systematic comparison of similarities and differences) the Roman Catholic and Protestant traditions, it also differentiated the different component traditions within Protestantism. However, the incoherence of its general analysis, like those of the other projects, was evident from the way it modulated in its use of 'culture' and 'tradition'. It was not unambiguously clear what was under investigation: one culture and one tradition or two? On the one hand, the project materials referred to 'the different strands and facets of Irish culture' and to 'the Christian tradition'. On the other hand, they referred to 'the division of our society in Northern Ireland into two cultures'.

In many respects *Looking at Churches and Worship* also anticipated Education Reform. In particular, the structure of its teaching materials fitted well with the way in which Cultural Heritage came to define culture in terms of artefacts, learned behaviour and ideas. However, the materials focused mainly on similarity and difference in the present. They paid little attention to historical development or assessment of continuity and change and did not broach the inter-connection of religion and politics.

The Religion in Ireland Project, 1974-85

The other 'religious' project was targeted at an older age group (11-16). It was based in the same university as the *Schools' Cultural Studies Project* at Coleraine, began in the same year and adopted the same 'reconstructionist' approach of Skilbeck, which it applied to the teaching of RE (McElhinney 1983). It shared with the previous projects the same general community relations aim of 'encouraging in pupils a sympathetic appreciation of differing traditions'; the same focus on classroom discussion as the main teaching strategy, with contact between Catholic and Protestant pupils an important element. With *Looking at Churches and Worship* it shared a common focus on the comparison of different religious traditions with visits to different church buildings as an important element.

Of all these projects, *Religion in Ireland* offered the most thorough analysis of its key concept, 'culture'. The project team were explicit in rejecting the argument of some church leaders and educators that the conflict is not primarily religious but political. They also rejected the subsidiary argument

71

that the conflict is not religious because Christian believers with personal faith (on both sides), who are to be distinguished from church-goers for whom religion is merely a social ritual, are not involved in the conflict (Greer and McElhinney 1985, 3; cf Mawhinney and Wells 1975, 213). They preferred Conor Cruise O'Brien's explanation that it is a 'conflict between groups defined by religion' and concluded:

> Whether they like it or not, the churches are part of the problem in Northern Ireland and there is a dual responsibility laid on their members to be faithful to their tradition of faith and at the same time to contribute in a constructive manner to the resolution of the conflict which surrounds them (Greer and McElhinney 1985, 8).

The concept of 'dual responsibility' in this context is closely related to the 'floating voter's' dilemma, which is hidden by paradigm or choice modulation.

Religion in Ireland, like *Looking at Churches and Worship*, skillfully accommodated the apparently conflicting confessional and community-relations requirements of RE. It made clear that it was ecumenical only in the weak sense of improving inter-church relations, not the strong sense of promoting church unity. So far as 'reconstructionism' was concerned, the project capitalised on the convergence of the 'secular' arguments of Skilbeck's school and those to be found in both Roman Catholic and Protestant documents on the role of RE (1985, 9-14).

This project was clear-sighted in anticipating 'not only a questioning of the organisation of the curriculum but a questioning of the organisation of the school', which came to pass with Education Reform, the introduction of EMU and Cultural Heritage and statutory encouragement of integrated schooling. As things were, the team concluded that: 'schools can only be expected to unfreeze a little in line with any general unfreezing in society at large' (1985, 41). Its major achievement was in recognising 'the importance of religion as a crucial factor in the clash of cultures' and in raising awareness of 'the role of the religious educator in helping to create understanding and respect for those who belong to another tradition' (Greer and McElhinney 1984, 342).

As the phrase 'clash of cultures' indicates, however, *Religion in Ireland* did not succeed in resolving the inter-related ambiguities of 'culture', 'tradition', 'community' and 'religion'. One the one hand, Northern Ireland was referred to as being part of one culture, as in: 'Western Culture'. On the other hand, it was referred to as consisting of 'two cultures', as in: 'the Protestant and Roman Catholic cultures'.

Similarly with 'community'. On the one hand, Northern Ireland was referred to in the teaching materials as one society and one community, as in:

'Northern Ireland Society Today: a Divided Society'; 'a divided community'; and 'the other side of the community'. On the other hand, it was referred to as consisting of two separate communities, as in: 'the two communities'; and 'both communities'.

Similarly with 'religion'. On the one hand, the 'two traditions' of Catholicism and Protestantism were referred to as constituting one religion, namely Christianity, as in: 'Christian traditions'; 'Christians of different traditions'; 'Christian divisions in Ireland'; 'various living forms of Christianity'. On the other hand, the two traditions were referred to as constituting two different religions, as in: 'the other religion'.

Even more confusingly, 'culture', as in 'the Protestant (or Catholic) culture' was sometimes, but not always, used as a synonym for 'community', 'tradition', or 'religion'. At other times, culture was differentiated from them, as in: 'the religion and culture of the community'; 'their respective communities, culture and religious traditions'. On other occasions, 'culture' was differentiated from 'school', as if school is a thing apart from the culture. In contexts where it was contrasted with 'school', 'religion' or 'religious tradition', 'culture' signified all the other 'non-school' or 'non-religious' aspects of one 'community' or the other.

Further confusion was added when in some of these contexts 'culture' or 'cultural' signified the 'political' as distinct from the 'religious' dimension, as in 'cultural setting', 'cultural context', while in others it signified the 'artistic and aesthetic' as distinct from the 'political' and 'social' dimensions, as in 'cultural, social, political outlook'.

Although this terminological modulation or confusion constituted a serious structural weakness in the project, it needs to be kept in perspective. The project team did turn to the already vast and expanding literature on the Northern Ireland conflict for guidance in constructing their cultural analysis. That literature had become vast partly because of the successively vain attempts to establish a consensus about the nature of the conflict. It would be unreasonable to expect that a team of educators should have cut through the manifold disagreements of the many professional analysts of different types and devise a satisfactory analysis of their own to mediate to schoolchildren. Indeed, the team unwittingly illustrated the difficulty of their task by modulating in their use of experts: in support of their project philosophy they cited both the work of the anthropologist, Rosemary Harris, which emphasises a 'common culture' and the work of the historian, F.S.L. Lyons, which emphasises 'the clash cultures' (1985, 3).

It was a strength of *Religion in Ireland* that, unlike the other projects, it did take up a position and address the inter-connection of religion and politics. Like *Cultural Studies* and *Looking at Churches and Worship*, however, it also neglected the historical dimension by focusing on the religious divide almost exclusively through comparison of similarity and difference in the present and not including a study of continuity and change as well.

The most serious weakness of *Religion in Ireland*, which it shared with the other projects, was that it aimed to engage pupils in a general analysis of culture without a clearly thought-out framework within which to set its teaching materials. The fundamental problem of ambiguity was not recognised. Much paradigm modulation obscured from view the basic questions (one community or two communities? - one religion or two religions?), with the result that pupils did not confront them.

Other projects

Four other cultural traditions projects which aimed at improving community relations may be mentioned more briefly. They were each focused on achieving better mutual understanding of religious traditions. (There have been no curriculum development projects with a comparable focus on political traditions.)

Teaching Religion in Northern Ireland, 1984-86 This project aimed at promoting contact between RE teachers in Catholic and Protestant schools and at improving their competence in the use of classroom discussion. *Religion in Ireland* had found discussion work to be 'teacher dominated ... narrow in scope, and limited to somewhat predictable question and answer exchanges' (Greer, Harris and McElhinney 1989, 92). This follow-up project reported some success in improving what it described as 'an essential teaching skill in dealing with controversial issues of all kinds', although it also noted that 'in some parts of Northern Ireland, the climate of suspicion and hatred made such cross-community ventures difficult, if not impossible (1989, 102).

Three Churches in Ballycastle, 1989 This was a relatively small-scale project which aimed simply at producing new materials which would encourage cross-community groups to use church buildings close to Corrymeela as educational resources (Greer et al. 1989). They emphasised the importance of local churches as among the most important components of the local heritage of pupils. As with previous projects, the main concern was to compare similarity and difference in the present. Attention was drawn to historical information only incidentally.

Irish Presbyterians, 1989 Unlike the teaching materials of the previous projects, *Irish Presbyterians* was a pupils' GCSE workbook that was specific to one denomination, not comparative in its approach. It was produced for the Presbyterian Church by a team of eight RE teachers, none of whom was from a Catholic school. Emphasis was on how Presbyterians practise their beliefs today. Historical information was only given incidentally and none of the pupil assignments focused on assessing continuity and change. Although its title suggested an historical approach, the accompanying video, *The Scottish Connection*, gave only a brief introduction to the development of the tradition from its origins in Scotland.

Viewpoint: What it Means to be a ..., 1989-90 In contrast with *Irish Presbyterians*, this project involved the collaboration of the four largest churches. Four twenty minute videos examined *What it Means to be A Presbyterian; A Methodist; A Roman Catholic; A Member of the Church of Ireland*, through the eyes and the largely unedited words of a young person from each tradition. A unique feature of this project was the subtlety of its approach in combining the views of 'outsiders' to the tradition with the views of 'insiders'. For example, the presenter of *On Being a Roman Catholic* was a young Presbyterian from Ballymena who travelled to Dublin to meet and learn from a young Roman Catholic and her family.

This project was also the first to use film of religious practices (worship) in progress. Film helps to get round the dilemma of the 'outsider' trying to investigate and interpret one religious tradition while being a committed member of another. In the case of *On being a Roman Catholic*, for example, the Presbyterian presenter, on the advice of his minister, declined to be present inside the Roman Catholic Church during filming of Mass. This illustrates the importance of distinguishing between the 'presentation' of a religious tradition and its 're-presentation'. Mere presence by an outsider at an actual religious service (its presentation to the tradition's insiders) may be interpreted as assent to what is taking place. By contrast, watching a re-presentation (film) of the same religious service in the classroom can be interpreted as a secular, not a religious act.

Again, as with all the previous projects, the main focus of the videos was on current belief and practice in the traditions, rather than on continuity and change in their historical developments. Two of the issues which pupils were encouraged to assess once they had viewed the four videos were: the closeness or otherwise of inter-church relations (in the present, not the past); and the extent of similarities and differences between the churches. This, probably, was the closest any of the projects came to challenging pupils with the basic 'one religion or opposite religions still?' question.

Education Reform: EMU and Cultural Heritage

The curriculum development projects mentioned above all aimed at improving understanding of cultural traditions. Most of them also aimed at improving community relations in schools through cross-community contact. To a greater or lesser extent, they were precursors of the kind of work which is now a statutory requirement in all schools in Northern Ireland. The Education Reform (Northern Ireland) Order 1989 has resulted in the most thorough-going reform of education in Northern Ireland since the Education (Northern Ireland) Act 1947. There is now a Northern Ireland Curriculum which is common to all schools across the religious divide. Two of its six compulsory cross-curricular themes, Education for Mutual Understanding (EMU) and Cultural Heritage, are intended specifically to address community relations objectives.

It is significant that both of these cross-curricular themes were afterthoughts. There was no mention of them at all in the first *Proposals for Reform*, issued by the Department of Education (DENI) in March 1988. They were first proposed, after the consultation period, in *The Way Forward*, which was issued in October 1988. How *The Way Forward* introduced the idea of Cultural Heritage to the public is particularly instructive [author's italics]:

> Several respondents suggested that there should be opportunities for pupils to gain awareness of *aspects of history, culture and traditions* which contribute to the *cultural heritage of Northern Ireland.* The Government welcomes and accepts this suggestion as a positive measure aimed at lessening the ignorance which many feel contributes to the *divisions in our society.*

The first thing to notice is that DENI distanced itself from any impression that it was imposing Cultural Heritage of its own initiative. Its long tradition had been one of non-interference with the *de facto* segregation of the education system into Catholic and Protestant sectors. The community relations work done in schools during the 1970s and 1980s, through projects like the ones mentioned above, had relied on schools participating voluntarily.

A second thing to notice is that DENI, as one would expect, committed itself clearly to the picture of Northern Ireland as one community ('our society'). It envisaged one 'cultural heritage of Northern Ireland'.

Thirdly, DENI made its definition of Cultural Heritage broad, not narrow: 'history', 'culture' and 'traditions' were used virtually as synonyms for cultural heritage. Their tautologous use ('aspects of *history, culture* and *traditions* which contribute to the *cultural heritage*') was intended, presumably, to emphasise that Cultural Heritage as a cross-curricular theme should be as all-embracing as possible. This implied a multi-cultural approach to the wider world, not just a narrow focus on 'the two cultures' of Catholics and Protestants. The eventual full definition of the Ministerial Working Group, set up to flesh out the proposal, made this clear:

Culture may be defined in various ways. In its *widest* sense it is the artefacts, ideas and learned behaviour which comprise people's way of life, and Cultural Heritage consists of those elements of culture which are inherited.

Modulation surfaced as a problem for the Cultural Heritage Working Group which did come close to articulating the issue of choice between separation and sharing. Its *Report* both posed and answered the 'one community or two communities?' question in this way:

Is Northern Ireland made up of one society or two? The Working Group inclined to the view that there is a single community, although a community rent by bitter division' (NICC 1989, 6).

The use of 'inclined', rather than 'committed' is indicative of how the Group (chosen to be representative of both communities) was not unanimous on the question. Some members were committed, others were uncertain - some to the point of tending to the 'two communities' view. In the consultation which followed the publication of its report, critics challenged the Group's 'inclination' to the 'one community' view. For example, the Social Democratic and Labour Party (SDLP) rejected it with the argument that:

The word 'community' implies shared beliefs, shared values and shared aspirations. It would be quite difficult to argue that a single community exists when such features of the concept are examined in Northern Ireland. ... [We recommend that] the term community not be used, but that the people of Northern Ireland be referred to as belonging to different (cultural) traditions, the beliefs, values and attitudes of which are, in some respects, shared, but in others not (McGlone, 1989).

This case illustrates how ambiguity can generate misunderstanding and mistrust. The Working Group had used 'society' and 'community' as synonyms (because of its ideological bias towards seeing them as exactly synonymous). Normally, they are not exactly synonymous. 'Society', as in 'the society of Northern Ireland' is not contentious. The existence of Northern Ireland as an entity is not in dispute. However, its validity is and 'community', as in 'the community of Northern Ireland', is contentious for the reasons given by the SDLP spokesperson.

In Northern Ireland (as in most places), 'community' is nuanced differently from 'society'. That is why it is common to hear 'community', as in 'the Catholic community' and 'the Protestant community'; but 'society', as in 'the Catholic society' and 'the Protestant society' is rarely, if ever, heard. Community can be synonymous with society but not always. That would imply a denial of the integrity of one or other of the separate communities which together make up the larger community. Society is the acceptable term generally for the larger unit which 'the two communities' in Northern Ireland indisputably constitute. In answering the 'one community or opposite communities?' question, the Working Group might have still made its point by repeating 'society' and not introducing 'community' as a synonym for it. This might have given the SDLP no grounds for objection.

Nevertheless, the enduring nature of the 'opposite communities?' problem was evident. After the consultation period on the Cultural Heritage Working Group's Report, the Northern Ireland Curriculum Council reported that:

> Mixed views were expressed on whether Northern Ireland is one community or two. Some of those inclined to the latter view felt that the report presented an approach designed to remove conflict dividing a single community rather than, as required, attempting to reconcile two commuities with diverse traditional and contemporary values (NICC 1989b, 6).

NICC responded to the criticism thus:

> Council recognises that there is divided opinion on whether Northern Ireland is one community or two, but it does not believe that the recommendations of the report would have been substantially different if a different viewpoint has been adopted .

This was one of the rare occasions on which the issue of paradigm modulation has surfaced and this response effectively buried it again. The Curriculum Council acknowledged the issue by recognising that 'there is divided opinion on whether Northern Ireland is one community or two' but concluded that it does not really matter either way.

Subsequently, the Council seemed to have recognised that it had a vested interest in the continuing ambiguity of 'community'. In documents such as the *History Guidance Materials* 'community' is used ambiguously, as for example: '... should enable pupils to see the history of *their own community and country* ...'. However, the Council's ideological slip could not be prevented from showing all the time. This is how NICC answered the question 'why have cultural heritage in the curriculum?' [author's italics]:

The tensions within *the Northern Ireland community* underline the need for a systematic and unifying programme of cultural heritage for young people ... Such a programme should help to dispel the myths and provide for the creation of tolerance and mutual respect. It will also ensure that all pupils, by the age of sixteen, will possess a knowledge, understanding and critical appreciation of *their cultural heritage* (NICC 1989b, 7).

'Their cultural heritage' is suitably ambiguous: it could mean one common heritage or two (or more) separate heritages. 'The Northern Ireland community', however, is unambiguous. The difficulty which this ideological bias causes is apparent when we consider the idea of 'a systematic and unifying programme of cultural heritage', which *is* ambiguous. On the surface it seems to mean that the programme will be unifying in the sense that all pupils are required to study the same aspects of culture. This is uncontroversial. However, some critics, like Farren, see a deeper meaning:

If the phrase [unifying programme] is intended to carry a deeper meaning i.e. that the curriculum should unify young people in a cultural sense, it invites the question 'Unify about what?' In Northern Ireland such a question immediately acquires a political connotation because of the fear that what is intended is the cultural assimilation of one community by the other. Given the Anglicisation of Ireland, on the one hand, and, on the other, the efforts to reGaelicise it, such fears have a very real basis (Farren 1991, 55-56).

It depends upon one's point of view whether one sees the NICC bias in favour of one community as tending in the direction of Anglicisation or reGaelicisation. While Farren feared the former, the Convenor of the Education Board of the Free Presbyterian Church, the Rev Ivan Foster, feared the latter:

If Protestant children were to be taught the truth about these matters [Irish culture and history] we would welcome it. We believe there is a sad ignorance amongst Protestants on many things Irish. But it will not be the truth that the children will be taught (*The News Letter* 14/6/89).

Others agreed that the government was attempting to indoctrinate pupils. Councillor Sammy Wilson of the Democratic Unionist Party called on parents to 'vigorously protest and remove children from these indoctrination sessions' (*The News Letter* 14/6/89).

Not surprisingly, the introduction of EMU (Education for Mutual Understanding) got a similarly mixed reception. For example, the Orange Order said:

> 'Underlying the Mutual Education Theory is an attempt to promote Ecumenism amongst the youth of the province. There are great dangers in any attempt to use education to undermine the traditions of the society in which they operate' (Belfast Telegraph 15/3/89).

Similarly, various commentators from a Catholic perspective saw a danger that EMU might impute to young people the responsibility for remedying the divisions of society which properly belongs with politicians and governments. There continues to be confusion about the difference between Cultural Heritage and EMU because the overlap between their objectives is so considerable. However, rather than rationalise them into one theme, the Department of Education introduced the concept of 'conjoined objectives' (DENI 1992, 9-11). In practice, teachers tend to think of Cultural Heritage as more about content and EMU as more about the process of learning. The introduction of Cultural Heritage to the Northern Ireland Curriculum required that the ambiguous meanings of 'culture' and of 'heritage' (one or two?) had to be addressed. As we have seen, all the parties involved, to a greater or lesser extent, have a common vested interest (the limiting of conflict) in condoning these ambiguities. So they remain integral to the network of related words through which and within which paradigm modulation takes place. This helps to explain the suspicion (noted especially amongst Protestants; see Pollack 1993, 37 and Dunlop 1995) with which documents such as the *Anglo-Irish Agreement*, the *Downing Street Declaration* and the *Frameworks Document* are usually greeted. 'Definitive' documents such as these are unwelcome because they threaten ambiguity (the environment of paradigm modulation) by seeming to pin down meanings authoritatively.

The story of the origins and development of Northern Ireland's 'cultural traditions industry' (a sector of the 'community relations industry') helps to explain why ambiguity is enduring generally, not just in the world of education, and why general agreement has yet to be reached on an intellectual framework within which 'culture' can be debated without mutual misunderstanding.

The origins and development of 'cultural traditions'

'Cultural traditions' in its special Northern Ireland sense can be traced back to 1988 (the year before the introduction of EMU and Cultural Heritage). The

80

Central Community Relations Unit of the Northern Ireland Civil Service drew together a number of people in education, the arts, and communications 'to explore ways of promoting a better understanding of, and a more constructive debate about, our different cultural traditions in Northern Ireland' (Crozier 1989, vii). This resulted in the formation of the *Cultural Traditions Group*, which operated under the aegis of the Institute of Irish Studies at Queen's University, Belfast. In 1990 this group was reconstituted as a sub-committee of the newly formed Community Relations Council.

The Cultural Traditions Group

Significantly, neither in the literature of *Cultural Traditions Group* before 1990 nor since has there been much discussion of the meaning of 'culture', or 'tradition(s)', or of the new coinage 'cultural traditions'. According to Crozier (1995, 38) the terms are 'virtually inextricable'. Hayes (1991, 7) embarks on an inconclusive definition of 'culture', and uses 'culture' and 'tradition' interchangeably. The lack of discussion and clear agreement on definition of these terms is best explained by a general assumption that, since they are so fundamental and so widely used (like 'church'), they require little or no critical examination.

Yet, on the face of it, the concept 'cultural traditions' is problematic. Given the broad definition of culture (way of life - as adopted for Cultural Heritage), it is tautologous: all traditions are cultural in the sense that necessarily they must be part of a culture (way of life). In other words, non-cultural traditions are inconceivable. If not on the broad definition, then cultural traditions must rely on the narrow definition which restricts culture to the artistic or aesthetic aspects of society (as distinct from the political, economic, social and, religious aspects). Which of the two meanings was intended by the Community Relations Council is apparent from the statement of aims of the Cultural Traditions sub-committee (despite the document's ambiguous use of communities, heritage and cultures):

> In the particular area of Cultural Traditions, the Council is working to ensure that *communities* can feel confident in the non-triumphalist expressions of *their heritage* through, for example commemorations, museums, music, language, and local history work ... and it also seeks to ensure that the existence of *differing cultures* should be accommodated within any relevant consititutional structures (author's italics, NICRC 1991, 9).

It is clear from the examples given that heritage (a collective term for traditions which form a distinct corpus) is intended in a narrow sense. Only certain aspects of what has been inherited from the past are included; artistic, aesthetic and social aspects ('commemorations, museums, music, language and local history') as distinct from political and economic aspects. It is clear also that *Cultural Traditions* is not intended to be merely tautologous (all traditions are cultural) because the cultural traditions referred to are those of at least two separate cultures, where culture clearly means that of the entire way of life of a community. The number of cultures (communities) is identified as two:

> The [Cultural Traditions] programme's aim has been to broaden the appreciation of cultural diversity in Northern Ireland as a means of fostering increased tolerance and mutual understanding between Protestant/unionist and Catholic/nationalist communities.

At the same time, however, the two communities are thought of as forming one community. As the Chairman of the Council put it: 'Community Relations, simply defined, endeavours to bring *the two sides of our community* towards greater understanding'. He envisaged that 'our infamous divide' will remain: 'No case is argued for a *common culture* but rather that the full spectrum should be explored and celebrated; there are many more colours than orange and green' (1991, 5).

To say that no case was being argued for a common culture was disingenuous. Elsewhere, the Chairman of the Cultural Traditions Group clearly makes the case for 'a common culture' of 'the general community' (Hayes 1991, 22). The very notion of one community, albeit divided infamously between two sides (or communities or cultures), presupposes a common culture in which diversity is unified (the spectrum which integrates all the colours). The Chairman's disclaimer is explained by the need to modulate between paradigms. The Council's underlying ideological bias towards the notion of a common culture is clear. However, the Council could not have nailed its colours to the mast without weakening its prospects for improving community relations. It would have drawn fire from the communities upon whose co-operation it was depending in much the same way that Cultural Heritage and EMU drew fire from the SDLP, DUP and others. As Frazer and Fitzduff (whose thinking was influential in the setting up of the NICRC) had explained:

> There are some in Northern Ireland who dream of a day when all peoples in the larger community of Northern Ireland will not only accord each other equality of rights and existence, but will be 'reconciled' with one another, sharing feelings of mutual understanding and respect, and will work to achieve these aims. Many others would settle for the less

idealistic goal of equitable arrangements between communities (1986, 16).

Not referred to here explicitly are those who favour separate (and not necessarily equitable) arrangements between communities; that is to say *apartheid* of the type formerly in South Africa. This is the far end of the spectrum across which core choice preferences (between sharing and separation) are ranged. Although Community Relations workers may be inclined to the common culture end of the spectrum, they cannot afford to be publicly committed to the core choice in favour of sharing rather than separation. For the sake of their work (which would be impossible if they did not), they modulate to the centrist position of qualified separation (or qualified sharing), which seeks to hold the balance between the alternatives of the choice. On the one hand the NICRC offers the reassurance that 'rejecting sectarianism does not require the sacrifice of cultural identity or the surrender of political convictions' (NICRC, *Community Relations*, 5/7/91). On the other hand, it holds out the prospect of the development of a new culture of Northern Ireland:

> Communities which have acquired a clear sense of their own cultural identity based on knowledge and understanding, as opposed to prejudices and myths, are in a much better position to engage confidently, and without menace, with others and are more likely to recognise the interdependence of cultural traditions. Culture is in any case not static and the richest cultures are those which have developed through contact with others. Diversity can be an asset, and not necessarily a threat (NICRC, *Community Relations*, 4/5/91).

Two ideas of key importance are implied by this argument: first, the interdependence and substantial common interest of the two cultures (Catholic/nationalist and Protestant/unionist) and second, the inter-relationship of continuity and change. Both of these underpin the appeal for diversity. The process of contact with 'the other side' in dispelling mutual prejudices will reveal common ground upon which good relations may be built in future. This is cultural change which makes one culture richer by developing contact with another. What is implied, but not stated, is that contact will result effectively in the emergence of a new unifying common culture, in which the two cultures are still diverse (that is, continuous with their past), but no longer opposite.

How self-aware was NICRC of the skillful use it was making of paradigm or choice modulation? Certainly, Frazer and Fitzduff had been aware of the difficulty of defining community and had hinted at paradigm modulation by drawing attention to the way definitions of community keep changing:

Definitions as to what constitutes a community are fraught with difficulty. Communities are often defined as those groups within which frequent social interaction occurs, common ties abound, and who often live within a common geographical area. But definitions keep changing, reflecting the complexity of ideas surrounding the notion of what constitutes a community.

While differences in groupings within Northern Ireland normally emphasise the two main groupings of Loyalists and Nationalists, most of us in fact function as part of many communities. While this study [a foundation document of the NICRC] addresses itself primarily to problems existing in the main between *these two major communities*, we feel there may be a danger to the basic rights of all not to acknowledge the existence of other groups in Northern Ireland, many of whom also suffer from prejudice and discrimination e.g. the Equal Opportunities Commission considers that in fact women are the community most at risk from discrimination in Northern Ireland. Similarly, disabled people, people of a minority sexual preference, senior citizens and itinerants have protested and documented discrimination against their particular communities (1986, 15-16).

The 'complexity of ideas surrounding the notion of what constitutes a community' describes well the network of words related to community (culture, tradition, church, religion) which constitute the environment of ambiguity within which paradigm or choice modulation takes place. Seeing the way definitions of community are continually changing as a reflection of the 'complexity of ideas' comes close to describing the operation of paradigm modulation. However, in the second section of this extract, Frazer and Fitzduff did not press their observation further. Rather, they came closer to identifying what Boyle and Hadden were later to call 'the third community' (constituted by those firmly committed to a religious and political identity which is neither Catholic/Nationalist nor Protestant/Unionist). Acknowledgement of the complexity (or ambiguous nature) of 'community' was sufficient for their purpose, leaving them free to justify their focus of attention on relations between the two 'major communities'.

The point can be made again. Like the Northern Ireland Curriculum Council, it suited the purpose of the Community Relations Council to sustain an impression of hopeless (and in the final analysis unimportant) theoretical complexity. Any attempt then to sort out an agreed framework within which to pin down the meaning of community would very likely have been doomed to acrimonious, intractable debate and nothing practical would have been achieved.

The focus of the *Cultural Traditions Group* of the NICRC on the divide between the two 'major communities' reflected the thinking of a precursor group, the *Two Traditions Group*. This had been formed in 1983 as a non-party political group, representative of different interests in Northern Ireland. One of its most influential members was Professor R.H. Buchanan, Director of the Institute of Irish Studies at Queen's University, which later hosted the *Cultural Traditions Group*. The *Two Traditions Group* based itself on a central insight:

> We are convinced that one of the most hopeful recent developments is the growing acknowledgement in Northern Ireland and Ireland as a whole of the relevance to our problems of violence and civil strife of the existence of *two distinctive traditions, cultures and communities*. The existence of these 'Two Traditions' is indisputable (Two Traditions 1983, 3).

There are three things to notice here. First is the general point that the Two Traditions Group was registering the shift to dominance of the internal conflict paradigm in place of the external conflict paradigm (as described by Whyte and discussed in Chapter 1). Second is the particular point that the Group used the three terms 'tradition', 'culture' and 'community' synonymously. Third, the existence of the Two Traditions is not indisputable.

The formulation of the Group's aims reflected both the ambiguity of fundamental terms (tradition, culture, community) and the apparently unavoidable need to modulate between their levels of meaning. The stated aims of the Group were:

> (1) to promote widespread acceptance of the legitimacy of *these distinctive traditions and cultures*;
> (2) to develop a deeper knowledge of what both have in common, and to foster a straightforward respect and tolerance for each other;
> (3) to stimulate a search for such understanding and comprehension of *both traditions and cultures* (their affinities and differences) as may encourage acceptance on 'both sides' of *the need for a multicultural society*;
> (4) to persuade those in positions of authority and influence to publicise and encourage the many opportunities that exist for bringing together *both traditions* in a variety of activities including those which *are social, economic, religious, political, **cultural** and educational* (1983, 3).

On the one hand, the first three aims use 'culture' in the broad sense of 'way of life'. On the other hand, the fourth aim uses 'cultural' in the narrow sense of artistic and aesthetic aspects only. It turns out, then, that tradition, culture and community are not exact synonyms. On the face of it, the Group might as well have called itself the Two Cultures or Two Communities Group. However, tradition was preferred and probably with good reason. The connotations of culture and community are such that, had they been preferred, they would more likely have suggested that the Group was in favour of keeping the Two Cultures or Two Communities separate, than that it was in favour of the opposite, namely 'the need for a multicultural society'.

There seems to be a scale against which fitness for the intended purpose can best be measured: the idea of Two Communities making One Community sounds better (less radical) than Two Cultures making One Culture; but better still is the idea of Two Traditions making One Tradition. As the 'community relations industry' grew, paradoxically perhaps, the tendency was towards greater, not less, ambiguity. The *Two Traditions Group* was much more up front about its commitment to the ideal of one multicultural society than its successor; a change which was reflected in the title change from *Two Traditions* to the more ambiguous *Cultural Traditions*.

Fairly interpreted, this change reflected not so much a loss of integrity as a gain in sophistication. There was movement forward from the relatively simplistic pioneering phase to a more sensitively modulated approach. However, its acknowledgement of complexity notwithstanding, the *Cultural Traditions Group* remains as firmly focused as its predecessor on the two traditions in the hope of strengthening the development of a third, all-embracing multicultural tradition.

Contrary to the assertion of the *Two Traditions Group*, the wisdom of its analysis has not proved indisputable. Buckley (1988), for example, has argued conversely for an analytical framework which gives prominence to a single Ulster culture which consists of a multiplicity of traditions, rather than to the two 'major' traditions:

> There is plenty of evidence to suggest that not only do Catholics and Protestants spend very little time and energy in affirming their cultural distinctiveness, but also that they frequently decide that such affirmation is undesirable. Thus do people avoid controversial subjects in mixed company and in other ways make an attempt to 'get on well' with people from 'the other side'. Ulster people tend to present themselves to others as Catholics or Protestants but only when it is socially or politically useful for them so to do. More generally, however, it is important to recognise that the overwhelming bulk of what people in Ulster (or Ireland) say or do is unconnected to their statuses as Catholics or Protestants (1988, 58-59).

There is clearly force in this argument for One (multi-traditional) Tradition. The difficulty is that the Two Traditions counter-argument seems equally forceful: just because not much time or energy is spent affirming cultural distinctiveness does not mean it is not important; and the convention of avoiding controversial subjects in order to 'get on well' with 'the other side' has manifestly failed to prevent protracted conflict. If both interpretations are convincing, they can only be partial. But that leaves the problem of integrating them: how can they both be true simultaneously?

Paradigm or choice modulation accounts for the apparent discrepancy. Buckley effectively describes its operation in showing how the affirmation by Protestants and Catholics of their distinct identities depends on (or is modulated according to) circumstance. Again the point can be made, the relatively small amount of time or energy spent by an individual in Protestant/Catholic mode as distinct from shared citizen mode is immaterial: paradigm modulation is no less effective for being momentary. It is probably true that most of the time most people in Northern Ireland perceive themselves to be participating in one community (society), or one common culture or tradition, in which all 'get on well' together. However, their experience of community harmony (unlike that of most of their western Euorpean neighbours) has not been continuous. Periodically, the underlying low discord of violent conflict has become dominant. At such times most people have perceived two hostile and opposed cultures (or communities, traditions, religions). Arguing about which perception is correct, therefore, is like arguing about whether the glass is half full or half empty. There are habitual optimists and pessimists and those whose mood modulates habitually. The protracted and violent conflict in Northern Ireland has been bad enough to leave few as habitual optimists but not bad enough to make many more habitual pessimists. It has made habitual modulators of most with, perhaps, an optimistic bias towards improving community relations (however that ambiguous term may be interpreted).

As seen in the various levels of meaning of key words such as culture and tradition, there is benefit in leaving well alone. Paradigm modulation flourishes best in a climate of vagueness. But, as we have also seen, the price to be paid for not having a commonly agreed intellectual framework is mutual misunderstanding and mistrust. Without such a framework, debate of the 'opposite cultures/traditions/communities/religions still?' question is ultimately intractable. One of the particular consequences is a limiting of the effectiveness of curriculum development in schools.

Is a commonly agreed framework for interpreting cultural traditions possible and, if so, would it be beneficial?

Cultural traditions: a framework for interpreting the meanings

The origin and development of 'culture' has been discussed by Williams (1981). Originally its meaning was agricultural: the cultivation of crops and the rearing of animals. By extension it came to be used of the cultivation (training and refinement) of the human mind. In the eighteenth century, it acquired the parallel meaning of the 'spirit' which informs 'a whole way of life'. The meaning of culture in this sense has further developed two aspects: the material and the non-material. The material aspect includes all the artefacts and activities (political, economic, social, artistic, aesthetic, religious etc) which constitute the way of life of a society. The non-material aspect refers only to certain specific activities (the arts, or humane intellectual works) which define the 'spirit' of a society in terms of ideology, nationality or religion.

In the second half of the twentieth century, the material (broad) and the non-material (narrow) meanings have converged. The narrow meaning has broadened from language, literature, the arts and philosophy to include, for example, journalism, fashion and advertising. Effectively, culture has been re-defined as the whole 'signifying system' through which a social order is created. The social order is created through four processes: communication; reproduction; experience; and exploration. These processes combine to produce the types of institution from which a society (culture) is constituted: political; economic; social; educational; artistic or aesthetic; and religious. It is possible to interpret the complex of inter-relations between them as a whole by using the concept of *organisation* (Williams 1981, 13).

What this convergence of the narrow and broad meanings of culture requires is that any separate interpretation of a particular aspect or dimension should be integrated ultimately within an interpretation of the whole organisation (culture, way of life). For example, the political and religious 'sides' or 'dimensions' of a culture need to be interpreted both separately and in relation to each other (and to the other dimensions). Their separate treatment, and no more, necessarily results in an incomplete and, therefore, inadequate interpretation.

This approach to interpretation is rooted in the metaphor of marriage; the idea that two separate entities can become one without either losing its individual identity. In the case of culture, as many as six or more distinct entities (the aspects/sides/dimensions of a society) are 'married' into one organisation (culture), while still being separately identifiable as such. Related to this view of culture is the modern view of cultural change in the form of the multicultural ideal of Two (or more) Cultures renouncing single life and 'marrying' to form One Culture. The one new culture is 'multi-cultural' in the sense that the distinctive identities of the parent cultures live on through their children.

Tradition is to be distinguished from culture. Although in Northern Ireland the Two Cultures means virtually the same as the Two Traditions, culture and tradition are not exactly the same. The origin and development of 'tradition' has been discussed by Gailey (1988). Like culture, tradition has developed two meanings. Its broad meaning is 'something which is carried or handed on from one generation to the next'. What distinguishes tradition at this level from culture is that it deals mainly with the reproductive process through which a society is constituted. Culture includes the reproductive process (tradition) as well as the other three processes (communication, experience, and exploration), which deal more with change and innovation than with continuity (the main concern of tradition).

Alongside the broad meaning of tradition is the narrow meaning which restricts it to non-material aspects such as 'oral tradition' in story or music or communal seasonal or life-cycle customs, rather than material aspects such as houses or household implements. Confusingly, experts on tradition (folklorists) themselves modulate between the broad and narrow definitions. Sometimes they intend tradition to mean lore in general and at others only a narrowly defined canon of lore. On the one hand tradition means comprehensively a body of information and practice transmitted through the generations. On the other hand, it means only particular modes of expression, as in 'oral tradition' or 'literary tradition' (Ben-Amos 1984).

In these ways culture, tradition and heritage (a body of traditions) are ambiguous and their ambiguity is compounded when they are combined (or married) in expressions such as Cultural Traditions and Cultural Heritage. It should not be surprising, therefore, that any interpretation of any particular aspect of culture (or tradition) within such an ambiguous intellectual framework should be misunderstood. When it comes to interpreting the role of religion within cultural traditions and in Cultural Heritage this is emphatically the case.

Ambiguity about the role of religion in Cultural Heritage

An example of how these ambiguities make for a shifting conceptual framework, which alters according to point of view, is provided by the RE Drafting Group of the four largest Churches, which prepared a core syllabus for Religious Education in the new Northern Ireland Curriculum. This Group dissented from the all-embracing definition of Cultural Heritage (made by the Cultural Heritage Working Group) by making clear that it regarded cultural heritage and religious heritage as separate entities. It reported that 'the whole process of working together to produce a common RE curriculum has been a valuable exercise in EMU and the appreciation of aspects of each other's *cultural and religious heritage*' (Churches 1991, 65). This narrow use of cultural (meaning non-religious) heritage, which probably reflected the Group's vested interest in promoting that particular aspect, was in spite of the Group's enthusiastic welcome for the cross-curricular theme of Cultural Heritage which explicitly included the religious dimension as part of culture (1991, 66).

It might be supposed that the RE Group was simply confusing the broad and narrow meanings of 'cultural' in seeming to imply that religious heritage is separate from and not part of cultural heritage. However, deeper issues were at stake. The Education Reform Order 1989 itself seems to separate the 'religious' (spiritual) from the 'cultural' by naming the five dimensions of education as *'the **spiritual**, moral, **cultural**, intellectual and physical development* of pupils'. Distinguishing religious (spiritual) heritage from cultural heritage it turns out was a function of the RE Drafting Group's laying claim to the spiritual (religious) dimension of education. But more than that, in the wider perspective, the view that religion is an aspect or dimension of culture is not uncontroversial. Religious believers, following Dawson (1948), may take the view that religion is something which stands over and above culture.

Like 'cultural', the word 'spiritual' is ambiguous. Its broad sense refers to the *spirit* or non-material aspects of a culture or way of life. Its narrow sense refers to that which is beyond the merely human and leads to the transcendent reality called God. The framework within which culture is thought about, therefore, may vary according to the individual's religious belief or non-belief: the broad meaning of spiritual includes religion within culture; the narrow meaning sets it apart.

Analysts like Dawson, who believe the universal truth claims of religion, tend to see the relationship between religion and culture as two-sided: the culture (way of life) influences the approach to religion and the religious attitude influences the culture. Dawson recognised that a synthesis takes place so that a religious dimension is an integral part of culture, but he insisted nevertheless on the distinction between culture and religion, which, as a believer, he regarded as being of a 'higher order' (1948, 206).

The absence of a shared framework for cultural analysis, then, is not simply a matter of imprecision of language. Underlying the ambiguity of spiritual are two radically opposed views of the relation between religion and culture. The four largest Churches in their joint promotion of RE in the Northern Ireland Curriculum part company with the secular approach of Cultural Heritage.

They go further in showing broad sympathy with Dawson's vision of a 'movement of spiritual regeneration which would restore that vital relation between religion and culture which has existed at every age and at every level of human development' (218).

On this view, the spiritual dimension of education is seen as permeating almost all the other subjects of the curriculum on the grounds that:

> Events which are conventionally seen as ordinary or 'secular' may, when looked at in depth, take on a religious dimension. If all truth is God's truth, then the pupils' search after truth in any subject is capable of including a religious dimension' (Churches 1991, 6-7).

Thus, clarification of the role of religion in the analysis of culture in general, and in the Northern Ireland conflict in particular, threatens to resolve itself into a battle between the godly and the godless. The attraction of leaving things as ambiguous and as vague as they are is understandable.

Ambiguity about the role of religion in Irish historiography

The tension of ambiguity about the role of religion in Cultural Heritage in the Northern Ireland Curriculum is paralleled in the writing of Irish history. Connolly (1983) has distinguished between the 'religious' and the 'secular' historian. They differ about the nature of spiritual experience, the one believing it to be genuine, the other understanding it as a form of expression of other mental energies. Connolly foresees a 'possibly unbridgeable gap' opening up between the two types, doubting that a historian who is also committed to religious belief within a particular denomination may successfully transcend his denominational commitment and conduct the new kind of historical enquiry which deals with the interaction of politics and religion (all traditions) in society as a whole.

The 'religious' approach to history writing of which Connolly is critical is illustrated by the following comments of two such historians:

> The Christian message can normally give to any society only a little more than what that society is disposed to receive (Corish 1981, 5).
> It may be impossible for the historian to measure the church's influence in the lives of men and women whom its preaching and teaching 'made glad to live and unafraid to die', and inspired 'to do justly, to love mercy and walk humbly with their God' (Holmes 1985, 75).

Both Corish and Holmes believe in the elusive 'little more', which Connolly doubts. Just as the four main Churches in their promotion of Religious Education part company with Cultural Heritage, so the 'religious' historian parts company with the 'secular' historian in believing that assessment of the importance of religion must in the end be theological. The approach of Corish and Holmes can be contrasted, for example, with that of Inglis (1987, 6-7) who has set out in purely secular terms to 'examine the reasons why Irish Catholics adhere to the Church in terms of rational, instrumental calculation of means towards more immediate, specific, material ends'.

The first generation of professional historians in Ireland from the 1930s onwards succeeded largely in their aim of 'exorcising passion' from Irish historiography, which had previously been dominated by the nature of Anglo-Irish relations. But they did so 'largely by evading the challenge of contemporary history' (Lee 1989, xiv). This evasion included the neglect of the religious dimension referred to in Chapter 1. The present generation of Irish historians are taking up this challenge with the result that, as one commentator puts it, a battle for possession of 'the heritage of Gospel faith' as a cultural resource is developing between 'religious' and 'secular' historians:

> The hope of Ireland is the honesty of its disaffected Catholics (or those clever enough to stay on as *à la carte* Catholics). The straight talk and penetrating analysis that has been pouring from their lips in recent years has greatly helped to clarify our religious situation. What needs to be urged, however, is that this critical movement not consider itself to be cut off from the heritage of Gospel faith. It should confidently claim the Gospel for itself, even against the Church. If it does do, it may bring about a wider religious and human vision, which could once more make our country's voice one of the respected voices in the concert of civilization (O'Leary 1988, 241).

The plea here for 'a wider religious and human vision' is for a vision which integrates religion as an important part of culture (rather than sets it apart). It recalls the line taken by Hickey and Bruce. However, it is in strong contrast both with the reductionist view, which minimises and marginalises the role of religion, and with the religious view, which sets religion apart from culture. Corish and Holmes give the alternative perspective of the 'religious' historian:

> The Irish Catholic inheritance - like all religious inheritances - can be understood only by co-operation between theology and the humanities. It is only this that will give us a real Irish theology, hard at the centre not only with the great central tradition but with the Irish tradition as well (Corish 1985, 258).
>
> If our Irish Presbyterian history inevitably uncovers faults and failures in our past, may they lead us to repentance in the present and a new commitment to Christ and his way for the future (Holmes 1985, vii).

Conflicting projects are in evidence here. Where Corish advocates a 'real Irish theology' common to all Irish Catholics, others like Inglis advocate 'an ethic of individual responsibility'. Whether or not these projects are reconcilable ultimately is not of concern here. What is of concern is that the interpretation of the religious inheritance (heritage) of Ireland is central to them both. The tension between their 'religious' and 'secular' approaches (hidden for the most part) also inhibits the emergence of an agreed, unambiguous framework for the analysis and discussion of culture in general and of the role of religion in culture in particular.

Ambiguity about culture in Irish historiography

Obscuring this fundamental point of disagreement between 'religious' and 'secular' historians is, once again, ambiguity of terminology. Like the educators who depend upon them, historians and social scientists are thoroughly ambiguous in their use of key terms. Culture, perhaps, is the prime case. For example, the title of a recent book about Northern Ireland, *Culture and Politics* (Hughes 1991), indicates that culture and politics should be thought of as separate entities, yet it contains an article entitled 'Political Culture'.

Foster (1988) is even more elusive in the way he modulates between the broad and narrow meanings of culture. On the one hand he refers to 'the culture' and 'Irish culture' as a whole. On the other hand, he uses culture in connection with each of the various dimensions of culture as a whole: the political dimension (as in, 'political culture'; 'political cultures'; 'civic culture'; 'landlord political culture'); the economic dimension (as in, 'factory culture'; 'merchant culture'; 'linen culture'; 'grazier-shopkeeper-publican culture'); the social dimension (as in, 'the culture of dining out'; 'the recreational culture of picnics'); the artistic and aesthetic dimension (as in 'middle-brow clubman culture'; 'the culture of exaggeration'; 'youth culture'); and of the religious (or religio-political) dimension (as in, 'the cultures of Catholicism and Dissent'; 'local Catholic culture'; 'Ascendancy culture'; 'Presbyterian political culture'; 'Catholic Nationalist culture'). Foster does not call any of these 'sub-cultures'. This, presumably, is to avoid any pejorative connotation since elsewhere he does use sub-culture, as in: 'the smuggling sub-culture' and 'the sub-culture of the Protestant gentry'.

Ambiguities such as these compound the fundamental point of disagreement between historians who are religious believers and those who are not. The net effect is to inhibit the emergence of a shared framework within which to debate the relation of religion to culture, without mutual misunderstanding or mistrust. It is as if there is an unconscious calculation at work: better all round to continue nursing the intractable disagreement about the role of religion in the conflict for fear of getting something worse.

Like 'community' and 'religion', the ambiguities of 'culture' and 'tradition' conform to Empson's seventh type of 'full contradiction'. At present they are satisfying only to the extent that they generate a climate of vagueness which obscures potentially divisive issues. At the same time they are preventing historians and others from providing educators with the kind of framework which they need in order to interpret cultural traditions coherently. The experience of curriculum development projects which have addressed cultural traditions with the aim of improving community relations in Northern Ireland bears this out.

The introduction of the cross-curricular themes of Cultural Heritage and Education for Mutual Understanding has gone a considerable way towards establishing a coherent framework, However, Cultural Heritage and EMU have yet to be connected with the issue of Boyle and Hadden's core choice. They remain inhibited by the hidden effects of choice modulation.

The next chapter describes a further curriculum development project which was concerned with improving community relations by interpreting cultural traditions. It focused particularly on the way schoolchildren perceive the role of religion in the conflict and it investigated choice modulation in the school population.

5 Opposite religions?

The previous chapter reviewed the series of curriculum development projects concerned with 'cultural traditions'. They preceded the watershed of Education Reform in 1989 and the introduction of the compulsory cross-curriculur themes of Cultural Heritage and Education for Mutual Understanding. This chapter describes a further project in the series, the first after Education Reform, which was centred on the choice between separation and sharing and on the question: opposite religions still?.

The *Opposite Religions? Project, 1988-92*

During the academic year 1989-90, the Department of Education for Northern Ireland (DENI) seconded a team of eleven primary and secondary school teachers to various cultural institutions. Their brief was to develop classroom materials across a range of subjects. These materials were intended to assist teachers in implementing the new cross-curricular themes of EMU and Cultural Heritage.

The present writer was seconded as one of the team and was based jointly at the Institute of Irish Studies in Queen's University, Belfast, and at the Ulster Folk and Transport Museum, Cultra. His specific brief was to write new teaching materials for use in History and Religious Education. These materials were to focus on comparing the historical development of Protestant and Catholic religious traditions and on the inter-connection of religion and politics in Northern Ireland. The production of these materials was the first part of what eventually became the *Opposite Religions? Project.*

Opposite Religions? was in three parts. The first was the production and trialing for DENI of the new teaching materials, under the title *Religion in*

Ireland: yesterday, today and tomorrow (Lambkin 1990). The second part was the evaluation of the trial and the revision of *Religion in Ireland: yesterday, today and tomorrow* for publication by DENI as *Opposite Religions?: Protestants and Catholics in Ireland since the Reformation* (Lambkin 1991). The third part was doctoral research by the writer for the University of Ulster at Coleraine. This studied the whole process of writing the *Opposite Religions?* trial materials, testing them out in a representative sample of 19 schools in the Easter Term 1989-90, and then evaluating and revising them for publication as *Opposite Religions?* (Lambkin 1993).

Religion in Ireland: Yesterday, Today and Tomorrow

The title chosen for the trial teaching materials, *Religion in Ireland: Yesterday, Today and Tomorrow*, was intended to reflect the way they built on the foundation of the previous similar projects discussed in Chapter 4. Two main strengths were identified in that tradition of curriculum development. Firstly, there was a sound educational rationale that benefited from the convergence of the aims of 'secular' reconstructionism and ecumenical theology (a convergence exploited most fully by the *Religion in Ireland Project*). Secondly, there was a teaching methodology consisting mainly of classroom discussion, contact between Protestant and Catholic pupils, and visits to church buildings. The approach in each case was through teaching materials that compare Protestant and Catholic religious traditions. The new project, *Opposite Religions?*, aimed to build on these strengths and facilitate the continuation and extension of the good practice that the previous projects had established. In doing so it would be new only in two senses: the general content of the teaching materials would be re-structured in line with the newly defined objectives of EMU and Cultural Heritage, and particular items of evidence selected for inclusion might be different from those used previously.

It was clear, however, that the new project should also be new in the sense that it would address three main weaknesses identified in previous projects. These weaknesses (discussed in Chapter 4) were:

- Lack of a comprehensive cultural analysis which describes adequately the role of religion in society,
- Lack of comparative teaching materials which are diachronic in their approach (concerned with continuity and change over time) as well as synchronic (concerned with similarity and difference in the present),
- Lack of co-operation between History teachers and RE teachers in dealing with the complexity of the inter-relationship of politics and religion in Northern Ireland.

96

The *Opposite Religions?* trial, like the *Religion in Ireland Project* and the *Teaching Religion in Northern Ireland Project* before it, gave a central place to discussion based on consideration of evidence as a teaching strategy. In the thinking behind these projects, openness was a prerequisite for successful classroom discussion of controversial questions such as: 'why is there distrust among Christians in Ireland?'; 'why is there such ignorance of religious beliefs and practices across the religious divide?'; 'why do Protestants have misgivings about marriage with Roman Catholics, and vice-versa?'; 'why do Protestant clergy become involved in the Orange Order?'; 'what should be the attitude of Christians to violence as a means of political action?' (McElhinney et al. 1987, 24). It is particularly noteworthy that these questions point to the two central mechanisms for maintaining the boundary between the two communities (endogamy and segregated education) and to the special inter-relationship of religion and politics in Northern Ireland.

An important issue which the *Opposite Religions?* trial and its discussion-based predecessors had to face was the extent to which attitude-change by pupils was a desired outcome. In some subject areas, notably health education with issues such as smoking, use of drugs, alcohol, and personal hygiene, the notion that attitude change should be an educational aim is not controversial (Stradling, Noctor and Baines 1984, 108). Attitude change as an educational aim for political or religious education, however, is controversial, precisely because it has no underpinning consensus of the kind that sustains educational programmes that are anti-smoking or anti-drug abuse. It is true there is a consensus that prejudice of all kinds (racial, political, religious) is wrong (Lynch 1987, 33). However, there is not usually a clear consensus about what actually constitutes prejudice in any given case. This is especially so with religion where many see the truth claims of various religions (and denominations within religions) as mutually exclusive.

There is a way through this problem if the teacher's task is defined as being 'to enable pupils to become morally autonomous as well as socially responsible' (Lynch 1987, xii). A distinction can be drawn between the teacher changing pupil attitudes directly and changing them indirectly. Direct attitude change is usually regarded as an unacceptable form of 'social engineering' that violates the freedom of the individual. On the other hand, the process of indirect attitude change preserves the moral integrity of pupils and teacher alike. It may (or may not) come about when the teacher 'challenges' pupils to reconsider existing attitudes and to consider choosing (autonomously) new ones.

Lynch writes of the urgent need for teachers to 'empower pupils to undertake social criticism and action in pursuit of democratic values such as justice, equality and the combating of prejudice'. He stresses the dual aspect of the teacher's role in cultural heritage: 'they are not ... mere servants of the status quo, and their role can be as much socially transformative as culturally transmissionist' (1987, 178-9). This recalls the approach of Skilbeck and the *Schools Cultural Studies Project* discussed in Chapter 3.

Both the *Religion in Ireland* and *Learning about Churches and Worship* projects were modest in their expectations of being socially transformative. McElhinney saw *Religion in Ireland* as being like the *Schools Cultural Studies Project* - a 'minimalist' rather than a 'maximalist' interventionist version of cultural reconstruction, which brought about 'some unfreezing' of attitudes rather than changes of attitude (1983, 431). Similarly, Richardson stressed in his study of the way teachers used the *Learning about Churches and Worship* materials that the aim of the teacher was to 'challenge' rather than 'change' attitudes (1992, 24).

The EMU Working Group (but not the Cultural Heritage Working Group) dealt with the question of attitude change. In a wide-ranging statement, it said that 'all teachers will be expected to develop in their pupils a range of skills and attitudes which will enable them to respect and value themselves and others, and to be sensitive to the views and attitudes of others (NICC 1989, 7, 9.2.2.). It is significant here that teachers are expected to 'develop' rather than 'change' attitudes. The implication is that acceptable attitudes are already inherent in all pupils, albeit in an under-developed form, and so the question of attitude change as such is avoided.

The *Opposite Religions?* trial adopted the position that the teacher should 'challenge' pupil attitudes and encourage individual autonomous choice after evaluation of relevant evidence. This position may be considered as intermediate between that of 'developing' attitudes already inherent in pupils (the EMU position) and that of 'changing' attitudes directly (by appeal to an adult consensus, as in the case of anti-smoking campaigns, and pressure to conform). This is what is meant by Education for *The Choice*; challenging pupils to consider, or re-consider, the choice between separation and sharing and the question: opposite religions still?.

The Opposite Religions? trial teaching materials

The *Opposite Religions?* trial teaching materials (called *Religion in Ireland: yesterday, today and tomorrow*) consisted of an illustrated *Pupils' Work Book* and accompanying *Teachers' Guide*. The *Pupils' Book* contained eight units of work, designed to last 6-8 weeks, as follows:

Unit 1. Religion out of doors - why?

Compares the present with the past. Today each religious group in a town or village usually has its own church building. At times in the past, only one religious group had its own church buildings and others had to worship in their homes or in the open air.

Unit 2. Two places for religion indoors: Drumcree, Co. Armagh and Kilmore, Co. Down

Case studies of two church buildings now relocated at the Ulster Folk Museum, Cultra. Compares their histories and invites comparison with the pupils' local area.

Unit 3. Catholics, Protestants and Others on the island of Ireland

Introduces the idea of types of history (political, economic, social, religious). Presents the evidence of membership of religious denominations from the 1981 Census and compares the distribution of the main religious groups in Ireland in 1911 and 1971.

Unit 4. Are funerals the same?

Focus on the moment when the body is committed to the grave.

Unit 5. Are weddings the same?

Focus on the moment when the Bridegroom gives the ring to the Bride.

Unit 6. Are baptisms the same?

Focus on the moment when water is used.

Unit 7. Is Communion the same?

Focus on the moment when bread and wine are given and received.

[Units 4-7 present for comparison extracts from Roman Catholic, Presbyterian, Church of Ireland and Methodist orders of service past and present. Each poses an open-ended question designed to stimulate investigation and assessment of features of similarity and difference and of continuity and change.]

Unit 8. Conclusions about Religion in Ireland

Encourages pupils to draw together their findings. Focuses on assessment of similarity and difference, and continuity and change from their comparison of Protestant and Catholic religious artefacts and practice. Introduces the inter-connection of religion and politics.

This final unit also presents for comparison and evaluation brief answers to the question 'is the fighting in Northern Ireland about religion?' given by: Cardinal T. Ó Fiaich (Roman Catholic Primate of All Ireland); Archbishop R. Eames (Church of Ireland Primate of All Ireland); Rt Rev Dr J A Matthews (Presbyterian Moderator 1989-90); Rev Dr G Morrison (Methodist President 1989-90); Mr J Molyneux (leader of the Ulster Unionist Party); Rev Dr I Paisley (leader of the

Democratic Unionist Party and Moderator of the Free Presbyterian Church); Dr J Alderdice (leader of the Alliance Party); Mr J Hume (leader of the Social Democratic and Labour Party).

Trial schools

A representative sample of 19 post-primary schools took part in the trial of the *Opposite Religions?* materials (*Religion in Ireland: yesterday, today and tomorrow*) in the Easter Term of 1989-90 (Lambkin 1993, 294-307). Classifying them loosely, 13 of the schools may be considered as urban and 6 as rural. They were distributed according to Education and Library Board Areas as follows: Belfast 6; South Eastern 6; Southern 4; Western 2; North Eastern 1. According to management type they were: Maintained Roman Catholic Secondary schools 6 (including 1 Comprehensive) and Controlled (Protestant) Secondary schools 6; Roman Catholic Voluntary Grammar schools 2 and Voluntary or Controlled (Protestant) Grammar schools 3; Maintained Integrated (Catholic and Protestant, Comprehensive) schools 2. Calculating on the number of schools, therefore, 42% of the sample were Roman Catholic, 47% were Controlled or Voluntary (non-Catholic) and 11% were Maintained Integrated. With the caveat that integrated schools were disproportionately represented, there was a good match between the sample of schools and the regional profile.

In the 19 schools there were 48 participating teachers who used the *Opposite Religions?* trial materials with 24 History classes and 24 RE classes. The teachers agreed to administer to each class a *Questionnaire* before starting work on the Pupils' Book and the same *Questionnaire* at the end. The results of the *Before Questionnaire* are reported on in this chapter. The results of the *After Questionnaire* are reported on in Chapter 6.

A total of 1014 pupils responded to the *Before Questionnaire*. Of these 475 (47%) were boys and 539 (53%) were girls. The youngest pupils were aged 11 and the oldest aged 16. The large majority (over 80%) were in the age range 12-14, that is in the second and third years of secondary education. The majority (53%) were in non-grammar schools, with 28% in grammar schools and 19% in comprehensive schools.

According to their self-descriptions, the pupils by religious denomination were 50% Roman Catholic; 24% Presbyterian; 14% Church of Ireland; 3% Methodist; 3% Other; 6% None. No religion other than Christianity was represented in the sample. The 28 pupils who described themselves as 'Other' represented 26 different religious denominations (none of which were non-Christian).

The main aims of the *Questionnaire*, given immediately before and after work on the trial teaching materials were as follows:

1. To investigate the knowledge, understanding and attitudes of pupils with regard to the role of religion in the present conflict in Northern Ireland.

2. To investigate their knowledge and understanding of the main religious denominations of Northern Ireland with regard to: similarities and differences between their artefacts and practices, beliefs shared and not shared by them, and continuity and change in the history of each.

3. To investigate attitudes to the religious dimension of Cultural Heritage.

4. To measure the extent of change, if any, in pupils' knowledge, understanding and attitudes brought about as a result of studying *Religion in Ireland: Yesterday, Today and Tomorrow.*

Apart from the personal information requested on the first page, the questionnaire comprised 83 questions in total (Lambkin 1993, 624-636). Counting subdivisions of questions, there were 102 items altogether. Of the 83 questions, 67 were of the Likert 5-point measurement of agreement type; 8 were of the multiple choice single answer type; 2 were of the rank-order type; and 1 required the respondent to grade on a 5-point scale. There were also 5 open-ended questions which asked respondents to write a short passage in answer. These various types of question were used to elicit four types of information about religious traditions: general knowledge and understanding; specific knowledge and understanding of the present; specific knowledge and understanding of the past; and personal attitudes.

The *Questionnaire* has a good pedigree in the tradition of evaluating research on religious education in Northern Ireland, established largely by Greer (1981) and McElhinney (1983, see 312-349). A range of evaluation procedures, both informal and formal, formative and summative (including classroom observation), were also used to elucidate and corroborate the findings (Lambkin 1993, 307-339).

This chapter describes and analyses the current state of pupils' knowledge, understanding and attitudes as shown by their responses to the *Before Questionnaire*. Changes in the state of pupils' knowledge, understanding and attitudes as measured by the *After Questionnaire* are considered in Chapter 6. For the purposes of general discussion, differences between boys and girls, or between Catholics and Protestants and Others, are considered significant at 5% or more.

The findings of the *Before Questionnaire*

The *Questionnaire* comprised questions of four main types. Type I questions (12 items) tested pupils' general knowledge (such as the relative proportions of Catholics and Protestants in the population of Northern Ireland as a whole). Type II (28 items) tested pupils' perception of similarity and difference when comparing the artefacts, practices and beliefs of the four largest churches in Northern Ireland (Roman Catholic, Presbyterian, Church of Ireland and Methodist). Type III (44 items) tested pupils' perception of continuity and change in those things over the last fifty years. Type IV (18 items) tested pupils' attitudes with regard to various aspects of religion and the inter-connection of religion and politics in Northern Ireland.

Not all the findings are reported on here. What appear to be the most salient have been selected. The question of whether school type or gender or religious denomination account for significant differences in pupils' responses is taken up in discussion of the findings of the *After Questionnaire* in Chapter 6.

When quotations are given below, they are taken from pupils' answers to the five open-ended questions. Quotation is extensive but not exhaustive. It is extensive in order to allow the full range of pupils' voices to be heard as clearly as possible. The answers of the 'less able' are well represented. Some changes to spelling, puctuation, and grammar have been made in the interest of clarity but have been kept to a minimum.

It would have been possible to allow more articulate answers to stand for the less articulate. However, there is benefit to be gained from setting out less articulate and more articulate answers of the same type and sub-type together. Very often answers from less able pupils are brief, or obscurely phrased, to the point that on their own they may be unintelligible. Given that a common idea can be identified, the more articulate answer can often help to elucidate the less articulate. Sorting and setting out representative examples of pupils' responses in this way is illuminating. It may be especially helpful to educators in revealing the thinking about the conflict that is going on in the school population at different levels.

The reader may identify the source of each quotation by the code number which is given. For example: **f1presb** identifies a pupil who was female, in the First Year of post-primary education (aged 11-12), and who described herself as 'Presbyterian'. Thus, **m2rc** identifies a male pupil in Second Year (aged 12-13) who described himself as 'Roman Catholic'. For **rc** read 'Roman Catholic', for **presb** read 'Presbyterian', for **ci** read 'Church of Ireland', for **meth** read 'Methodist', for **freepresb** read 'Free Presbyterian'.

In the discussion of project data which follows, the terms 'catholic' and 'protestant' (lower case) are used to differentiate pupils who responded to the *Questionnaire* as two groups and to avoid implying that their perceptions are necessarily those of Catholics and Protestants generally. 'Catholic' and 'Protestant' (upper case) are used refer generally to the Churches and their members in wider discussion.

Perceptions of the role of religion in Northern Ireland

How do schoolchildren see the role of religion in Northern Ireland? Chapter 1 showed that the conflict about the interpretation of the conflict among adult commentators centres on the role of religion. Schoolchildren do not seem, at first sight, to be in conflict about this issue.

The overwhelming majority of schoolchildren in Northern Ireland (84%) agree that religion is an important part of life, whether we like it or not (Table 5.1). The level of agreement is marginally higher in girls than boys (1%) and significantly higher in catholics than in non-catholics (7%). This contrasts strongly with the perception of their peers in England and Wales. There a recent survey of 13,000 13-15 year olds found that only 27% disagree with

Table 5.1   Openness to religion

	Agree %	Don't Know %	Disagree %
Religion is an important part of life in Northern Ireland today, whether we like it or not	84	8	8
We should try to understand religion better whether we believe in it or not	78	10	12
History and RE in schools should help us to understand those who are different from us	78	12	10

the reverse proposition that the church seems irrelevant to life today (Francis and Kay, 1995, 187).

A further indication of how seriously schoolchildren in Northern Ireland take religion is their openness to learning about religion. A large majority (78%) agree that we should try to understand religion better whether we believe in it or not. The level of agreement is slightly higher in girls than boys (2%) and more so in catholics than non-catholics (6%). This openness contrasts with the finding of Francis and Kay that only 33% in England and Wales agreed that religious education should be taught in school.

Similarly, most schoolchildren in Northern Ireland are open in their attitutde to the basic aim of the cross-curricular themes of Cultural Heritage and EMU. A majority of 78% agree that History and RE in schools should help us to understand those who are different from us. The level of agreement was higher in girls than boys (2%) and in catholics than non-catholics (7%).

Perceptions of the origins of the Protestant / Catholic divide

How do schoolchildren see the origins and historical development of the divide between Catholics and Protestants? A substantial majority (63%) gave the correct answer or target response (TR) that the original Reformation split took place about 500 years ago. Slightly more boys than girls know this (2%) and more non-catholics than catholics (7%).

Table 5.2   Perceptions of the Reformation

Roughly how long ago would you say people in Europe split into religious groups called Catholics and Protestants?

	%
100 years ago	16
500 years ago	**63**
1000 years ago	16
2000 years ago	5

However, only a small majority (53%) know more or less accurately what were the main things that the first Protestants were 'protesting' about. The approximately accurate open-ended responses to the question of Table 5.3 were grouped into three categories: those which referred to the Pope; to issues of doctrine or liturgy; and those which combined reference to the Pope with reference to doctrine or liturgy.First were answers which referred to the Pope or to the nature or exercise of papal authority (21%). For example:

Protestants did not like the Pope (m4presb).
About how the Pope was a Roman Catholic and this was unfair (f3rc).
Because they thought the Pope wasn't good enough to be God's representative on earth (m2rc).
About the Pope of Antichrist (m3presb; f3ci).
King Henry wanted to get a divorce but the pope wouldn't let him so he formed his own church. Many people followed the king (m3rc).
The way the Catholics ran the church, they thought they were wrong in paying for their sins to be forgiven (f2presb).

Table 5.3   Perceptions of the original Protestants

What would you say were the main things that the first Protestants were 'protesting' about?

	%
The Pope	**21**
Doctrine and Liturgy	**25**
The above combined	7
Conditions in Ireland	25
Don't Know	22

Lower level (less sophisticated) answers referred simply to 'the Pope' as the main thing which the first Protestants were protesting about. Higher level answers identified the authority of the Pope as the issue. Some answers specified claims to authority by the papacy while others specified one or more ways in which the papacy exercised authority.

Answers referring to the Pope or papal authority in general terms were shared evenly between catholics and protestants. There was a tendency for catholics to specify the issues of greed for money, corruption of the clergy, and Henry VIII's divorce and for protestants to specify the sale of indulgences.

The second type of accurate answer referred to matters of doctrine and/or liturgy. For example:

Because they had idols in their chapel (f3presb).
About having to go to Mass (f2rc).
The right to have their own religion (f2presb; m2none; m2rc).

Because they did not like the Catholic religion and because they could do most of the things they wanted when they had their own religion (m2rc).

Martin L. King [sic] broke away from the main Roman Catholic denomination after the Pope refused to back down (m2rc).

The Prods [Protestants] used to be Taigs [Catholics], then a man who read the Bible said that the Catholics were wrong about Confession and other things like that (m2ci).

Answers which made general reference were shared evenly between catholics and protestants. Protestants tended to specify the worship of statues; complicated ritual; lack of freedom of worship; prayer to the Pope instead of God; and compulsory church attendance at services in Latin, not the vernacular. Catholics tended to specify belief in God; in transubstantiation; the Real Presence; and insistence on clerical celibacy. There was a strong tendency for protestants to specify the Bible (freedom to read it in the vernacular as a direct access to God with no intermediary) and for catholics to specify the prohibition on divorce.

There were contrasting tendencies for catholic answers to use the formula 'the protestants didn't do x' and for protestant answers to use the formula 'the catholics did y'. This was particularly evident with regard to veneration of Mary. Catholics specified (in some cases anachronistically) what protestants did not believe about Mary (e.g Virgin Birth, Immaculate Conception, Assumption) while protestants specified what unacceptable things Catholics believed about Mary (e.g that she is more important than Jesus).

Answers which referred to the Reformation of the Church (the lack of religious freedom, tension which needed to be resolved, the following of named Protestant leaders, the desire to create a new religion) were for the most part shared evenly between catholics and protestants. There was a tendency for protestants to specify the strictness and the error of the Catholic Church and there was a tendency for catholics to specify the desire of the Protestants to reform the church (rather than make a new religion).

The third type of accurate answer, which combined reference to papal use or abuse of power with reference to disagreement about doctrine or liturgy, was the most sophisticated. For example:

Bowing down to idols, drunk priests, lazy nuns and the Bible was in Latin so the ordinary person could not read it (f2ci)

Corruption in the Church (the selling of indulgences), Catholic doctrine concerning Eucharists (m3rc)

The Catholics' religion, the way of services, and the way God was worshipped, and about having the Queen as leader (f2presb).

There were too many rules all made by the Pope. They didn't believe in
the principles of the Church (m2rc).

Answers were shared evenly between protestants and catholics for the most part. There was a tendency for protestants to specify the worship of statues and the prohibition on translation of the Bible into the vernacular and for catholics to specify veneration of Mary.

Almost half (47%) of schoolchildren, however, were unable to give even a partially accurate answer to this question. More than a fifth (22%) were uncertain and 25% gave inaccurate anwers which were anachronistic in that they attributed the protest of the original Protestants to post-Reformation conditions. Almost invariably these were particular conditions in Ireland. For example:

> That they won the Battle of the Boyne. They wanted to have a religion of
> their own. (f3rc).
> The Catholics wanted to be in Derry but the Protestants didn't want them
> so they started fighting (f3ci).
> About the Church of Ireland making other religions pay rates [tithes?]
> (m3rc).
> Keeping Ulster British, keeping Catholics out of N. Ireland (m3ci).

Between them answers of this type pressed into service most of the main events in Irish history from the Plantation of Ulster to the Anglo-Irish Agreement. Anwers of almost all sub-types came equally from protestants and catholics. The only observed (weak) tendencies were for catholics to cite superiority of numbers and discrimination in employment as reasons, and for protestants to cite keeping Catholics out of Northern Ireland as a reason.

Perceptions of population balance

As Table 5.4 shows, most pupils had a more or less accurate perception of the balance between Catholics and Protestants in the population of Northern Ireland today (in the range 30-50%). However, pupils' awareness of the historical explanation for the Protestant majority was not as strong (Table 5.5). In anwer to the question about Protestants in Ireland (as distinct from Protestants in Europe), only two in five (39%) identified the Plantation of Ulster as the best of the explanations on offer as to why there are more Protestants than Catholics today in Northern Ireland. More boys than girls knew this (6%) and more catholics than non-catholics (3%).

Table 5.4   Perceptions of population balance

Roughly how much of the population of N. Ireland today is Catholic?

	%
20%	8
30%	**21**
40%	**44**
50%	**14**
60%	13

Table 5.5   Explanations of the Protestant majority in N. Ireland

Which of the following do you think best explains why there are more Protestants than Catholics today in Northern Ireland?

	%
The Norman Invasion	3
The Plantation of Ulster	**39**
The Battle of the Boyne	32
The Great Famine	3
The Troubles	23

This indication of a low level of historical knowledge contrasts with the ability of the majority of schoolchildren (79%) to estimate accurately (within the range 30-50%) the proportion of the population of Northern Ireland today which is Catholic. Accurate estimation was slightly higher in boys (2%) and in non-catholics (3%).

Churches burning: perceptions of 'other' religious buildings

If Protestant and Catholic schoolchildren in Northern Ireland are well aware of the relative sizes of their communities, how do they see each other's church buildings? These are the most concrete expressions of 'the other's' religious heritage in the environment and are important markers of territory. (In the summer of 1995 a large number of churches, Catholic and Protestant, and Orange halls were deliberately burned throughout Northern Ireland.) Pupils were asked to write a passage in answer to the open-ended question 'How do you think you would feel if one of the churches in your area (not your own) was burned down?'. Answers were sorted into five categories (see Table 5.6). The following are examples of answers of each type:

'*Upset*':

If it was a person of a different religion did it I would be angry because they just don't like Catholics or Protestants (m2rc).

Appalling, that the people who burnt the church down couldn't tolerate a different religion (m1none).

Very disappointed and sad and hope that our minister would invite the members of the church that was burned down to worship with us (f2presb).

'*Concerned*':

Annoyed because whoever burned it down was probably the opposite religion (f2congregational).

'No feelings/Uncertain': It was either youths or people of the opposite religion burning it down (f3rc).

'*Unconcerned*':

I wouldn't care because they wouldn't care if ours was burnt so why should we? (m3rc).

'*Pleased*':

If it was a Protestant church I would be very angry and rebellious but if it was a Catholic church I wouldn't mind really and hope that there were Catholics in it (f2presb).

Table 5.6   Churches burning

How do you think you would feel if one of the churches in your area (not yours) was burned down?	%
Upset	37
Concerned	37
No feelings / uncertain	15
Unconcerned	9
Pleased	2

A large majority of pupils (74%) indicated, by giving answers sorted as 'Upset' or 'Concerned', that they attach positive value to religious buildings other than their own in their local area. Most expressed an appreciation of what the building must mean to its members both in material and emotional or spiritual terms. Some expressed an appreciation of the aesthetic and historical value of the building. Given that pupils had a clear and safe opportunity to express anti-Catholic or anti-Protestant feelings, it is encouraging that only a small minority (11%) indicated, by giving 'Unconcerned' (9%) or 'Pleased' (2%) answers, that they attach a negative value to the other side's religious buildings. Most were 'Pleased' because of a personal antipathy towards members of the church affected or towards religion as a whole. A slightly larger minority (15%) indicated, by giving 'No feelings/Uncertain' answers, that they attach neutral value to other religious buildings in their area. It is noteworthy that the level of 'Upset' or 'Concern' was higher in girls (11%) and in catholics (7%).

Perceptions of the fighting

In answering the question about churches burning, many pupils assumed that the probable motive was sectarian. To what extent do schoolchildren in Northern Ireland see the fighting there as being about religion? A substantial majority (66%) agreed that the fighting is about religion. Agreement was higher in girls (6%) and in non-catholics (12%).

Given that a majority believes that the fighting is about religion, what role is there for the religious leaders in resolving the conflict? Almost half (49%) believed that the religious leaders could end the fighting by working together. Only 30% disagreed. Belief in the effectiveness of ecumenical co-operation was higher in girls (9%). Curiously, although more non-catholics believed that the fighting was about religion, more catholics (11%) believed in the effectiveness of ecumenical co-operation in ending the fighting.

Table 5.7 Perceptions of the fighting

	Agree	Don't Know	Disagree
	%	%	%
The fighting in Northern Ireland is about religion	66	11	23
The religious leaders could end the fighting by working together	49	22	29

110

The *Before Questionnaire* tested the extent to which pupils' perceive a range of religious practices in the Roman Catholic and Protestant Churches to be more similar to each other than different or vice versa. The practices asked about were: baptisms, weddings, communions, and funerals. Due to pressure of space, only baptisms and weddings are reported on here. They have been selected because (following the argument of the preceding chapters) attitudes to them are particularly strong indicators of the state of inter-church relations.

Baptism This is the 'rite of passage' by which the four largest Churches in Northern Ireland, and others in the Christian tradition, induct individuals into formal membership. Since Vatican II (1962-65) there has been formal recognition by all four Churches of each other's baptism, that is baptism into the Christian Church is regarded as conferring shared membership of the one Christian Church.

To what extent do schoolchildren see the Protestant and Catholic Churches as being fundamentally similar or different in their practice of Baptism? A majority (56%) is uncertain as to whether or not Catholic and Protestant practice of Baptism are very different. Although there are differences in practice (for example the use of oil and candles), the Churches themselves do not regard these as indicative of fundamental difference. Only 15% indicated this perception by disagreement. Disagreement was slightly higher in girls (2%) and in catholics (2%). A larger majority (65%) were uncertain as to whether or not Church of Ireland and Presbyterian practice of Baptism are

Table 5.8   Baptism practice: similarity and difference

	Agree %	Don't Know %	Disagree %
Catholic priests baptise babies in a very different way from Protestant ministers	29	56	15
Church of Ireland ministers baptise babies in a very different way from Presbyterian ministers	11	65	24

very different. In this case, a higher proportion (24%) disagreed that they are very different. Disagreement was higher in girls (5%). Predictably, it was much higher in non-catholics than in catholics (24%).

Marriage This is the 'rite of passage' by which the four largest Churches formally witness before God in public (and on behalf of the state) the mutual promise which the couple makes. There are differences in practice (notably the Catholic practice of the wedding service normally taking place during Mass). To some extent differences in practice reflect that the Roman Catholic Church and the Church of Ireland share a sacramental understanding of marriage which is not shared by the Presbyterian and Methodist Churches. However, the four main Churches do not regard the differences between them on marriage as being fundamental. Each is generally prepared to recognise as valid the other's form of wedding service (including mixed marriages, provided that certain conditions are met).

Do schoolchildren see the Protestant and Catholic Churches as being fundamentally similar or different in their conduct of weddings? Almost half (44%) are uncertain. The rest divides fairly evenly between those who see them as very different (34%) and those who see them as more similar (22%). Slightly more girls (1%) and catholics (3%) see them as being more similar. A clear majority (60%) is uncertain whether Church of Ireland and Presbyterian wedding practices are very different or not. However, the division of the rest is less even. Only 10% see them as being very different, while 30% see them as being more similar.

Table 5.9   Marriage practice: similarity and difference

	Agree %	Don't Know %	Disagree %
Catholic priests perform weddings in a very different way from Protestant ministers	34	43	23
Church of Ireland ministers perform weddings in a very different way from Presbyterian ministers	10	60	30

Baptism To what extent do schoolchildren recognise that Roman Catholics and members of the three largest Protestant churches share a common baptism into one Christian Church? Almost half (48%) believe that the Catholic Church does not recognise Protestant baptisms (indicated by agreement that re-baptism is necessary to become a Catholic). Almost a third (30%) were uncertain. Only 22% indicated, by disagreement, understanding of a common baptism. This perception is slightly higher in girls (1%). It is also higher in non-catholics (5%).

Pupils are more evenly divided when it comes to Protestant recognition of Catholic baptisms. More than a third (38%) believe that the Protestant Churches do not recognise Catholic baptisms. A further 37% are uncertain. Only 25% think that the Protestant Churches do recognise Catholic baptisms. This perception is slightly higher in boys (3%). It is slightly higher also in non-catholics (2%).

Table 5.10 Baptism belief: similarity and difference

	Agree	Don't Know	Disagree
	%	%	%
If a Protestant becomes a Catholic, they have to be re-baptised by a Catholic priest	48	30	22
If a Catholic becomes a Protestant, they have to be re-baptised by a Protestant minister	38	37	25
If a Church of Ireland person becomes a Presbyterian, they have to be re-baptised by a Presbyterian minister	17	47	36
If a Presbyterian becomes a member of the Church of Ireland, they have to be re-baptised by a Church of Ireland minister	18	47	35

As to the mutual recognition by the Church of Ireland and the Presbyterian Church of each other's baptisms, almost half (47%) are uncertain. Almost a fifth (17%; 18%) believe that they do not recognise each other's baptisms. However, over a third (36%; 35%) believe that they do, which is actually the case. This perception is substantially higher in girls (11%;12%). Again not surprisingly, it is very much higher in non-catholics than in catholics (35%; 30%). This is strong indication of a gap in mutual understanding between Protestants and Catholics.

Marriage Officially, all four of the largest churches recognise as valid each other's form of wedding service. Although they may have argued the point in the past, the sacramental understanding of marriage by the Roman Catholic and Anglican Churches no longer makes them fundamentally different from the Presbyterian and Methodist Churches. To what extent do schoolchildren see Catholic and Protestant understandings of marriage as being very different?

Fewer see the differences as being fundamental than in the case of baptism. More show awareness that there is a common understanding of essentials. Only 23% believe that the Catholic and Protestant wedding promises are very different (compared with 48% who believe that Catholics do not recognise Protestant baptisms). Only a third (34%) is uncertain - compared with the 47% who are uncertain about Catholic recognition of Protestant baptisms. Two in five (43%) disagree that Catholic and Protestant wedding promises are very different from each other. This perception is considerably higher in girls than in boys (10%) and slightly higher in non-catholics than in catholics (2%).

By contrast, there is greater awareness that the Church of Ireland and Presbyterian wedding promises are not very different from each other. Exactly half (50%) disagree that they are very different and only 9% agree that they are. However, the level of uncertainty is higher (42%). The perception that Catholic and Protestant wedding promises are more similar than different is higher in girls than in boys (10%). The perception that Church of Ireland and Presbyterian wedding promises are more similar than different is very much higher in non-catholics than in catholics (26%). This is another strong indication of the gap in mutual understanding between Protestants and Catholics.

Table 5.11 Marriage belief: similarity and difference

	Agree %	Don't Know %	Disagree %
The promise which a Catholic couple make at their wedding is very different from the promise which a Protestant couple makes	23	34	43
The promise which a Church of Ireland couple make at their wedding is very different from the promise which a Presbyterian couple makes	9	41	50

Perceptions of continuity and change: baptism and marriage practice

The concept of 'development' in church history was pioneered in the nineteenth century by Newman and others. Self-understanding by the churches of 'development' in their worship and doctrine is therefore a relatively recent phenomenon. To what extent are schoolchildren aware that in religious practice some things continue the same and others change? Pupils were asked if there had been any change in Protestant and Catholic baptism and wedding practices over the last fifty years.

Baptism Over the last fifty years some changes have been made to the words and actions prescribed in Protestant and Catholic orders of service for baptism. For example, the words of baptism in the Roman Catholic rite have changed from Latin to the vernacular, from 'Ego te baptizo' to 'I baptize you'; in the Church of Ireland rite 'I baptize thee' has been changed to 'I baptize you'; in the Presbyterian order 'I baptize thee' remains unchanged but there have been other changes, such as the dropping of the requirement that the minister should put formally the question 'What is the name of this child?'. To what extent are schoolchildren aware that such changes can and do take place?

Only 15% are aware that there has been change in the Roman Catholic practice of baptism. A majority (53%) are uncertain. Almost a third (32%) believe that here has been no change. Awareness of change is very slightly higher in girls than in boys (1%) but it is considerably higher in catholics than in non-catholics (13%), again indicating a gap in mutual understanding. Fewer (9%) are aware that there has been change in the Church of Ireland practice of baptism. More are uncertain (64%). Less than a third (27%) believe that there has been no change. In contrast with the perception of Roman Catholic practice, awareness of change in Church of Ireland practice is slightly higher in boys (4%) and in catholics (7%). Perception of change in Presbyterian practice is almost identical to that of change in Church of Ireland practice, except that awareness of change is only 1% higher in boys and 2% higher in non-catholics.

Table 5.12 Baptism practice: continuity and change

	Agree %	Don't Know %	Disagree %
What Catholic priests say and do when they baptise babies has changed	15	53	32
What Church of Ireland ministers say and do when they baptise babies has changed	9	64	27
What Presbyterian ministers say and do when they baptise babies has changed	9	63	28

Marriage There have also been changes in the Protestant and Catholic wedding services over the last fifty years. For example, the bridegrooms' formula 'With this ring I thee wed' has been changed in the Roman Catholic service to 'Wear this ring as a sign of our love and fidelity'. In the Church of Ireland service 'With this ring I thee wed' has been changed to 'I give you this ring as a sign of our marriage'. The formula 'With this ring I thee wed' was not used in the Presbyterian order of service. However, the comparable words prescribed for the minister have been changed from 'In token of these covenants you give and receive this ring' to 'As a token of the covenant into which you have entered, this ring is given and received'. To what extent are schoolchildren aware that such changes can and do take place?

Perception of continuity and change in Protestant and Catholic wedding practice is very similar to that of baptism practice. Only 16% are aware that there has been change in Roman Catholic practice. Almost a half (48%) are uncertain. More than a third (36%) believe that there has been no change. Awareness of change is slightly higher in boys (2%) and, as might be expected, much higher in catholics (11%). Fewer are aware of change in Church of Ireland and Presbyterian practice (8%; 9%). Well over half (60%; 58%) are uncertain. About a third (31%; 33%) believe that there has been no change. Awareness of change in the Church of Ireland is marginally higher girls (1%) and in non-catholics (1%) and for the Presbyterian Church it is marginally higher in boys (1%) and in non-catholics (1%).

Table 5.13 Marriage practice: continuity and change

	Agree %	Don't Know %	Disagree %
What Catholic priests say and do at the wedding service has changed	16	48	36
What Church of Ireland ministers say and do at the wedding service has changed	10	60	30
What Presbyterian ministers say and do at the wedding service has changed	9	58	33

Perception of continuity and change: baptism and marriage belief

This century there have been significant doctrinal developments or changes in way the Roman Catholic and Protestant Churches understand each other's baptisms and mixed marriages. These understandings have become more ecumenical, that is less exclusive and more inclusive. For example, on becoming a Catholic, a Protestant is no longer required to be conditionally re-baptised; and mixed marriages in a Catholic church are no longer required to be conducted in the sacristy without Mass. All four of the largest Churches take a certain amount of pride in the ecumenical progress that they have made through their mutual recognition of baptism and joint pastoral care of mixed marriages, especially since Vatican II. To what extent are schoolchildren aware of these changes in the religious traditions of Protestants and Catholics in the direction of less hostility and greater friendliness between them?

Baptism Exactly 50% of pupils are aware that Catholics used to believe that baptism into their Church was necessary for salvation. Only 28% are uncertain if this was so. Only 22% do not believe it to have been the case. However, only a third (34%) think that Catholics no longer have this exclusivist understanding. A third (34%) is uncertain. The other third (32%) believes that Catholics retain their old exclusivist understanding unchanged. Awareness of the way things used to be is higher in girls (9%) and in catholics (8%). Awareness of how things have changed in an ecumenical direction is higher in boys (8%) and much higher in catholics (17%).

In contrast, only 20% of pupils are aware that Protestants used to believe that baptism into one of the Protestant churches was necessary for salvation. Almost half (46%) are uncertain if this was so. A third (34%) do not believe it to have been the case. Two out of five pupils (40%) think that Protestants no longer have this exclusivist understanding. Almost a half (48%) are uncertain.

Table 5.14   Baptism belief: continuity and change

	Agree %	Don't Know %	Disagree %
Catholics used to believe that unless a person was baptised into the Catholic Church they would not go to heaven	50	28	22
Most Catholics still believe this	32	34	34
Protestants used to believe that unless a person was baptised into one of the Protestant churches they would not go to heaven	20	46	34
Most Protestants still believe this	12	48	40

Only 12% believe that Protestants retain their exclusivist understanding unchanged. Awareness of the way things used to be is slightly higher in boys (1%) and in non-catholics (3%). Awareness of how things have changed in an ecumenical direction is higher in girls (8%) and very much higher in non-catholics (28%).

Marriage A substantial majority (67%) is aware that Catholics used to believe that it was wrong for a Catholic to marry a Protestant. Only 15% are uncertain that this was so. Only 19% do not believe that this used to be the case. However, less than half (42%) think that Catholics no longer have this exclusivist understanding. About a fifth (22%) are uncertain. Over a third (36%) believe that Catholics retain their exclusivist understanding unchanged. Awareness of the way things used to be is higher in girls (11%) and in non-catholics (7%). Awareness of how things have changed in an ecumenical direction is higher in girls (3%) and very much higher in catholics (20%).

Pupils have a similar perception of changes in Protestant understanding of mixed marriage. A substantial majority (61%) is aware that Protestants used to believe that it was wrong for a Protestant to marry a Catholic. Only 20% are uncertain that this was so. Only 20% do not believe that this used to be

Table 5.15 Marriage belief: continuity and change

	Agree %	Don't Know %	Disagree %
Catholics used to believe that it was wrong for a Catholic to marry a Protestant	67	15	18
Most Catholics still believe this	36	22	42
Protestants used to believe that it was wrong for a Protestant to marry a Catholic	61	20	19
Most Protestants still believe this	34	26	40
Presbyterians used to believe that it was wrong for a Presbyterian to marry a Church of Ireland person	15	46	39
Most Presbyterians still believe this	9	48	43

the case. However, less than half (42%) think that Protestants no longer have this exclusivist understanding. About a fifth (22%) are uncertain. Over a third (36%) believe that Protestants retain their exclusivist understanding unchanged. Awareness of the way things used to be is higher in girls (11%) and in non-catholics (7%). Awareness of how things have changed in an ecumenical direction is higher in girls (3%) and very much higher in catholics (20%).

Perceptions of the Catholic / Protestant divide

In the past Protestants and Catholics thought of the differences between them as so fundamental that they regarded each other as belonging to two rival or opposite religions. More recently there has been an unfreezing of hostility and a growing ecumenical emphasis on the elements of religious practice and belief which are shared rather than those which divide. This change has been particularly evident in changes in practice and belief relating to baptism and to mixed marriage. Attitudes to both of these are key indicators of the state of Protestant Catholic relations. Attitudes to baptism (the practice by which membership of the Roman Catholic and Protestant Churches is conferred) have been becoming less exclusivist. Attitudes to mixed marriage (the more or less strict discouragement of exogamy) with consequent attitudes to segregated education are central in determining the boundaries between the Catholic and Protestant communities (see Chapter 1).

How, then, do schoolchildren see the division between Protestants and Catholics? Do they see it as an impermeable barrier segregating two opposing religions? Or do they see it as a permeable internal barrier within the one religion? At first sight it appears that most pupils see two opposing religions. The overwhelming majority (89%) thinks that 'there are two main religions in Northern Ireland, Catholic and Protestant'. This perception is very slightly

Table 5.16 Perceptions of the Catholic / Protestant divide (1)

	Agree %	Don't Know %	Disagree %
There are two main religions in N. Ireland, Catholic and Protestant	89	4	7

higher in girls (0.2%) and in non-catholics (1%). Only 4% are uncertain and only 7% disagree.

However, when the same proposition is phrased differently, only half (50%) think that 'Catholics and Protestants belong to two different religions'. The other half thinks that 'Catholics and Protestants belong to the same religion'.

Table 5.17   Perceptions of the Catholic / Protestant divide (2)

Which of the following two statements do you prefer?

	%
A. Catholics and Protestants belong to two different religions	50
B. Catholics and Protestants belong to the same religion	50

Why responses to these two formulations of (apparently) the same proposition should be so markedly different is best explained by core choice modulation. Most agree that there are 'two religions' but half do not agree that they are two different or 'opposite religions'. This key response is discussed further in Chapter 6. The perception that Catholics and Protestants belong to the same religion is higher in girls (8%) and in catholics (6%). What seems clear is that the school population in Northern Ireland is evenly split: half sees one divided religion, the other sees two different or opposite religions.

Effects of the Protestant / Catholic divide on personal belief

If schoolchildren have two radically different ways of seeing the religious divide in Northern Ireland, how do these perceptions affect their own personal religious belief? Does seeing the division between Protestants and Catholics in a particular way make Christianity easier or harder to accept?

Almost half of pupils (47%) say that they find Christianity hard to accept because of the way Catholics and Protestants are divided amongst themselves. Only 20% are uncertain. A third (33%) disagrees that division makes Christianity harder to accept. Belief that division does make Christianity harder to accept is much higher in girls (16%) and in catholics (19%).

Table 5.18 Effects of the Protestant / Catholic divide on personal belief

	Agree %	Don't Know %	Disagree %
I find Christianity hard to accept because of the way Catholics and Protestants are divided amongst themselves	47	20	33

How do schoolchildren explain why they do or do not think that the divide makes Christianity harder to accept? Their open-ended answers fell into five categories. They focused on: violence or fighting; the religious (ecumenical) ideal of Christian unity; religious segregation for doctrinal reasons; social segregation for secular reasons; pluralism for secular reasons.

Types of answer were fairly evenly divided (see Table 5.19). About a quarter in each case gave answers focused on violence (27%); on religious integration (ecumenism) (24%); and on religious segregation (fundamentalism) (22%). About one in seven gave answers focused on social segregation (13%) or on social integration (14%) from secular (non-religious) points of view.

Table 5.19 Perceptions of the Catholic / Protestant divide on personal belief: reasons

This is why I answered the question (Table 5.18) the way I did Reasons	%
Fighting	27
Religious sharing (ecumenical)	24
Religious separation (fundamentalist)	22
Community separation (secular, separatist)	13
Community sharing (secular, pluralist)	14

Type 1 answers, fighting Answers of this type focused on political or social violence (27%). They were much higher in boys than in girls (15%) and somewhat higher in catholics than in non-catholics (5%). They related present divisions between Catholics and Protestants to the violence that was then taking place in Northern Ireland. Answers fell into four sub-types: fighting; causes of the fighting; hypocrisy; ways the fighting might end.

Answers of the 'fighting' sub-type simply referred to violence as the reason for agreeing or disagreeing that the religious divide makes Christianity harder to accept. For example [author's italics]:

> It is terrible when you go somewhere and you get constant abuse from *the other religion* and I have seen quite frequently my brother get beat up by a number of Protestants who get our bus (we are the only Catholics) (f2rc).
>
> Because Catholics like the IRA are bombing and shooting us down and the UVF is doing the same thing. All they are doing is killing one another. I think it is stupid and should stop (f2none).
>
> Because I don't like it and I think it is stupid the way the fighting *between the religions* is still going on after so many years (f2ci).
>
> Because there is always fighting between *the two religions* (f2rc)
>
> Because the community is always at each other's necks. And *no one religion* will become friendly (f2rc).

Only one answer of this sub-type disagreed that division makes Christianity harder to accept 'because not all Christians are fighting' (m2rc).

Answers of the 'hypocrisy' sub-type referred to the discrepancy between the actual fighting and the doctrine of Christianity which forbids fighting. Answers that agreed with the question centred on the notion of hypocrisy. For example:

> Because *the two religions* are fighting and killing and they are breaking the laws of God (f3rc).
>
> Catholics and Protestants are meant to be good Christians but each church is at the other's throat all the time, yet both are meant to be of *the same main religion* (m3rc)
>
> Christianity is about loving and caring for other people not fighting with them. So why should we accept Christianity when there is a lot of fighting going on? (f3ci).

Some answers (from non-catholics only), however, countered the implied charge of hypocrisy by drawing a distinction between the fighting and 'true' Christianity. For example:

> The divide shouldn't affect Christians. These people who pretend to be Christians and fight about it are not really Christian and just want to fight (f4ci).

Answers of the 'causes of the fighting' sub-type attributed, or tried to attribute, a cause or causes to the violence. Some think the fighting to be either without cause or incomprehensible. For example:

> I don't know why Catholics and Protestants fight (f2meth).
>
> Why does everyone fight over religion when everyone wants to get to the same place - heaven? (f1rc).
>
> I find it hard to understand any religion. I mean what is the point of *different religions* fighting with *other religions* when there is no such thing as God to fight about (sorry God) (f1none).

Some pupils were clear that the divisions between Catholics and Protestants themselves were the cause rather than the effect of the fighting. For example:

> The way they are divided makes them fight (f2rc).
>
> If Protestants and Catholics weren't divided there would be no fighting (f2presb).

Some thought that fighting is intrinsic to religion and a reason why many reject religion. For example:

> The Catholics believe in a different way and they always want to fight us (m2presb).
>
> People are living apart and fighting over religion for no real reason. People don't believe in Christ because of the fighting going on in Northern Ireland (f3rc).

Some connected God with responsibility for the fighting. For example:

> I think God is the cause of the fighting and murder between Catholics and Protestants (m3rc).
>
> If God was good there would be no more fighting (m3none).
>
> If us prodsins [sic] are going to win this war we have to look up to Jesus and ask for help (m3freepresb).

Others were equally concerned to distance God or religion itself from any responsibility for the fighting. For example:

> If people fight and become more divided, I don't really blame their religion. I blame the person themself. So therefore I have no need to find Christianity hard to accept because there are good and bad people in the world on every side and I suppose I take it for granted (f3rc).
>
> I think it gives you worries about Christianity but that doesn't mean you should not believe in God and find him hard to accept. It's our fault

we are fighting. God cannot do anything about it. His son already died for us and our sins (m3meth).

Far from being responsible for the violence, some (protestants only) thought that religion was being used as an excuse for it:

Most of the men causing the problems are using their religion as an excuse to murder (f4presb).

Some were clear that the violence is the responsibility of a small minority:

'There are only a few elements in society who hate members of *the other religion*' (m4presb).

Some were explicit in finding the cause of the fighting in a connection between religion and politics. For example:

It is mainly due to the fact that we are not divided by religion but by our beliefs on nationalism and religion is used as an excuse (m4rc).

With all the troubles in N. Ireland, fighting politics and faith, religion is a combination. People are too much into fighting and winning battles to take the true meaning of Christianity into consideration. Their religion is just an excuse (f4presb).

Some identified land as the cause of the fighting for which religion was being used as an excuse. For example:

They are fighting about who should own the land. The Catholics say they own it because they were first on it and the Protestants say the same reason (m2rc).

Years ago many kings quarrelled and nations were at war but this does not mean that Christianity is hard to accept (f2presb).

The violence in N. Ireland led me to agree with this because *2 religions* fighting over who owns what is stupid (f3rc).

Answers of the 'ways the fighting might end' sub-type suggested how the violence might stop and what might happen if it did. Some were clear that it is within the power of people to bring about an end to the fighting. For example:

It is our generation that will say if the troubles stop or carry on into the 21st century or be stopped in the 1990s. They can be stopped if the people wants them to (f3rc).

People should know more about their religion and if they did they would not fight so much (m2presb).

The people who are divided strongly and who support either Nationalists or Loyalists aren't true Christians. They should be rejected by both sides and if this happened they would both die away (m4rc).

Some, however, doubted this. For example:

Well you hear about Christians being one or joined altogether. Well I do not see this happening in N. Ireland. All I see is fighting. Protestants and Catholics will mix sometime but until then my answer is certain (f1presb).

Some thought that individual effort to be a better Christian would be the answer. For example:

If everyone was a true Christian there would be no fighting and troubles (f2presb).
I feel everyone should be a Christian and leave the fighting. Everyone can be a Christian and I cannot forgive the people who fight and kill others (m3rc).

And finally, some thought that unity between Christians would be the answer. For example:

If everybody went to church together it would help stop the troubles and Northern Ireland would become more peaceful (m2presb).
I would prefer Catholics and Protestants to be one and fighting in Northern Ireland to stop before everything gets out of hand (f4rc).
I think they should be in *one religion* and then there would be less fighting (f1presb).

These various sub-types of answer were shared evenly for the most part between protestants and catholics. Some slight differences were observed. Only protestants drew explicitly a distinction between nominal and 'true' Christianity when justifying the religion in terms of the discrepancy between fighting and Christian doctrine. In the light of this it is probably significant that only protestants argued explicitly that religion was being used as an excuse for the fighting.

Type II answers, religious sharing (ecumenical) Answers of this type focused on the religious idea of unity between Protestants and Catholics (ecumenism). They accounted for almost a quarter (24%) of the total. They were very marginally higher in boys (0.1%) and significantly higher in catholics (5%). Five sub-types were identified which focused on: the argument for unity (based on shared humanity and shared belief in the one God); the ecumenical imperative (God's intention for his people to be united as one family or

126

church); the distinction between religious doctrine and practice; hope for greater unity; and the prospects for future unity.

Answers of the 'argument for unity' sub-type were concerned with unity between Catholics and Protestants based on common humanity and common belief in one God. At the simplest level, some answers stated an opposition in principle to division: 'I am totally against Catholics and Protestants being separated' (f2ci). One foundation for this principle seemed to be the common humanity of Protestants and Catholics: 'I don't see what being Protestant or Catholic matters about being a Christian as they are still people all the same' (f2congregational). A related foundation was common belief in the one God:

> There is no difference between Catholics and Protestants. We are all human. We just have different ways of doing things in our services. We all believe in the same God (f3rc).

Some (catholics only) expressed lack of understanding at why, given common belief in God, there should be a division:

> I don't know why at the start people separated into *different religions* (f3rc).
> They are both Christians and pray to the same God. But why are we still fighting about something that happened many centuries ago? (f3rc).

Others were clear that the problems of division were 'man-made' and were anxious that God should not be blamed: 'The founder and central figure of Christianity, Jesus Christ, was not responsible for the rift in the Christian Church. This rift is a man-made problem (m3rc)'. Some thought that common belief in God entailed no important differences between Protestants and Catholics:

> We are all the *one religion* that believes in God (m2rc).
> *The religions* are no different. They both believe in the same God so why can't they live together? (f2rc/meth).

Some (non-catholics only) saw unity in common belief in God but did not think that this necessarily entailed common religious beliefs or practices:

> *Both religions* worship God and even if they worship in different ways it is no reason to fight (m3none).
> *Both religions* believe in the one God so it is very easy to accept Christianity not just slightly but deeply. To me it seems that the Bible has been changed so that they worship the Virgin Mary more than God (f3presb).

127

I believe that God is the Head of the Church and your culture is unimportant (f4christianfellowshipchurch).

Some identified the importance of common belief in Jesus:

> Christianity is getting harder to accept because what is the sense in fighting over, practically Our Lord Jesus Christ. It wasn't his wish that we murder and squabble over him. Sure we all believe basically in Our Lord. It's a puzzle (m3rc).

Answers of the 'ecumenical imperative' sub-type focused on the idea that it is the intention of God that his people should be united. Some answers focused in particular on the idea of Catholics and Protestants belonging to the same family. For example:

> Christians are 'supposed' to love each other but that is not how people are going about it (f2ci).
> Catholics and Protestants are so far apart as if they were *two totally different kinds of people* but they are the same. God made them and we are all *one family* (m3rc).
> I try to be a good Christian but I think that the Church should be a whole, not little sections (f1presb).
> This I feel is not being part of God's family. God said that he wanted us all to become *one family* in his home. This is not what we are doing - in fact it is *totally the opposite* (f4rc).

Answers of the 'doctrine/practice distinction' sub-type addressed the perceived discrepancy between what Christians are taught to do and what they actually do. Some found this to be a problem: 'I find it hard to be a proper Christian as Northern Ireland is divided between Catholic and Protestant' (f2ci). Others did not find it a problem. As one put it, apparently paradoxically: 'It doesn't matter what religion you are, you can still be a good Christian' (f2ci). This line of argument stressed the individual rather than the communal nature of Christianity. It drew a distinction between social practice or membership of a particular Church and the relationship of the individual with God and the unchanging nature of Christian teaching. For example:

> Christianity remains the same no matter who is fighting. The people fighting are not 'Protestant' or 'Catholic'. They've probably never been inside a church in their lives (m4ci).
> Some people in *Catholic or Protestant religions* say they are Christians but do not work like Christians. Just going to church doesn't mean you are a Christian. I think it involves a lot more than that. So it is hard to accept Christianity (f3rc).

Answers of the 'signs of hope for unity' sub-type argued that the cause of Christian unity was not hopeless. For example:

> It is harder because of *the two religions*. If they all joined together it wouldn't be so hard to believe in Christianity (m3rc).
>
> If Catholics and Protestants joined together it would make life easier (f2ci).
>
> If everyone was friends I would find it easier to accept Christianity between *the two religions* if there were no religious barriers between the two (f2rc).
>
> It is hard to pray and be in *the Catholic religion* and other people in *some other religion*. It would be easier if we were all in *the same religion* (f3rc).

Some did not find division amongst Christians a problem personally but recognised that it might be so for others: '*Both religions* believe in God. They are *both Christian religions* ... I agree that some people would find it easier if there wasn't a division but *the basic religion* is the same in both' (f3rc).

Some identified signs of hope for greater Christian unity based on personal experience. For example:

> I find it easy to accept because I was brought up in a Christian house and my Mum is a Protestant and my Dad is a Catholic (f2p/rc).
>
> I go to the Community of the King where both Protestant and Catholic worship God happily and freely together. We think everyone is the same! (In God's eyes it's true.) (m3presb).
>
> I wish Catholics and Protestants would join up because I love a Catholic but my Mum wouldn't allow me to go with him. I'm in love !! (f2presb).

Others based their hope on observation of the current state of inter-church relations. For example:

> The Christian churches still promote good relations and are growing closer together (m3ci).
>
> There may be a chance that Protestants and Catholics may come together. As long as I believe that I can accept Christianity (f2ci).

Answers of the 'prospects for unity' sub-type looked forward to greater unity between Christians in the future. Some saw Christian unity being brought about by individual effort: 'I am a Christian and I feel the divide between the churches could be healed if everyone in the churches were more Christian' (m4presb). Being a Christian in this sense is seen to require personal commitment: 'A Christian means you should love everyone and even your enemies. Protestants should love Catholics and Catholics should love Protestants. This is the way it should be' (m3rc). One pupil anticipated that if people became better Christians there would be implications for church structures: 'If everyone who went to church were Christians, then they should hold no grudges against *the opposite religion* and this is why I would like mixed churches' (f3presb).

Some were quite clear that individual effort would not be enough. We should make concerted efforts to break down divisions: 'Jesus came down to earth to die for us but I think that Catholics and Protestants should try and break the division between them' (m1presb). A start could be made by appealing to an original state of unity:

> We were once all one. Why can't we be again? (m2rc).
> At one time they were all Christians and I believe they can all be the same one day (m2meth).

Mutual ignorance and mistrust were identified as obstacles to be overcome. For example:

> I think that Catholics and Protestants could join together into one group because I don't know why the Protestants don't feel the same way about God as Catholics do (f3rc).
> I am a Christian and would love for the two churches to become friendly. I do not know very much about the Roman Catholic church but I do think it is wrong to pray to saints as it says in the Bible. But as I am a Christian I obviously do accept it but find the present situation stupid (f3meth).

The problem of differences of belief was also identified. Some wished it were possible to make a fresh start. For example:

> Why can't all the religions be scrapped and people have no religions and we all go to the one mass? (m2rc).
> I would like to see more people become Christians and leave the Catholic and Protestant beliefs but I see that it will not be as easy as this (m3interdenominational).

Others thought that compromise would be necessary. For example:

> I wish Catholics and Protestants would meet each other half way (f4presb).
> The divide can be healed if people accept their mistakes and come together in peace (m4ci).

Compromise might involve acceptance of guilt and seeing points of difference in clearer perspective. For example:

> Both sets of religious groups did wrong. Protestants did wrong to break away from the leadership of Jesus but Catholics should have proved themselves worthy of the name by doing more to prevent the split (m3rc).
>
> As both Catholics and Protestants accept the same God, they both believe in Mary and in Jesus Christ. The only difference is the Pope but I don't think this should separate people into *separate religions* (f4none).

There might also be scope for diversity of belief: 'Christianity is something everyone should follow together without one church's beliefs trying to overrule the other church's beliefs' (f4rc). And finally, a tangible outcome of unity ought to be worship together. For example:

> If there is one God everybody should believe in one God and worship him together (f2presb).
>
> I would feel a lot happier to become a joint parish with *other religions* (f4rc).

Answers of Type II were shared more or less evenly between protestants and catholics across the range of sub-types. A few slight tendencies were observed: for catholics to admit to a lack of understanding of why, given a common belief in God, there should be division; for protestants to see unity in a common belief in God but not to think that this necessarily entails common religious belief or practice; and for protestants not to see the Protestant / Catholic divide as an obstacle to the individual being a good Christian.

Type III, religious separation (fundamentalist) answers Answers of this type contrasted with those of the ecumenical type in focusing on religious segregation or separation; referring to the Catholic / Protestant divide as something given and fixed, either desirably or inevitably so. They accounted for almost a quarter of the total (22%). They were higher in boys (4%) and very marginally higher in non-catholics (0.5%). Three sub-types of answer were identified as those which focused on: the religious divide in general terms; the nature and extent of the divide; and the problem of choosing which side of the divide is right and which is wrong.

Answers of the 'religious divide' sub-type referred to either the desirability or inevitability of the religious divide in general terms. For example:

> We have *our religion* and the prods have *theirs* (m3rc).

> Prods want to believe *one religion* and Catholics want to believe *another* which will bring us further apart (f2presb).

> Catholics prefer *their religion* and Protestants will like *their religion* so it looks like no joining together (m3rc).

> Catholics and Protestants will probably never mix together because of the fighting that goes on and that is why it would be hard to accept it [Christianity]. If they went to church together riots would probably start (f2meth).

> Living in a very divided town it is hard sometimes not to be bitter but you have to control this as your parents teach you. I feel my religion is right for me although it mightn't be for other people (f3rc).

Answers of the 'nature of the divide' sub-type were more specific about the nature of the religious divide in terms of belief and practice. Some expressed a resigned sense of inevitability. For example:

> I don't think about protestants because they are the same as us only they don't believe in the Virgin Mary (m3rc).

> I have some friends in school who are Catholic but this doesn't change the way I think about Christ. When it comes to religion I'll let Catholics stick to *their religion* and I'll stick to *mine* (m2presb).

> *Both of the religions* believe in different things and shall probably always fall out about what they believe in (m2rc).

Others expressed themselves more forcefully. For example:

> Because Catholics worship the Virgin Mary and we worship Jesus and the way they try to change everything. Catholics say that you should believe in *their religion* and not the Prod's because it is a pile of shit! (f3ci).

> Because Catholics worship different things like the Virgin Mary and we worship Jesus. Catholics are trying to get us to worship *their religion*. This is the cause of the bombing because the prods wanted change and the catholics can't take it (f3presb).

Some thought the religious divide to be positively beneficial:

> This is the best way that there is *2 religions* (m3rc).

> I find it much more easier with them split up (m3ci).

> Catholics are Catholics and Protestants are Protestants and they should both stay to *the religion* they know best because it is a lot easier that way (m3rc).

Others saw a down-side. For example:

132

I personally do not find Christianity hard to accept at all but I think that other people might not accept Christianity because they think if this is the way it makes you (not liking others of *a different religion*) it is not worth having at all (f3presb).

Answers of the 'right and wrong sides of the divide' sub-type assumed that there is a right and a wrong side to the religious divide and focused on the problem of choosing between them. Some expressed strong conviction in the choice which they had inherited or made themselves. For example:

The Catholics way of religion may be right but I agree more with *the Protestant religion* (f2presb).

I find that *one of the two religions* is wrong so I just accept *my religion* and don't worry about it (m2ci).

We worship God and not Mary. We do not believe *their religion* (their being Catholics) as it is wrong (m2brethren).

I think Christianity has nothing to do with Catholics because they don't understand. Christianity is committing yourself to Jesus and not just going to church and reading the Bible. It is more than that (f3presb).

The Catholic Church is run by Satan himself. They don't realise this. They worship idols. They send people to hell. The Protestant faith is *the true religion* otherwise Martin Luther would never have formed it (m4independent meth).

Others perceived the choice to be less clear-cut and expressed their dilemma:

I don't know which to believe (f2presb).

With the Catholics telling you one thing and the Protestants another you don't know which one to listen to (f2ci).

There are that many *religions* you just don't know which one to go to (m4ci).

People consider Catholics and Protestants as being *separate religions*, so how can *both religions* be Christians? (f3meth).

Who is really right? Are we doing what God wants us to do or are we in the wrong? We were brought up as Catholics and so we believe in the Catholic church. But Protestants believe in their own church (f3rc).

We don't know which church to believe because Catholics, well some, want a united Ireland and use *their religion* to say they agree with it. And Protestants don't (m2rc).

Some Catholics think they are better than Protestants and the other way round. Children now don't know *which religion* to choose (f2presb).

Some pupils noted the further complication of divisions between Protestants: 'The way Protestants are divided and say different things makes you think if they all use the Bible they should be the same' (f3pentecostal). Some pupils, expressing the position of Boyle and Hadden's 'third tradition', resolved the dilemma their own ways:

> It is not only Catholics and Protestants who are Christians!! I am a Christian. I am neither Catholic or Protestant (f4none).
> I wouldn't really want to be a Catholic or a Protestant even if I was a Christian because I wouldn't want to be on either side (m2none).

Other pupils, however, predicted a bleak future for Christianity. One said:

> Many different religions say different things and you end up not knowing what to believe. I think many people will forget about the Holy Bible and what it says, especially in Northern Ireland because of the religious disputes (f3presb).

These various sub-types of answer were shared more or less evenly between protestants and catholics. The few differences observed were that only protestants made reference to inter-Protestant divisions and only protestants were explicit about the errors of Catholicism (Catholics were not explicit about the errors of Protestantism).

Type IV answers, community separation (secular, separatist) Answers of this type focused on the division between Catholics and Protestants in terms of social (ethnic, or socially religious as distinct from doctrinally religious) segregation or separation. They accounted for 13% of the total. They were barely higher in girls (0.2%) but significantly higher in catholics (8%). Six sub-types of answer were identified which focused on: social segregation in general; segregated housing; mixed marriage; segregated education; segregated employment; and the inter-connection of religion and politics. Answers across the range of sub-types were evenly divided between protestants and catholics.

Answers of the 'social segregation' sub-type referred to the social segregation of Catholics and Protestants in general terms, reflecting a range of sometimes unexpected perceptions. For example:

> I done Disagree Strongly [that I find Christianity hard to accept because of the way Catholics and Protestants are divided amongst themselves] becous we are *two complet diffrent people* [sic] (m3rc).
> I think it is awful the bitterness between *the religions*. We treat each other like aliens (f3presb).
> I am a Presbyterian. I do not hate RCs but I don't want to learn all about them (m4presb).

I don't think religion should come into Christianity at all. Division is the way it is. You learn to live with it (f3presb).

People should just accept the world as it is and not the way they want it to be (f2rc).

Answers of the 'segregated housing' sub-type focused on segregation in housing and the effects that this has on contact between Protestants and Catholics. There was a range of perceptions. Some preferred segregation, some were resigned to it, others positively deplored it. For example:

I couldn't care about the Fenians and I can accept it [the divide] alright just as long as there are no Fenians about. Some Fenians are alright though others are really Fenians (m2non-subscribingpresb).

People have lived like this for hundreds of years (m2rc).

If Catholics and Protestants are divided then we can't get to know each other (f3rc).

If they were not divided it would solve a lot of problems like boys of *Protestant religion* calling boys of *Catholic religion* names like Fenianes [sic] (m3ci).

Others, however, did not see a problem:

I have lots of Catholic friends and we get on fine. We don't let *different religions* get in the way (f2presb).

I know most of the Protestants and I really like them and I get on well with them (f2rc).

Protestants and Catholics can be Christians in *their own religion* and still get on as friends without bringing up religion (f3presb).

Answers of the 'segregated education' sub-type saw segregated education as a barrier to friendship. For example:

In a lot of schools they are strictly Catholic or Protestant and we don't get the chance to mix and get to know each other (f3ci).

It would be a much better world if Catholics and Protestants were combined in schools and churches (f3ci).

Answers of the 'mixed marriage' sub-type extended focus on barriers to friendship in housing and education to include attitudes to mixed marriage. For example:

Why should we not be friends? (f2rc).

It is hard with a Catholic and a Protestant to become friends and their parents won't like it. I hate the way they think they should stick to *their own kind* (f3presb).

> I feel we should play together, go to school together, and then maybe live together (f2ci).
>
> I find it hard as Protestants are not supposed to marry Catholics. This is not the way it should be. I believe Catholics and Protestants should come together (f3ci).

Answers of the 'segregated employment' sub-type saw segregation in leisure and employment becoming less of a problem:

> In most of Northern Ireland the Catholics and Protestants work together and are making life better and reducing fear in *our community* (m3rc).
>
> Some Protestants work with Catholics in every way, football, charity work and all ways in games and clubs (m3rc).

Answers of the 'religion and politics' sub-type identified the inter-connection of religion and politics in Northern Ireland as a problem:

> The pulpit in my view is just another political platform. Religion has divided and split this country and murdered over 2,500 people (m3presb).
>
> In Northern Ireland Protestants and Catholics are divided not because they all want to but because, due to the way the different political leaders act and with the example they set them, they have no other choice (m3rc).
>
> Politics as well as religion play a major role in life between Catholics and Protestants and that is why Christians remain separated from each other (m4rc).

Type V answers, community sharing (secular, pluralist) Answers of this type focused on the idea of tolerance of diversity (pluralism as distinct from ecumenism) from a secular rather than a religious perspective. They accounted for 14% of the total. They were marginally higher in girls (1%) but significantly higher in non-catholics (14%). Two sub-types were identified which focused on tolerance derived from: personal indifference to religion; and the civil liberty of freedom of religion. These answers were shared evenly between catholics and non-catholics.

At the simplest level, answers of the 'personal indifference' sub-type were those which declared no interest in or knowledge of religious matters. (It is worth noting that no such examples were collected from pupils describing themselves as catholic):

> Nothing to do with me (m4protestant).
>
> I don't care and I never ask anyone about *their religion* (m2none).

I don't care about religion (m4protestant) [but note that this respondent also said that he would be 'annoyed' at the burning of a church 'because it is a part of our protestant heritage'].

Others implied a commitment to tolerance based on a secular rather than a religious evaluation of Christianity:

It doesn't matter whether you are Catholic or Protestant as long as you believe in what you want (f2brethren).

Catholics say *their way* is right and Protestants say *their way* is right but I think you should believe in what you want and not what people want you to (f2presb).

One pupil was explicit about the difficulties caused by the inter-connection of religion and politics:

I find it hard [to accept Christianity because of the way Catholics and Protestants are divided amongst themselves] because people tend to think if you are a Protestant you are a Unionist (and it's the same with Catholics and Nationalists). Also I get mixed up in *the religions* (e.g. what Methodists and what Church of Ireland do (f2presb).

Answers of the 'civil liberty' sub-type were more explicit in referring to the idea of religious liberty as a civil right. For example:

If people want to be Protestants or Catholics let them. It's their own decision (f4rc).

I think that everyone is equal. *What religion* they are doesn't matter to me anymore. People are people no matter what they are (f3presb).

I think that everyone should be allowed to worship their own God in *their own way*, so I do not mind the religious division as long as other people can see that and accept that we are different. This shouldn't stop mixed marriages (f2rc).

I feel it is unfair that so many discriminations are made towards one party by the other party. Why can't we all live together in peace? In Northern Ireland it would be really good if we could because so many people suffer due to the conflict between *the 2 religions* (f4presb).

Setting out the pupils' thinking about the causes and effects of the religious divide in this way is very revealing. It shows that individually their thinking is perceptive but fragmentary. Taken collectively, the fragments are impressive in their comprehensive range and potential coherence. It is hard to find missing reference to any major aspect of adult interpretations of the internal conflict.

Conclusions

What overall picture, then, do schoolchildren in Northern Ireland have of religion and its role in the conflict? The responses to the *Before Questionnaire* reveal sufficient fragments of the picture at least to give a broad outline. What emerges is that although pupils experience the same phenomenon, some perceive it so differently from others that they seem be seeing two different pictures.

The detailed items of the full questionnaire were designed to be combined in order to answer a set of major questions. In this section, some corroborative use is made of findings of the *Before Questionnaire* that were not reported on above. The major questions were: is religion important to schoolchildren?; do they think the conflict is about religion?; do they perceive the divide between Catholics and Protestants as partial or complete?; do they see the divide as unchanging or not?; do they see Protestants and Catholics as belonging to the same religion or to opposite religions still? In short, have schoolchildren made the core choice decisively in favour of sharing or separation, or are they subject to choice modulation?

Is religion important?

Clearly, it is very important. Schoolchildren in Northern Ireland need to have a picture of the way religion is in their own country. The large majority (84%) see religion as being an important part of life, both social and individual. The religious dimension of culture is not one that they feel at liberty to ignore. Most schoolchildren consider themselves to be a member of one of the four largest churches. When asked to name the religious denomination to which they belong, only 6% answer 'none'. Further confirmation of the importance of religion was the positive attitude of most of the pupils surveyed to completing the *Questionnaire*. Almost 60% took the trouble to state that they had found it useful or very useful.

Pupils perceive religion as an important part of their cultural heritage. A large majority (74%) would be 'upset' if one of the other churches in their local area (not theirs) was burned down and 57% said they would be 'upset' if the other churches in their local area (again not theirs) had to be closed down.

That a majority of pupils assign positive value to buildings of religious traditions other than their own indicates an 'open' attitude towards 'the other side'. It also implies that their own religious traditions are very important to them since *a fortiori* they would be upset if their own church were to be burned down. Conversely, only a minority of pupils indicate strong feelings of indifference or hostility towards religion in general. Only 15% would be 'indifferent' if another church in their area were burned down. And only a small minority expressed a 'bigoted' point of view towards 'the other side': no more than 11% would be pleased if an 'other' church were burned down.

Some of these perceptions of schoolchildren can be compared tentatively with those of some adults. During the *Opposite Religions?* trial, a limited survey of adults was undertaken using a reduced version of the *Questionnaire* (Lambkin 1993, 547). The sample of adults was representative of certain groups only, not the population as a whole. It consisted of serving History teachers, trainee teachers, and adults voluntarily attending seminars on the teaching of Religious Education and on integrated education. All were residents of Northern Ireland. Like the schoolchildren, the overwhelming majority of adults surveyed (93%) saw religion as being important.

Generally, however, the overview which schoolchildren (protestant and catholic) have of religion in Northern Ireland and in the wider world is weak. There were 12 general knowledge items in the *Before Questionnaire*. Only three were answered correctly by 50% or more of pupils: the proportion of Catholics in Northern Ireland (79%); the approximate date of the Reformation (63%); and the nature of the protest of the original Protestants (53%). These items, therefore, may be regarded as central to the picture which schoolchildren have of religion. In contrast, a majority of pupils were not able to place in correct rank order of size the four largest Churches and the Free Presbyterian Church. They were not able to estimate approximately the proportion of Protestants in the Republic of Ireland or in Europe. Most underestimated significantly the number of different Protestant denominations in Northern Ireland.

In other words, a majority of pupils have a distorted mental picture of the way things actually are. It is striking, for example, that the majority of pupils underestimates the size of the Roman Catholic Church and overestimates the size of the Free Presbyterian Church.

This is not a matter of random guesswork. The distorted mental picture which pupils have is affected by the way they perceive politics. In the political context, Catholics are generally perceived as the minority community, not the single largest church. The Free Presbyterian Church is perceived, through its connection with the Democratic Unionist Party (both of which are led by the Rev. Ian Paisley), to have an influence commensurate with that of the DUP - an influence out of all proportion to the size of its membership.

How does the pupils' picture compare with that of the sample of adults? As one might hope, the adults were found to have a more accurate, or less distorted, mental picture. Whereas 61% of pupils underestimated the size of the Roman Catholic Church and 59% overestimated the size of the Free Presbyterian Church, a majority of adults estimated correctly in both cases (71%; 78%). By contrast, pupils were almost as good as the adults at estimating correctly the proportion of Catholics to Protestants in Northern Ireland (79% compared with 84%).

However, pupils are markedly weaker in estimating the proportion of Protestants in the Republic of Ireland: less than half of pupils (48%) estimated accurately, compared with 79% of adults. Pupils and adults were found to be equally poor at estimating (from 10% to 20%) the proportion of Protestants in Europe: 88% and 81% respectively failed to estimate accurately. Pupils and adults were also equally poor at estimating (from 30 to 40) the number of different religious denominations in Northern Ireland: 66% and 69% respectively underestimated (Lambkin 1993, 827-8).

The disparities between the pupils' and the adults' pictures of religion suggest a process of development. There is a hierarchy of general knowledge items about religion: some are of greater practical importance than others. The most important (or useful) are probably those which a majority of young people acquire correctly before going on to acquire other items. The more inaccurate the collective perception of any given item, the less important or useful it must be.

For example, two items that appear to be fundamental to the schoolchildren's picture of religion are the approximate date of the Reformation and the reason for the protest of the original Protestants. A majority (63%) knows that the Reformation took place about 500 years ago. A smaller majority (53%) knows that the protest of the original Protestants was to do with the Pope or with the doctrine or liturgy of the Catholic Church. In contrast, only a minority (39%) are aware of the connection between the Plantation of Ulster and the present Protestant majority in Northern Ireland. The weaknesses in knowledge of both pupils and adults (about the proportion of Protestants in Europe for example) probably indicate the limits to which the mental picture of religion is normally developed.

Religion is important to schoolchildren in this sense: as well as requiring certain basic general knowledge about it to function socially, they also need to acquire the skill of being able to tell Catholics and Protestants apart according to criteria which are religious in character. The overwhelming majority of pupils (91%) are confident of their ability to recognise churches (religious buildings) in the environment as such. A substantial majority (63%) are confident of their ability to tell whether a church is Roman Catholic or Protestant from looking at its interior; and 40% are confident that they can tell just from looking at the exterior. A majority (61%) are confident of their ability to tell Roman Catholic priests apart from Protestant ministers in public by the way they dress. In contrast, only 15% are confident about being able to tell Church of Ireland and Presbyterian ministers apart by their dress (Lambkin 1993, 830).

While most pupils appear confident about being able to tell Roman Catholic and Protestant churches apart, they are not confident about being able to tell different Protestant churches apart. Only 24% are confident about being able to distinguish between the interiors of Church of Ireland and Presbyterian churches and only 18% are confident about being able to distinguish them by looking at the exteriors (Lambkin 1993, 830). This suggests that pupils regard the skill of distinguishing between Roman Catholic and Protestant churches as important but not the skill of distinguishing between different Protestant churches.

Fighting about religion?

One of the main reasons that religion is important to schoolchildren in Northern Ireland is that they see it is central to the conflict. A majority (66%) thinks that the fighting is about religion and almost half (49%) thinks that the religious leaders could end the fighting by working together. This is in stark contrast to the sample of adults: only 16% of them think that the fighting is about religion, and only 17% think that the religious leaders could be so effective in ending it.

Why should the perceptions of pupils and adults be at such variance? The obvious explanation is that the majority of adults disagree that the fighting is about religion because they think such a simplistic explanation fails to do justice to the complexity of the conflict which involves other equally, if not more important, political, economic and social elements. The level of pupils' understanding is clearly naive in that it takes account only of what appears superficially to be the main cause. This is confirmed by pupils' unrealistic expectations of the power of religious leaders to alter the situation for the better.

This explanation has some merit. Most pupils are not able to articulate a sophisticated account of what the fighting is about. Almost half (47%) are unable to identify an even partially accurate religious issue which contributed to the original Reformation conflict. They appear to deduce that the fighting is about religion from little more than the titles which they use most frequently for the contending sides - the religious titles, Catholics and Protestants.

This begs the question of why Catholics and Protestants (not Nationalists and Unionists or Republicans and Loyalists) are the titles most frequently used by schoolchildren (and indeed by adults). The answer is probably that, because the conflict includes willy-nilly everyone living in Northern Ireland, fully inclusive titles for the opposing sides are needed and only Catholics and Protestants fits the bill. They include everyone. There is a serious side to the old joke that, even if you are an atheist, you must be either a Protestant or a Catholic atheist. Translated into political terms, the joke does not have the same force.

That said, it should not be altogether surprising that so many pupils have naive or inadequate understandings of the conflict. As Chapter 1 showed, there is no adult consensus on a sophisticated account of the conflict from which pupils may be expected to learn. Remarkably, the evidence shows that pupils between them possess an appreciation of most if not all the main elements which adults have advanced in explanation of the conflict. Many pupils, albeit mistakenly (when answering the question about the original Protestants), deployed contentious events from Irish history and contentious current social and economic issues such as segregated housing, education and employment when articulating their understanding of the conflict. They seem to posses explanatory fragments rather than a complete and coherent explanation.

Closer investigation indicates that adult thinking may not be much more complete or coherent. The large majority of adults (84%) disagreed that the fighting is about religion but only 60% disagreed that religious leaders might end the fighting by working together. If most adults think that the fighting is definitely not about religion, it is hard to see why some should think simultaneously that religious leaders have the power to stop it. Yet this seems to be the case for a significant number of adults. They seem to think that the religious divide between Catholics and Protestants is not the cause of the conflict but the fighting could be ended by bridging the divide religiously. Paradigm or choice modulation may account for this discrepancy.

Most schoolchildren, however, think that the fighting is caused by the religious divide and almost half think it could be ended by bridging the divide religiously.

A partial or complete divide?

How do schoolchildren see the religious divide in Northern Ireland? Do they see it as partial or complete? The first thing to notice is the obvious point that the Catholic / Protestant divide is perceived to be much wider than inter-Protestant divisions. The confidence level of pupils is much higher when comparing Protestant with Catholic religious traditions (artefacts, practices and beliefs) than when comparing those of the different Protestant Churches. This is illustrated by the level of uncertainty (Don't Knows) about similarity and difference: on average it is 14% higher for inter-Protestant comparison than for Catholic / Protestant comparison.

Pupils are split three ways, more or less evenly, in comparing Catholic and Protestant religious beliefs. When responses are aggregated and averaged out, 33% see them as fundamentally different; 35% are uncertain; and 32% see them as fundamentally similar. This contrasts with pupils' comparisons of beliefs between the Protestant Churches: only 12% see them as fundamentally different; 45% are uncertain; and 43% see them as fundamentally similar (Lambkin 1993, 840).

Pupils show greater confidence in responding to comparative questions about religious belief than about religious practice. For example, the levels of uncertainty about Catholic/Protestant wedding practice averaged out at 44%, whereas for wedding belief they averaged out at 34%. The levels of uncertainty for inter-Protestant wedding practice averaged out at 60% and wedding belief averaged out at 41% (Lambkin 1993, 831).

Why pupils should be more confident about the detail of religious beliefs than about religious practices is not immediately obvious. Probably, pupils are more predisposed to guess in the case of belief than of practice (or more predisposed to admit ignorance in the case of practice than of belief).

If, say, a Presbyterian has never actually been to a Catholic baptism, she will probably feel unable to compare Catholic and Presbyterian baptism services and so will choose Don't Know. When it comes to belief about baptism, she may not know the correct answer. But if she already holds a strong general position on the fundamental similarity (or difference) of Catholics and Protestants, she may be prepared to induce from that generalisation that their beliefs about baptism are similar (or different).

In other words, those who see the Catholic / Protestant divide as complete will be predisposed, in cases of comparison where they are ignorant of the detail, to assume fundamental difference, whereas those who see the divide as partial will be predisposed to assume fundamental similarity.

How influential is 'picture choice' on perceptions of the Catholic / Protestant divide? When comparing religious beliefs, picture preference seems to be a strong determinant. In the case of uncertainty about the detail of a particular, basic belief such as about baptism, someone who is strongly committed to seeing the one-religion picture will be correspondingly predisposed to assume similarity rather than difference, and vice-versa for someone committed to seeing the opposite-religions picture.

It is not clear that picture choice is so influential in the case of Catholic / Protestant comparison of religious practices. Suppose a Presbyterian, who is committed to seeing the opposite-religions picture, has no knowledge of how Presbyterian baptism practice compares with Roman Catholic practice. His grounds for assuming that they are more different than similar are much weaker than for assuming the same about baptism belief. There is logical force to the argument that, because Catholicism is a different 'religion' from Protestantism, Catholic and Protestant belief about the validity of each other's baptism must be very different.

However, it does not follow necessarily that Catholic baptism practice must be very different. According to the opposite-religions picture, Catholicism is a 'false' religion (a perversion of 'true' Christianity) so Catholic practices might well appear similar (although the content of the belief which the practice reflects *must* be different). Such a pupil might well be unwilling to guess as to similarity or difference and prefer the Don't Know option since he has no strong indication of which possibility is the more likely. The same would be true *mutatis mutandis* for pupils of whatever denomination and committed to either picture of the Catholic / Protestant divide.

By the same token, picture choice cannot be strongly influential in the case of inter-Protestant comparison of practices (as distinct from beliefs), although for a slightly different reason. Take the case of comparing Presbyterian and Church of Ireland baptisms. At first thought, the likely assumption is that they must be more similar than different. Since they are both 'Protestant' their beliefs about each other's baptism must be more similar than different. However, there must be important differences between the two Protestant traditions otherwise they would be identical. It may occur to the uncertain pupil that the practice of baptism constitutes one of the important differences. Unable to reconcile the general likelihood of similarity with the possibility of difference in this particular case, the uncertain pupil will probably opt for Don't Know.

Pupils split three ways in comparing Catholic and Protestant religious beliefs. About 32% see them as fundamentally similar, 35% are uncertain, and 33% see them as fundamentally different. The 35% of uncertain pupils may be considered as floating voters, modulating between the one-religion and the opposite-religions paradigms. This even three-way split must be related to the even two-way split (which sorted the floating voters) over choice between seeing Catholics and Protestants as belonging to one religion or to two different religions.

An unchanging divide?

If pupils split evenly in their assessment of the extent of the current Catholic / Protestant divide, how do they see it as having developed over time? Have things always been the way they are today or have things changed? There is a close relationship between the way pupils perceive similarity and difference and the way they perceive continuity and change. A similar three way split is observed. When responses to questions of continuity and change in Catholic and Protestant religious beliefs about each other are aggregated and averaged out, 39% are more inclined to be aware of change; 36% are uncertain; and 25% are more inclined to be aware of continuity.

In contrast, there is a much higher level of uncertainty about continuity and change in the Protestant Churches' beliefs about each other. Only 29% are more inclined to be aware of change; 47% are uncertain; and 24% are more inclined to be aware of continuity.

Take the example of marriage: 66% think that Roman Catholics used to believe that inter-marriage with Protestants was wrong and 36% think there has been no change. This compares with the 15% who think that Presbyterians used to believe that inter-marriage with members of the Church of Ireland was wrong and the 9% who think there has been no change.

Again, it seems probable that pupils are predisposed to assume continuity or change according to whether they hold a strong general position on the fundamental difference or similarity of Catholics and Protestants. If they see fundamental difference, they will be predisposed to assume continuity; if they see fundamental similarity, they will be predisposed to assume change.

One religion or opposite religions?

How do pupils formulate their perception of the Catholic / Protestant divide? Pupils who see a partial divide see Catholics and Protestants as belonging to the same religion (Christianity). Those who see a complete divide see them as belonging to two opposite religions (Catholicism and Protestantism). Superficially, by agreeing that 'there are two main religions in Northern Ireland', the large majority (90%) appears to prefer the opposite-religions picture.

As was shown in Chapter 3, however, 'religion' in this kind of context is ambiguous. It can mean either 'exclusive religious system' or 'Christian denomination'. When the choice between the opposite-religions picture and the one-religion picture is put unambiguously - 'Catholics and Protestants belong to two different religions' or 'Catholics and Protestants belong to the same religion' - pupils polarise evenly: 50% prefer the one statement and 50% the other. It is clear, therefore, that most of the 50% who prefer the one-religion picture must help to make up the majority of 90% who see 'two main religions in Northern Ireland'. They do this by 'modulating' to the opposite-religions picture. They are able to do so without mental discomfort because, in this context, 'religion' is conveniently ambiguous.

145

Although there is a tendency for catholics (particularly catholic girls) to prefer the one-religion picture, it is not strong: preference is only 6% higher in catholics than in non-catholics. Therefore, perception of the religious divide between them is not an issue which polarises catholics and protestants as such. It is an issue which divides catholics and protestants amongst themselves.

It is the case, however, that catholics and protestants are polarised in their mutual understanding. Not surprisingly, catholics tend to be better informed about the Roman Catholic Church than protestants, who tend to be better informed than catholics about the Protestant Churches. The most striking illustration of this is the finding that the Roman Catholic Church was identified as the largest religious denomination in Northern Ireland by 31% more catholics than protestants. Similarly, but less dramatically, the Presbyterian Church was correctly identified as the second largest religious denomination by 7% more non-catholics than catholics.

Finally, there is the question of how strongly pupils are committed to seeing the one-religion or opposite-religion picture of the Catholic / Protestant divide. Although all respondents did indicate preference for one picture or the other, it seems probable that in many cases the preference was not strong. Pupils did not have available to them the Don't Know/Uncertain option. Given the high levels of uncertainty (from 35% to 52%) across the range of questions, a substantial number of pupils, given the chance, might well have opted for Don't Know/Uncertain about picture choice. In other words, some pupils are 'floating voters'. They account largely for the high levels of uncertainty. Because they are not strongly committed on picture choice one way or the other, they are not as strongly predisposed as those who are to guess in cases of uncertainty.

The next chapter examines the effectiveness of the trial of the *Opposite Religions?* materials in improving the accuracy of pupils' understanding of religion and its role in the conflict in Northern Ireland. It also examines the effectiveness of the *Opposite Religions?* trial in challenging pupils' attitudes to the core choice between sharing and separation. It reports on the findings of the *After Questionnaire* which pupils completed at the end of about eight weeks work on the project teaching materials. In particular it looks at what happened to the modulators or 'floating voters' when challenged to reconsider the question: opposite religions still?

146

6 Opposite religions still?

This chapter maps the changing state of schoolchildren's perceptions of religion in Northern Ireland. In particular it maps how their perceptions of four aspects of Catholic and Protestant religious traditions changed as a result of working on the trial materials of the *Opposite Religions?* project. These four aspects were: the origins and development of Catholic / Protestant divisions; similarity and difference; continuity and change; and attitudes towards 'the other side'. Just how effective was this curriculum development project in improving the accuracy of pupils' knowledge, in developing their understanding of the role of religion in the conflict, and in clarifying their attitude toward *The Choice* between sharing and separation? Did pupils change in their preferences for the one-religion and opposite-religions pictures?

The concluding part of the chapter widens the discussion to assess the extent to which Protestants and Catholics in Northern Ireland are still seen in terms of the opposite-communities, opposite-religions picture. It does so by examining how these pictures and modulation between them are indicated by the use of key terms ('culture', 'tradition' and 'community') in the *Joint (Downing Street) Declaration* (1993), and the *Frameworks Document* (1995).

Improving accuracy of knowledge

The accuracy of pupils' knowledge at the beginning of the trial was weak generally. Their overall mental picture was distorted or inaccurate. For most questions the proportion of pupils giving the 'correct answer' or target response was 45% or less. Weakness of knowledge in most cases was a matter of self-admitted ignorance or uncertainty (indicated by the Don't Know response) rather than the possession of incorrect information. To what extent did accuracy of knowledge improve?

Taking responses to three of the four main types of question together (general knowledge - 12 items; perception of similarity and difference - 27 items; perception of continuity and change - 3 items), the improvement in pupils' knowledge was substantial. From being secure for less than a quarter (21%) of questions before, it improved to being secure for almost half (45%). Improvement was most dramatic in cases of basic general knowledge such as the relative sizes of religious denominations in Northern Ireland (Table 6.1). Improvement was greater for the similarity and difference type of question than for the continuity and change type. In the tables which follow, B means 'Before' (that is responses to the *Before Questionnaire*), and A means 'After', (responses to the *After Questionnaire*).

Table 6.1   Perceptions of relative sizes of Churches
(RC, Presb, CI, Meth, Free P)

		%	
		B	A
Roman Catholic Church: the largest		39	**61**
	Boys	42	**63**
	Girls	36	**58**
	Catholics	55	**71**
	Non-Catholics	23	**51**
	Presbyterians	21	**48**
	Church of Ireland	28	**49**
	Methodists	16	**50**
	Others	30	**62**
Free Presbyterian Church: the smallest		41	**58**
	Boys	44	**63**
	Girls	39	**54**
	Catholics	41	**53**
	Non-Catholics	41	**63**
	Presbyterians	41	**65**
	Church of Ireland	39	**59**
	Methodists	63	**79**
	Others	46	**58**

There was one marked exception to the general trend for the level of knowledge to increase from a weak initial level. The only item which was 'very secure' at the start was knowledge of the proportion of Catholics to Protestants in Northern Ireland: that is, most pupils (79%) are aware that Catholics are the minority community but substantially so (in the range 30-40%).

However, this was the only item for which there was no significant change at the end of the trial. This suggests that the project was ineffective in improving the general knowledge of a hard core of about 20% of pupils taking part. This group probably corresponds with the 19% who thought the *Before Questionnaire* 'useless'.

Did gender or religious denomination make a difference?

Taking responses to the fourth type of question (attitude) together with the other three, there was a general trend for differences between catholics and non-catholics to be higher than those between boys and girls. Also, knowledge tended to be higher initially in girls and in non-catholics. This is accounted for by the structure of the *Questionnaire*. More items referred to inter-Protestant comparison than to Roman Catholic / Protestant comparison (of similarity and difference and continuity and change). It is not surprising, therefore, that non-catholics (especially non-catholic girls) should have been more knowledgeable than catholics about inter-Protestant comparisons at the start of the project.

Girls and boys and non-catholics and catholics were fairly evenly divided in their knowledge of religious traditions to begin with. However, there were some significant (5%+) differences. The level of knowledge in girls was higher initially than in boys for 58% of the knowledge questions by an average difference of 6%. This compares with knowledge in boys being higher initially than in girls for 42% of questions by an average difference of 4%. By contrast, knowledge in non-catholics was higher initially for 60% of questions by an average difference of 11%. This compares with knowledge in catholics which was higher initially for 40% of questions by an average difference of 7%.

Reassuringly from the point of view of teachers, initial differences between boys and girls and non-catholics and catholics tended to even out. The level of increase in knowledge was higher in boys than in girls for 68% of questions by an average difference of 5%. It was higher in girls for 32% of questions by an average of 3%. Increase in knowledge was higher in catholics than in non-catholics for 71% of questions by an average difference of 7%. It was higher in non-catholics for 29% of questions by an average difference of 5%.

A useful way of showing the main differences between boys and girls and between catholics and non-catholics is to highlight questions where there were differences of 10% or more, taking each type of question in turn.

Type 1 questions, general knowledge For this type of question, the level of knowledge tended to be higher in boys initially and tended to remain so. For example, the target response for the proportion of Protestants in Europe (10-20%) was 19% higher in boys initially.

There was a higher increase of knowledge in girls of 13% but not sufficient to close the gender gap completely. Also, knowledge about Roman Catholics tended to be higher initially in catholics than in non-catholics and knowledge about Protestants tended to be higher in non-catholics initially. In both cases it tended to remain higher. For example, the target response for the relative size of the Roman Catholic Church (the largest denomination in Northern Ireland) was 31% higher in catholics initially. There was a higher increase of knowledge in non-catholics of 12% but not sufficient to close the gap between non-catholics and catholics. Similarly, knowledge of the relative size of the Presbyterian Church (the second largest denomination) was 7% higher initially in non-catholics. There was a marginally higher increase of knowledge in catholics of 1% so the gap between catholics and non-catholics remained virtually unchanged.

Type 2 (similarity and difference) These questions compared four religious services (see for example Table 6.2). Pupils initially expected similarity to be more evident in weddings and funerals and difference to be more evident in baptisms and communions. The main gender difference was that knowledge tended to be higher initially in girls and tended to remain so. Girls' initial level of knowledge was 10%+ higher for 8 of the 27 items. It should be noted that 6 of the 8 related to inter-Protestant comparison.

Catholics tended to be more knowledgeable initially about Roman Catholic / Protestant comparison and to remain so. For example, knowledge of the position of the Protestant Churches on giving communion to Roman Catholics (policy of an open table) was 15% higher in catholics initially. (The statement was: 'If a Catholic goes to communion in a Protestant church, the minister won't give them communion'.) There was a marginally higher increase in non-catholics of 1% so the gap remained virtually unchanged. On the other hand, non-catholics tended to be more knowledgeable initially about inter-Protestant comparison. Their initial level of knowledge was 10%+ higher for all 14 items of inter-Protestant comparison (35% higher in the case of the position of Presbyterians on re-baptism). Although increase in knowledge for 4 of these items was higher in catholics by more than 10%, in no case did catholics close the gap between them and non-catholics completely.

Table 6.2   Perceptions of similarity and difference: marriage

Practice and Belief	Agree %		Don't Know %		Disagree %	
	B	A	B	A	B	A
Practice						
Catholic priests perform weddings in a very different way from Protestant ministers	34	**37**	43	**17**	23	**46**
Church of Ireland ministers perform weddings in a very different way from Presbyterian ministers	10	**14**	60	**28**	30	**58**
Belief						
The promise which a Catholic couple makes at their wedding is very different from the promise which a Protestant couple makes	23	**21**	34	**14**	43	**65**
The promise which a Church of Ireland couple make at their wedding is very different from the promise which a Presbyterian couple makes	9	**9**	41	**29**	50	**71**

Type 3 (continuity and change) For this type of question (see Table 6.3), girls tended initially to be more knowledgeable than boys. For example, level of knowledge of the present Protestant position on intermarriage with Roman Catholics was higher in girls than boys by 26%. Increase in knowledge of this item was higher in boys by 23% so the initial gap was narrowed but not closed completely.

Table 6.3   Perceptions of continuity and change: marriage

	Agree %		Don't Know %		Disagree %	
	B	A	B	A	B	A
What Catholic priests say and do at the wedding service has changed	16	**43**	48	**18**	36	**39**
What Church of Ireland ministers say and do at the wedding service has changed	10	**33**	60	**25**	30	**42**
What Presbyterian ministers say and do at the wedding service has changed	9	**31**	58	**25**	33	**44**

There was a tendency for catholics to be more knowledgeable initially about continuity and change in the Roman Catholic tradition. Twelve questions referred to continuity and change in RC practices and beliefs. Initial knowledge was 10%+ higher in catholics for six of these. There was a tendency for non-catholics to narrow the gap but not completely. For example, knowledge of change in RC practice of baptism was initially 13% higher in catholics and increase in knowledge was 11% higher in non-catholics.

Similarly, there was a tendency for non-catholics to be more knowledgeable initially about continuity and change in Protestant traditions. Eighteen questions referred to continuity and change in Protestant practices and beliefs. Initial knowledge was 10%+ higher in non-catholics for four of these. For example, knowledge of change in the Protestant position on attendance at Mass in a Catholic church was 17% higher initially in non-catholics. Increase in knowledge was 18% higher in catholics, so the gap in this case was closed completely.

The evidence suggests that pupils tend to assume continuity in religious traditions rather than change. In answer to a question about perception of change in the various dimensions of culture (political, economic, social and religious) pupils rated religious change lowest of all (Lambkin 1993, 743-750).

If pupils felt confident about their perception of a particular religious practice or belief in the past or the present, they tended to assume continuity by projecting that practice or belief forward into the present or back into the past as the case might be. Overall, there was evidence that pupils developed a greater awareness of change within both Roman Catholic and Protestant traditions.

It is noteworthy that non-catholics were more confident, both intially and finally, about their skill of distinguishing between Roman Catholic and Protestant churches by looking at their interiors.

Type 4 (attitudes) In contrast to questions of types 1, 2 and 3, a different pattern emerged from the responses to Type 4 questions which were concerned with pupils' attitudes. There were 17 items of this type. Four of these related to the importance of religion in Northern Ireland and the need to understand it better (Table 6.4).

Table 6.4   Perception of the role of religion in Northern Ireland

	Agree %		Don't Know %		Disagree %	
	B	A	B	A	B	A
Religion is an important part of life in Northern Ireland today, whether we like it or not	84	**93**	8	**3**	8	**4**
We should try to understand religion better whether we believe in it or not	78	**81**	10	**8**	12	**11**
History and RE in schools should help us to understand those who are different from us	78	**86**	12	**8**	10	**6**

The target response was 'very secure' (75%+) in each case. This means that before (B) the trial there was a strong consensus amongst all pupils and that after (A) the trial the consensus had gained in strength. By contrast the intial consensus that 'there are two main religions in Northern Ireland' and that 'the fighting is about religion' got weaker in both cases (see Tables 6.9 and 6.5). So unlike the knowledge-type questions where the general trend was from a low level of knowledge to a higher level of knowledge, the main trend with

153

the broad attitude-type questions was for some (relatively minor) modifications of a strong initial consensus. The main trend for the other attitude-type questions was for some (again relatively minor) modifications of a pronounced lack of consensus. In short, over the course of the trial change in knowledge was more dramatic than change in attitudes.

There was a tendency for girls to express more positive attitudes initially: that is, girls were more likely than boys to give the targeted responses. There was also a tendency for increase in positive attitudes (targeted responses) to be higher in boys. The initial levels of target response (TR) were higher in girls for 78% of attitude questions by an average difference of 7%. Increase in levels of TR was higher in boys for 63% of attitude questions by an average difference of 4%. In other words, differences between boys and girls tended to even out. For example, the initial level of agreement that Christianity is hard to accept because of Catholic / Protestant divisions was 16% higher in girls and the increase in agreement with this was 15% higher in boys.

There was a tendency for catholics to express more positive attitudes initially and also for increase in levels of TR to be higher in catholics. Unlike the process of evening out which took place between girls and boys, this difference between catholics and non-catholics persisted. The initial level of TR was higher in catholics for 54% of attitude questions by an average difference of 10%. The increase in levels of TR was also higher in catholics for 54% of attitude questions by an average difference of 4%. For example, the intial level of agreement that Christianity is hard to accept because of Catholic / Protestant divisions was 19% higher in catholics. The general increase in agreement with this was only 3% higher in non-catholics.

Perceptions of the fighting

The trial had an impact on the way pupils relate their thinking about religion and about the conflict to each other. The initial majority of 66% believing that the fighting is about religion was reduced by 10% (Table 6.5). This 10% represents floating voters who changed their minds for two possible reasons. Either they changed their view about the involvement of religion in the conflict (that is, decided that the cause of the fighting is political or economic or social, not religious) or else they developed a more sophisticated view according to which they were no longer prepared to accept religion being described as the sole cause of the conflict.

Table 6.5   Perceptions of the fighting

	Agree %		Don't Know %		Disagree %	
	B	A	B	A	B	A
The fighting in Northern Ireland is about religion	66	**56**	11	**7**	23	**37**
The religious leaders could end the fighting by working together	49	**53**	22	**15**	29	**32**

Given this reduction, it seems surprising to find that there was no parallel reduction in the proportion (49%) of those believing that the religious leaders could end the fighting by working together. Quite the reverse. This proportion increased to form a majority (53%). However, this is probably explained by the level of uncertainty about the effectiveness of the religious leaders in solving the conflict being twice as high initially as for belief that the fighting is about religion. The higher initial proportion of uncertain pupils in this case decided finally in favour of the religious leaders' effectiveness rather than against it.

Initially, the level of disagreement that the fighting is about religion was higher in boys than in girls (9%). However, this difference tended to even out rather than persist. There did not appear to be a correlation between agreement that the fighting is about religion and preference for the opposite religions-picture. More girls than boys (6%) initially preferred the religious explanation of the conflict and also the one-religion picture (14%).

Protestants tended to prefer the religious explanation of the conflict more than catholics. This tendency was equally pronounced among Church of Ireland and Presbyterian pupils (even though the tendency to prefer the opposite-religions picture was more pronounced in Presbyterian than in Church of Ireland pupils). At the end of the project, catholics were still more likely than protestants to disagree that the fighting is about religion but less so than initially. In other words, an effect of the project was to bring protestant and catholic perceptions more in line with each other.

This aligning effect of the project is demonstrated clearly by the responses to questions which differentiate the pupils who were most 'enlightened' from those who were most 'prejudiced'. For example, the small minority of pupils who disagreed that 'there are two main religions in Northern Ireland' may be fairly described as the most 'enlightened' since the only grounds for disagreeing is an unwillingness to accept the implication that Catholics and Protestants belong to two different religions. Their disagreement indicates their sensitivity to core choice modulation. This 'enlightened' group was balanced evenly, both at the start and at the end, between boys and girls and between catholics and non-catholics.

The small minority of pupils who said they would feel 'unconcerned' or 'pleased' if one of the other churches in their local area (not their own) was burned down may be regarded as representing the most 'prejudiced' group (Table 6.6).

Table 6.6   Perceptions of churches burning

How do you think you would feel if one of the churches in your area (not yours) was burned down?

Feelings	%	
	B	A
Upset	37	**32**
Concerned	37	**42**
No feelings / Uncertain	15	**12**
Unconcerned	9	**11**
Pleased	2	**3**

Like the most 'enlightened' group, the most 'prejudiced' group was balanced evenly between boys and girls and between catholics and non-catholics. Overall we may conclude that no group, boys or girls, catholics or protestants, are typically more 'enlightened' or more 'prejudiced'.

Perceptions of similarity / difference and continuity /change

In the case of both Catholic / Protestant and inter-Protestant comparison, the proportion of pupils with 'correct' awareness (TR) increased from roughly a third to a half. (The level of uncertainty remained proportionately higher for inter-Protestant comparison.) The pattern of change was almost identical for both aspects of comparison of continuity and change. The fact that the levels of uncertainty about inter-Protestant comparison remained proportionately higher than for Catholic/Protestant comparison confirms that pupils remained more aware of the latter.

Marriage The pupils' perception of wedding traditions provides a good test case for illustrating the detail of how change took place. Given the importance of endogamy (marriage within the community) as one of the two most important mechanisms for maintaining the boundary between Protestants and Catholics, it may be supposed that, of all the aspects of religious traditions which the *Before and After Questionnaire* examined, this aspect is the one most central to the improvement of community relations. If endogamy is to continue being as effective as it undoubtedly has been in the past, it would seem reasonable to expect that pupils should be developing during their adolescent years an awareness at least that mixed marriage (Catholic/Protestant) is normally regarded as unacceptable.

Further, it might reasonably be expected that there would be a close relationship between attitudes to inter-church marriage and preference for the one-religion picture or the opposite-religions picture. This was the case. A majority of pupils agreed that mixed marriage between Catholics and Protestants in the past was regarded as wrong (see Table 5.15). This majority exceeded that preferring the opposite-religions picture (see Table 5.17). So we may conclude that some pupils who prefer the one-religion picture see that Catholic / Protestant relations in the past were 'bad', at least in so far as they regarded intermarriage as wrong. In contrast, only a small minority of pupils agrees that mixed marriage between Protestants in the past was regarded as wrong. So we may conclude that, whether they prefer the one-religion or opposite-religions picture, pupils are agreed that relations in the past between the Protestant Churches were relatively 'good'.

These appear to be the main premises upon which pupils' thinking about religious traditions is based: Catholic / Protestant relations in the past were bad and inter-Protestant relations were relatively good. However, pupils diverge on the assumptions which they make about the relationship of the past to the present. Some conclude that Catholic/Protestant and inter-Protestant relations today are better than they used to be and others conclude that they are more or less the same as they ever were. The former tend to be those who see the one-religion picture and the latter tend to be those who see the opposite-religions picture.

The trial did have an impact in increasing the awareness of pupils that inter-Protestant relations in the past were not as friendly as they thought. However, because the base of awareness was so low in the first place, a majority of pupils continued to believe that inter-Protestant relations in the past were friendlier than they actually were. The majority of pupils continued to project an awareness of good inter-Protestant relations in the present back onto the past, notwithstanding evidence to the contrary.

The most important change which took place with regard to wedding traditions was in pupils' perception of the acceptability of mixed-marriage between Catholics and Protestants (Table 6.7).

Table 6.7   Perceptions of continuity and change: marriage

	Agree %		Don't Know %		Disagree %	
	B	A	B	A	B	A
Catholics used to believe that it was wrong for a Catholic to marry a Protestant	67	**76**	15	**10**	18	**14**
Most Catholics still believe this	36	**35**	22	**13**	42	52
Protestants used to believe that it was wrong for a Protestant to marry a Catholic	61	**74**	20	**13**	19	**13**
Most Protestants still believe this	34	**34**	26	**16**	40	**50**
Presbyterians used to believe that it was wrong for a Presbyterian to marry a Church of Ireland person	15	**27**	46	**28**	39	**45**
Most Presbyterians still believe this	9	**12**	48	**29**	43	**59**

Those believing that mixed marriage was no longer regarded as wrong (that is, that there had been a change in both traditions from greater difference to greater similarity) increased from about 40% to about 50%. In other words, at the end of the trial pupils were split more or less evenly on the question of whether mixed marriage between Catholics and Protestants is acceptable or not.

If there were a strong correlation between the way pupils perceive particular aspects of religious traditions and their preference for either the one-religion picture or the opposite-religions picture, one would expect the level of those believing mixed marriage to be acceptable today to have increased disproportionately to about the same level as those preferring the one-religion picture. This does not appear to happen. Rather, increases in awareness about particular items tend to take place in step with each other. While pupils are probably predisposed by their picture preference to make particular assumptions about details of practice or belief, they are not prepared to generalise simply on the basis of it. If they begin by being more confident about one particular item than another, they tend to remain so, albeit usually at a higher level. So we find that 50% of pupils initially, and 59% finally, see the one-religion picture; however, only 42% initially and 52% finally believe that mixed marriage with Protestants is acceptable to Catholics today.

In pupils' thinking, their perception of the unacceptability or otherwise of mixed-marriage in the past seems to have priority over all the other items related to wedding traditions. Perceptions of similarity/difference and continuity/change in particular cases are subordinate to it. This is not surprising. It is clearly more useful to pupils to know whether mixed marriage is now acceptable or whether it is still unacceptable than it it is to know whether Catholic and Protestant wedding practices and beliefs are more similar than different or whether they have changed or not. These items are secondary because they are not essential in themselves, but they do help to make intelligible the primary item.

The pattern of change in the attitude of pupils towards the acceptability of mixed-marriage, apart from some relatively small differences, was similar in boys and girls and in catholics and protestants. Girls were more aware initially of the unacceptability of mixed-marriage in the past (11%) and remained more aware than boys (9%). Girls were also more aware initially that mixed-marriage is acceptable today but only marginally so (4%). Non-catholics were more aware initially of the unacceptability of mixed marriage in the past (7%). This suggests that there is a tendency for catholics (especially catholic boys) to have a slightly rosier view than non-catholics of Catholic / Protestant relations in the past. In turn, this is probably connected with catholics being marginally more aware than non-catholics of the acceptability of mixed marriage now.

The most noteworthy inter-Protestant difference was a tendency for Church of Ireland and Methodist pupils to be more aware than Presbyterian pupils (16% and 10% respectively) that mixed marriage is now acceptable. This is probably connected with the tendency for Presbyterians to be more likely than Church of Ireland or Methodist pupils to prefer the opposite-religions picture (13% and 24% respectively).

Perceptions of the Catholic / Protestant divide

At the start, there was an exactly even balance between those preferring the one-religion picture and those preferring the opposite-religions picture. The single most important effect of the trial was a shift of 9 points in favour of the one-religion picture (Table 6.8). The pupils, therefore, moved closer to the position of the sample of adults referred to in Chapter 5.

Table 6.8   Perceptions of the Catholic / Protestant divide (1)

Which of the following two statements do you prefer?	%	
	B	A
A. Catholics and Protestants belong to two different religions	50	**41**
B. Catholics and Protestants belong to the same religion	50	**59**

The trial also had the effect of making more pupils sensitive to the phenomenon of core choice modulation. This was indicated by the increase of 7 points in the proportion of pupils disagreeing with the proposition that 'there are two main religions in Northern Ireland'.

Table 6.9   Perceptions of the Catholic / Protestant divide (2)

	Agree %		Don't Know %		Disagree %	
	B	A	B	A	B	A
There are two main religions in N. Ireland, Catholic and Protestant	89	**83**	4	**3**	7	**14**

The most likely grounds for their disagreement is an unwillingness to accept the statement's implication that Catholics and Protestants belong to two different religions in the sense of mutually exclusive religious systems.

Taken together, these two effects confirm the explanation of core choice modulation advanced in Chapter 3. That is, a substantial number of pupils are 'floating voters' in the sense that they are not firmly committed to seeing either the one-religion picture or the opposite-religions picture. The trial appears to have had the effect of enabling some at least of these floating voters, who previously felt themselves more inclined towards the opposite-religions picture, to switch preference to the one-religion picture. It seems reasonable to conclude that their switch was a result of being challenged by the teaching of the trial materials to reconsider their initial preference.

Effects of the Protestant / Catholic divide on personal belief

Strikingly, the proportion of pupils who said they found Christianity hard to accept because of the divisions between Catholics and Protestants remained constant at 47% (Table 6.10).

Table 6.10   Effects of the Protestant / Catholic divide on personal belief

	Agree %		Don't Know %		Disagree %	
	B	A	B	A	B	A
I find Christianity hard to accept because of the way Catholics and Protestants are divided amongst themselves	47	**47**	20	**13**	33	**40**

In view of the trends towards a more accurate awareness of comparisons of similarity/ difference and continuity/change and of preference for the one-religion picture, it may seem surprising that there was not also a comparable decrease in those finding Christianity hard to accept because of Catholic / Protestant divisions. It might have been expected that greater awareness of the nature of Christian divisions and greater preference for seeing the one-religion picture would have left fewer pupils feeling that lack of unity is an obstacle to accepting Christianity.

A decrease was observed but it was amongst those who were initially uncertain about what they thought on this issue. The number disagreeing that lack of Christian unity was a difficulty increased in proportion as the level of uncertainty decreased.

However, division between Catholics and Protestants clearly remains a stumbling block in the way of acceptance of Christianity for almost half of pupils. In giving reasons why they had answered this question the way they had, pupils at the end of the project made less reference to 'ecumenical' reasons and more reference to 'violence' (Table 6.11)

Table 6.11 Effects of the Protestant / Catholic divide
on personal belief: reasons

This is why I answered the question (Table 6.10) the way I did

Reasons	%	
	B	A
Fighting	27	35
Religious sharing (ecumenical)	24	17
Religious separation (fundamentalist)	22	26
Community separation (secular, separatist)	13	12
Community sharing (secular, pluralist)	14	10

From this it seems reasonable to conclude that the trial had an effect of focusing pupils' minds more closely on the inter-relationship of religion and conflict in Northern Ireland.

Schoolchildren after the project: opposite religions still?

On the basis of the *Opposite Religions?* trial, the following summary statement can be made about the thinking of Protestant and Catholic schoolchildren in Northern Ireland about each other's religious traditions and about the inter-relationship between religion and the conflict in Northern Ireland.

Most pupils:
- think that religion is an important part of life in Northern Ireland,
- appreciate positively the religious buildings in their local area and the people who use them,
- know more about their own religious traditions than those of others,
- respond positively to opportunities to develop their awareness of their own religious tradition and those of others,
- think that relations between the Catholic Church and the Protestant Churches in the past were bad,
- think that relations between the Protestant Churches in the past were relatively good,
- believe religion to be the cause of the conflict in Northern Ireland,
- believe the religious leaders could end the fighting by working together,

162

- are independent in their attitudes to their own and to other religious traditions (that is, they do not rely on a classroom peer group attitude).

Pupils are more or less evenly divided between:
- those who prefer the one-religion picture and those who prefer the opposite-religions picture,
- those who are more aware of similarity between Catholic and Protestant traditions and those who are more aware of difference,
- those who are more aware of change (towards mutual sharing) within Catholic and Protestant religious traditions and those who are more aware of continuity with the past (on-going separation),
- those who believe that inter-marriage between Catholics and Protestants is acceptable and those who do not,
- those who find that divisions between Catholics and Protestants make Christianity hard for them to accept and those who do not.

Few pupils:
- are sensitive to the phenomenon of core choice modulation,
- are prejudiced against 'the other side' to the extent of wishing them harm,
- are able to give an adequate account of the original Reformation division between Catholics and Protestants,
- have an adequate understanding of the inter-connection of religion and politics in Northern Ireland.

The evidence suggests that there are no perceptions or ways of seeing the inter-connection of religion and politics in Northern Ireland which are typically male or female, Catholic or Protestant, Presbyterian, Church of Ireland, Methodist or other. All these groups share the same diversity of perceptions, although not in identical proporitons (See for example Table 6.12).

After going through the common learning experience of investigating the same evidence, the groups tended to become more, rather than less, similar to each other in the proportions of the different perceptions which they shared.

Generally, learning took a positive direction towards the objectives of Cultural Heritage and EMU. There were many points of detail concerning comparison between religious traditions about which a majority of pupils were uncertain at the start of the trial of the *Opposite Religions?* materials. Levels of uncertainty about many questions were dramatically reduced.

By contrast, most pupils were confident at the start about their personal position regarding the central issues (core choice preference and the

Table 6.12 Perceptions of mixed marriage

		Agree %		DK %		Disagree %	
		B	A	B	A	B	A
Most Catholics still believe it is wrong to marry a Protestant		36	**35**	22	**13**	42	**52**
	Boys	36	**35**	24	**12**	40	**53**
	Girls	36	**36**	20	**13**	44	**51**
	Catholics	31	**28**	17	**10**	52	**62**
	Non-Catholics	41	**42**	24	**14**	35	**44**
	Presbyterians	41	**44**	28	**16**	31	**40**
	Church of Ireland	28	**41**	25	**11**	47	**48**
	Methodists	34	**39**	25	**13**	41	**48**
	Others	39	**39**	31	**22**	30	**39**
Most Protestants still believe it is wrong to marry a Catholic		34	**34**	26	**16**	40	**50**
	Boys	35	**34**	30	**18**	35	**48**
	Girls	33	**34**	24	**14**	43	**52**
	Catholics	30	**27**	30	**20**	40	**53**
	Non-Catholics	40	**40**	22	**12**	38	**48**
	Presbyterians	46	**46**	21	**11**	33	**43**
	Church of Ireland	33	**41**	22	**8**	45	**51**
	Methodists	22	**30**	19	**13**	59	**57**
	Others	34	**32**	26	**18**	40	**50**

acceptability of intermarriage) on which the trial found them to be more or less evenly split. Most pupils did not change their minds. For these pupils the trial may have performed a useful function in challenging them to think through more clearly their reasons for continuing to hold their chosen positions. More importantly, perhaps, the trial identified a group of between 10% and 20% of pupils who were 'floating voters', uncertain about their position on most issues. Most of these had made up their minds by the end of the trial. This is the central measure of the effectiveness of *Opposite Religions?*: 10% of pupils changed their minds by deciding against the opposite-religions picture and in favour of the one-religion picture.

Pictures of religion in transition

The school trials part of the *Opposite Religions? Project* indicates how Catholic and Protestant schoolchildren in Northern Ireland think about each other's religious traditions and about how religion and politics are inter-connected. How should this be interpreted as fitting into the wider picture described in Chapter 3?

Briefly, the Reformation and Counter Reformation brought about a paradigm shift in thinking about religion in western Europe. A majority of people changed from seeing themselves in terms of a one-religion picture to seeing an opposite-religions picture. Catholics and Protestants perceived the division between them as so complete that each regarded the other as 'outside the Church', to the extent that they were prepared to fight each other to death in the name of 'true' religion. This revision of core choice had profound implications: most people had become fundamentally predisposed to prefer political, economic and social (as well as religious) structures for separation rather than for sharing.

Since the Reformation there has been a further paradigm shift in western Europe from the opposite-religions picture to a new one-community, one-religion picture. The twin processes of secularisation and ecumenism have gradually brought about consensus in favour of it. The vision of a single European community is predominantly secular but it is strongly reinforced by the religious vision of ecumenism. Full organic church unity has not been restored but it is at least an ideal shared. A majority of the greatly reduced numbers of Protestants and Catholics now regard each other as belonging within the same religion, Christianity. Most non-Christians see them this way also.

Judging by the perceptions of its schoolchildren, Northern Ireland is distinctive because it does not yet seem to have passed through the critical stage when consensus in favour of the old western European opposite-religions picture shifts in favour of the new one-community, one-religion picture. The school population at least (and probably the adult population as

165

well) is evenly split between those who continue to prefer the opposite-religions picture and those who prefer the one-religion picture. Characteristic of the even balance is the group of 'floating voters' who 'modulate' between the two pictures. Modulation for most people is an unconscious process which may take place in a single conversation according to a change in circumstances. It seems probable that in the adult population only minorities are firmly committed to seeing either the one-religion picture or the opposite-religions picture and that the majority are modulators or floating voters.

This is what is meant by the 'deep structure' of the Northern Ireland conflict. Here lies the explanation as to why the conflict about the conflict has been so protracted and consensus about the nature of the conflict so elusive: its deep structure has not been understood.

The internal conflict in Northern Ireland is still between two groups which are religiously 'closed' or mutually exclusive. Virtually all schoolchildren are enculturated into either the Protestant community or the Catholic community. They receive powerful signals that their community prefers the opposite-religions picture: Catholics and Protestants are qualitatively different. They are sent to separate schools and learn that inter-marriage with 'the other side' is not normally acceptable. It is probably misleading to describe such a fundamental belief about 'the other side' as either religious or political: no religious or political commitment is necessarily entailed by it. To avoid giving the impression that one is promoting the religious dimension above the political we may call it 'proto-religious'.

Within limits, it is irrelevant to the community (Catholic or Protestant) whether or not an individual develops a community-based religious or political commitment, provided that he or she assents to the opposite-communities picture. Even though individuals become secularised (or never become religious), the process of secularisation in itself does not necessarily undermine their sense of belonging to the community in which they grew up and from which they derived their social identity. What self-identification with one's own community does entail (implicitly if not explicitly) is acceptance, if not approval, of its opposite-communities picture. Obviously, a critical point may be reached eventually when too few are committed religiously and politically to the opposite-commuities picture for it to be sustained any longer as the view of the majority.

The situation for schoolchildren at present is confusing. As well as receiving strong signals that indicate their (Protestant or Catholic) community's preference for the opposite-communities picture, they are also receiving counter-signals from two different directions which indicate preference by 'the wider community' for, not surprisingly, the one-community picture. From one direction, the leaderships of the four largest Churches encourage to a greater or lesser extent ecumenical co-operation between each other as Christians together. From the other direction, government community relations policy encourages 'cross-community' contact. Caught in this cross-fire, the result is tension of a kind which one might expect of a society at a critical stage of transition. Tension between the one-community picture and the opposite-communities picture produces the phenomenon of picture or choice modulation, which is having it both ways without being aware of the contraction.

It is important to emphasise that community preference (core choice in favour of separation or sharing) is an issue for everyone, regardless of personal religious or political commitment. If the outcome is eventually consensus in favour of the one-community picture, it will probably be achieved through an informal coalition of religious believers whose viewpoint is ecumenical in the religious sense and non-believers whose viewpoint is ecumenical in the secular, pluralist sense.

The polarised nature of Northern Ireland society makes the core choice of community an issue for all. If individuals do not themselves articulate the issue, or if they are not challenged by having the issue presented to them, they will make no conscious choice. In which case, they will tend to adopt sub-consciously as their own the choice of the group, or sub-group, in which they have been brought up. Since neither the Protestant nor the Catholic communities are homogeneous in this respect, the individual Protestant or Catholic may do one of three things: become committed to the one-community choice; become committed to the opposite-communities choice; modulate or float uncertainly between the two, according to prevailing influences.

The core choice of community, therefore, is not an issue which divides Catholics as a whole from Protestants as a whole. Certainly, the evidence of the *Opposite Religions?* trial shows that Catholic schoolchildren are almost as evenly divided amongst themselves as Protestant schoolchildren (see Table 6.13). This is both disturbing and reassuring.

It is disturbing because it calls into question the commonly-held belief that Catholics and Protestants perceive the conflict differently. Whyte has summed up the orthodox interpretation: 'Protestants fear the Catholic religion and the consequences of living in a State dominated by the Catholic Church, while Catholics object not to the Protestants' religion but to their political outlook and their grip on power' (1990, 106). This is true, but only up to a point. Perhaps as much as half of the Catholic community has yet to shift to preference for the one-community or one-religion picture. A substantial proportion of Catholics retain the traditional Catholic objection to 'the Protestants' religion' (as Whyte puts it) in spite of their Church's official commitment to ecumenism. While it may be true that their objection does not surface in the rhetoric of conflict, it is none the less real for being unspoken. Catholics who still prefer the opposite-religions picture have no need to manifest their objection to the Protestants' religion because they conveniently interpret ecumenism as meaning 'the return of the lost sheep to the fold of Rome'. Given that the religious tide in western Europe is running (albeit

Table 6.12   Perceptions of the Catholic / Protestant divide

	One religion %		Two religions %	
	B	A	B	A
	50	**59**	50	**41**
Boys	46	**60**	54	**40**
Girls	54	**59**	46	**41**
Non-catholics	47	**56**	53	**44**
Catholics	53	**62**	47	**38**
Presbyterians	40	**53**	60	**47**
Church of Ireland	53	**56**	47	**44**
Methodist	64	**53**	36	**47**
Others	51	**60**	49	**40**

sluggishly) in favour of ecumenism, the religious battle to these Catholics seems as good as won. Their sort of ecumenism does not involve them necessarily in surrender or sacrifice. However, one may imagine *mutatis mutandis* that these Catholics would find such a view of ecumenism as objectionable as most Protestants do.

On the other hand, it is reassuring to find that Catholic pupils as a whole are almost as evenly divided as Protestants as a whole in their choice between the one-religion and opposite-religion pictures. It is strong evidence that both sets of pupils are fundamentally similar. This comes at a time when a growing body of evidence from the research of Greer and others has pointed increasingly to important differences between the religious attitudes of Catholic and Protestant pupils (Greer and Long 1990). It is well established that Catholic pupils are more positive in their religious commitment than Protestant pupils and that Catholic girls are more positive than Catholic boys.

Greer and Francis have given a stern warning. Since real differences in pupils' religious profiles which result from the system of segregated schools have been confirmed, this evidence 'could be used by protagonists to argue in support of a separate Catholic culture or of a separate Protestant culture which needs its own schools through which distinctive values and beliefs are transmitted to the next generation' (Greer and Francis 1992a and 1992b, 23). These protagonists may be said to be commited to the opposite-religions picture and consequently to a policy of separate development in education. The more different the religious profiles of Catholic and Protestant pupils are shown to be, the less wise seems a policy of integration.

So far as core choice of community is concerned, the most important aspect of difference in religious profile is Greer's finding that 'openness' to 'the other side' is greater in Catholic pupils (1985, 288). By 'openness' Greer means willingness to value members of the other traditions as neighbours, relatives, workers and people worth knowing and understanding. *Opposite Religions?* provided further evidence of greater openness amongst Catholic pupils. They are more 'ecumenical' in their thinking. They show greater awareness of similarity between Catholic and Protestant religious traditions and greater awareness of change in an ecumenical direction in inter-church relations, for example in the mutual recognition of baptism and the acceptability of mixed-marriage.

However, *Opposite Religions?* suggests that 'openness' is not a matter of fundamental difference between Catholic and Protestant pupils; rather it is a matter of degree. In structure their religious profiles are basically similar. Both groups are divided more or less evenly on the issue of core choice. Difference in degree of openness between the two is accounted for simply by the shift towards the one-religion picture being more advanced in Catholics than in Protestants. After engaging in the common *Opposite Religions?* learning experience, the attitudes of Protestants tended to become more rather than less similar to those of Catholics. Most importantly for religious ecumenism and community relations policy in education alike, the attitudes of both groups shifted in the direction of the one-community, one-religion picture. Teachers still need to take account of important differences in the religious profiles of Protestant and Catholic pupils. Nevertheless the same educational strategy is appropriate for both.

The *Opposite Religions?* trial demonstrated that 'Education for *The Choice*' is a viable educational strategy. If schoolchildren have the core choice of community or religion (separate or shared) articulated for them; if they are presented with relevant evidence and challenged to reconsider the attitudes which they hold, then they respond positively. They become more 'open' than 'closed' towards 'the other side'. Given the opportunity to improve their understanding of similarity and difference, continuity and change, and conflict resolution, they do so - which is the main purpose of the Cultural Heritage and EMU initiative in the Northern Ireland Curriculum.

Teachers of Religious Education need to take into account that almost half of pupils (Catholic and Protestant) believe that the lack of unity between Protestants and Catholics makes it hard for them to accept Christianity. Of course, this is only one factor among many which makes it hard for them to accept (see Greer 1988). It is an important one nevertheless. The difficulty of these pupils is the perennial one of reconciling the Christian message with the apparently contradictory behaviour of its messengers.

The other half of pupils have either not perceived this contradiction or else they have resolved it. If they have resolved it (to their own satisfaction at least) they have done so in either a religious (ecumenical or fundamentalist) way or in a secular (pluralist) way. They reason as follows: either we are all basically the same (as children of God or as human beings) and therefore we should live together; or we just have to accept that we are different and therefore we should live separately. The first line of argument derives from preference for the one-religion picture; the second from preference for the opposite-religions picture.

Adult perceptions after the ceasefires

If the *Opposite Religions?* trial gives some insight into the thinking of schoolchildren and the direction in which it may develop or change as a result of curriculum development, to what extent is the thinking of schoolchildren a reflection of thinking in the adult population at large? Is adult thinking changing, especially in the new political context after the ceasefires? Further research is required to answer that question. However, some indication of thinking at the highest level can be found in the *Declaration* of December 1993 by the British and Irish Prime Ministers and the subsequent *Frameworks for the Future*, published in March 1995. They are the defining documents of the ceasefires. They set the context for political negotiation and they are open to examination for the evidence they contain about the British and Irish governments' position with regard to the core choice for Northern Ireland after the conflict. Can it be said that the governments at least have chosen finally in favour of sharing rather than separation, or do they modulate still?

The Joint (Downing Street) Declaration

In the *Joint Declaration*, modulation between the one-community and two-communities picture is evident. On the face of it, Northern Ireland is described unambiguously and consistently in terms of the two-communities picture: the final paragraph refers to 'both communities in Northern Ireland' (12) and there is no reference to Northern Ireland as 'one community'. One of the two communities is referred to specifically as 'the Unionist community' (6). 'Tradition' is used as a synonym for 'community'. The phrase 'both communities' (5) is echoed by 'both traditions' (6, 7).

'Community' and 'tradition' are not exact synonyms in the *Joint Declaration*: 'both communities in Northern Ireland' (12) is echoed by 'both traditions in Ireland' (2, 4, 11). There is a subtle difference. In Ireland as a whole there are 'two main traditions' (6). Only in Northern Ireland do these two traditions constitute two communities. The expression 'Northern Unionists' (6, 7) implies 'Southern Unionists' but Southern Unionists are not thought of as constituting a separate community inside the Republic of Ireland as Northern Nationalists are inside Northern Ireland. Although the document does not use the term 'culture', the two communities are thought of as two cultures: the 'Unionist community' has its own 'way of life and ethos' (6), i.e. culture.

However, the *Joint Declaration* does modulate to the one-community picture. The term most frequently used to describe the various groups is 'people', not 'community' or 'tradition'. Although they are not referred to as constituting a single community, the inhabitants of Northern Ireland are referred to as 'the people of Northern Ireland' (4, 5, 7). On the face of it, this expression does not disturb the two-communities picture; on its own it might be nothing more than neutral description of the way things are at present but it is clear that more is intended. Also referred to as entities are 'the people of Britain' (4) and 'the people of Ireland' (9). The meaning of the latter becomes clearer when set with its variations: 'the people of Ireland, North and South' (1, 2, 12), 'the people living in Ireland' (4), 'all the people who inhabit the island' (4), 'the people of Ireland as a whole' (5), 'all the people of Ireland together' (6), 'the people of the island' (8). The effect of this rich series of synonyms is to emphasise the oneness of the inhabitants of the island. The common interest of all the inhabitants of the island is specified as:

> the desire to preserve those inherited values that are largely shared throughout the island or that belong to the cultural and historical roots of *the people of this island* in all their diversity (6).

In this way, the *Joint Declaration* modulates from a two-communities picture towards a one-community picture. It is a one-community picture of Ireland as a whole rather than of Northern Ireland as a whole. The peoples (communities, traditions) of the island are not described explicitly as constituting a single community but the inherited values which they share imply a single community of interest at least.

Further than this, the oneness of the inhabitants of both islands is emphasised: 'the peoples of both islands' (1), 'both their peoples' (2, 12), 'the peoples of Britain and Ireland' (9), 'the people of these islands' (12). By extension, the inhabitants of Britain may be thought of as sharing also in 'those inherited values that are largely shared throughout the island [of Ireland]'.

Here can be seen the dynamics of paradigm modulation. On the one hand the *Joint Declaration* recognises the separateness of 'the two traditions in Ireland' dividing people 'on the issue of whether they prefer to support the Union or a sovereign united Ireland' (4). It also recognises the separateness of 'the two communities in Northern Ireland' (12). On the other hand, it recognises the oneness of two traditions in Ireland and the two communities in Northern Ireland. They share inherited values, not only with each other but also with the people of Britain.

The *Joint Declaration*, therefore, does not resolve the issue of core choice by deciding unambiguously in favour of sharing rather than separation. Rather than move Northern Ireland from its precarious point of balance between the options of the core choice, it deliberately seeks to modulate between both: 'the time has come to consider how best the hopes and identities of all can be expressed in more balanced ways, which no longer engender division and the lack of trust' (7).

Balance is the key concept. The document expresses dissatisfaction with the precarious balance of the past. There has been too much 'bitter division' and 'lack of trust' (7) and not enough 'harmony' and 'partnership' (4). There is need for a 'new departure' which will 'break decisively the cycle of violence' and realise the 'full potential for prosperity and mutual understanding' (12). At the same time, the validity of separateness is acknowledged: 'that step would compromise no position or principle, nor prejudice the future for either community' (12). What is sought is a 'balanced constitutional accommodation' (7) and a 'balanced approach to all the problems which for too long have caused division' (8).

The Frameworks Document

Modulation is also evident in the *Frameworks Document*. What is most remarkable is the difference between the way the key term 'community' is used in Parts I and II. Part I sets out the British Government's 'Framework for Accountable Government in Northern Ireland'. In contrast to *the Joint Declaration*, Part I describes Northern Ireland in terms of the one-community picture. There is no specific reference to 'the two communities'. Northern Ireland is thought of consistently as one community: 'the community in Northern Ireland'(iii). There is acknowledgement of 'the main community division'(3). The community is split into two 'sides', 'parts' or 'sections' as in: 'both sides of the community'(3); 'both the main parts of the Northern Ireland community'(3); 'both main sections of the Northern Ireland community'(23). The effect of the avoidance of 'community' in Part I as a synonym for 'side', 'part' or 'section' is to emphasise the oneness of the divided Northern Ireland community. Other variants are used to the same effect: 'all parts of the community'(iii); 'all sections of the community'(iii); 'the wider community'(vi); 'the community at large'(13).

Part II sets out 'A New Framework for Agreement' which is 'a shared understanding between the British and Irish Governments to assist discussion and negotiation involving the Northern Ireland parties'. In marked contrast to Part I, Part II describes Northern Ireland in terms of the two-communities picture. There is no specific reference to 'the community in Northern Ireland'. Neither is there any specific reference to the two 'sides', 'parts' or 'sections' of Northern Ireland. They are referred to consistently as 'both communities in Northern Ireland' (10, 13, 19, 20, 22; cf 'either community' 7) and particularly as 'the unionist and nationalist communities in Northern Ireland' (19, 52). Conversely, the effect of avoidance in Part II of forms such as 'the wider community', 'the community at large', 'the community in Northern Ireland' is to emphasise the twofold division rather than the oneness of Northern Ireland.

In short, the *Frameworks Document* modulates between an emphasis on sharing in Part I and on separation in Part II. Since it took two years of careful preparation to produce, the question of 'studied ambiguity' arises. The theory of conflict intractability proposed in Chapter 3 would suggest that its ambiguity is not 'studied' or deliberate; rather it is accidentally a manifestation of the all-pervasive 'hidden effect' of paradigm or choice modulation.

Accidental ambiguity or not, either way the evidence of both the *Joint Declaration* and the *Frameworks Document* indicates that the British and Irish Governments have not pre-empted the core choice between separation and sharing by committing themselves unequivocally to either. There are both negative and postive aspects to this. The negative aspect is that, by modulating (consciously or unconsciously) and not making a definitive choice jointly in favour of sharing, the Governments may have entrenched the intractable conflict still further. The positive aspect is that, for all the people in Northern Ireland, *The Choice* between separation and sharing is still open.

After the ceasefires: opposite religions still?

If in politics there is still modulation between the one-community and two-communities pictures of Northern Ireland, what is happening in the Churches? Is there still modulation between the one-religion and the two-religions pictures of the Churches in Ireland? The *Joint Declaration* and the *Frameworks Document* set out the joint position of the British and Irish Governments. In the absence of comparably definitive documents published jointly by them, it is harder to assess the current position of the four main Churches.

The position of the Methodist Church, for example, became clearer in September 1995 with the launch of a framework-type document called *Biblical Perspectives on the Peace Process* (McMaster, 1995) aimed at helping the Churches in Northern Ireland to boost the peace efforts. It highlights the 'kairos moment' (a moment of opportunity for critical reflection and decisive action which does not last for ever). Then it challenges members of the Churches to make the core choice in favour of sharing rather than separation:

> What might it mean for unionists and nationalists to ... create an arrangement of power that serves rather than dominates? Each tradition in Northern Ireland fears domination by the other. ... The key question (for local churches) is not merely what can we think of the present but what do we do in the present. Kairos calls us to action.

However, the two-religions picture still has force as the following letter from a District Secretary of the Independent Loyal Orange Institution indicates:

> While we have no difficulties with being good neighbours to all creeds and classes, we wish to record our opposition to the planned Protestant/Roman Catholic 'prayer breakfast' which is partly organised by the Grand Master of the Orange Order.
>
> It is somewhat hypocritical for the Rev M Smyth to stand one night in an Orange lodge which terms Roman Catholic worship (correctly in our judgement) as "unscriptural, superstitious and idolatrous' and then attend a 'prayer breakfast' where practising RCs are accepted as fellow Christians.
>
> Surely it is time for Mr Smyth, Mr John Taylor, and any other Orangeman who will be attending this function to reconsider their membership of the Orange Order. (*Belfast Telegraph* 11/9/95).

Not only does the writer express commitment to the two-religions paradigm by refusing to accept Roman Catholics as 'fellow Christians', he criticises

Martin Smyth and others for modulating between paradigms: attendance at a prayer breakfast with Roman Catholics is interpreted as commitment to the one-religion paradigm, whereas membership of the Orange Order is interpreted as commitment to the two-religions paradigm. The term used here to describe the modulation is hypocrisy.

Ambiguous use of 'religion' is still widespread in Northern Ireland. For example, the Labour MP, Kate Hoey, described recently going to the Ulster College of Physical Education at Jordanstown in 1964 when there were only 60 students on campus:

> Out of the 20 girls entering in my year, eight were Catholics, which was the highest proportion they ever had. It was, for many, the first time they had contact with anyone from *another religion* (*Belfast Telegraph* 11/9/95).

Similarly, a recent graduate of the Catholic teacher training college in Belfast said at interview in 1995:

> It is hard to take when the very people who are supposed to be spreading peace, love and togetherness are sometimes the very ones who promote that training for the teaching profession must take place in one institution for *one religion* and *members of another religion* should not attend it.

Further research is needed to investigate the ambiguous usage of 'community' and 'religion' in both the school and adult populations and to test the theory of choice modulation. Now, in the light of the evidence currently available, what are the implications for interpreting Northern Ireland after the conflict?

7 Interpreting Northern Ireland after the conflict

For whatever may be yet to come of the 'endgame' or final stage of the Northern Ireland conflict, there remains the problem of interpretation - the conflict about the conflict. Since conflicts are often 'settled' without agreement as to their nature, the problem of interpretation will probably be with us still after the conflict proper. How then will all the parties to it explain the twenty-five years or more of communal violence? Will they deliberately set about interpreting it to each other (jointly or separately), to their children, to visitors and to the rest of the world, or will they try to forget?

The aftermath of traumatic, shameful, 'best-forgotten' periods in the history of peoples generally raises such questions. The experience of many countries this century suggests that in the long run it is better to remember the past and wrestle with the problem of its interpretation, rather than to suppress its memory. In the United States, Germany and Japan, for example, centres for the interpretation of the history of slavery, the Holocaust, and the bombing of Hiroshima and Nagasaki are now highly respected and increasingly popular with schools and with the general public.

In Northern Ireland the conflict to be interpreted is not quite over. While it is possible for conflicts to be settled without agreement as to their nature, such settlements are not likely to be long-lasting. If the fundamental issues are not identified, agreed upon and dealt with, the integrity of the quarrel remains intact. Dormant for now, it may re-erupt later.

As Boyle and Hadden have identified it, the fundamental issue for people in Northern Ireland is *The Choice* between sharing and separation, between living together as one community and living apart as opposite communities. The opposition between sharing and separation, between integration and segregation, puts the choice very starkly. While this has the merit of focusing attention clearly on the fundamental issue, there is also danger in describing a complex situation so crudely: to contrast a possible integrated future with a segregated past is simply bad history. The theory of conflict intractability proposed here shows how the original core choice at the time of the Reformation in favour of segregation has been overlain subsequently by modulation to forms of sharing and integration. Before challenging people to make *The Choice* definitively, the educational task is to interpret how the present point of precarious balance between sharing and separation in all its complexity has been reached.

This chapter considers the practical implications of a programme for 'Education for *The Choice*' and the need for new resources to enable people to address the challenge of the core choice.

Education for *The Choice*

The *Opposite Religions?* project approached the way schoolchildren see the core choice by mapping an outline of their perceptions of each other's religious traditions and their perceptions of the inter-connection of religion and politics. It showed that curriculum development projects can be effective in improving community relations by challenging pupils to re-evaluate their core choice.

The map of pupil perceptions derived from *Opposite Religions?* is by no means complete or fully detailed. The investigation addressed only a limited range of points of comparison. However, it seems unlikely that further investigation would alter substantially the broad outlines. The evidence presented in Chapters 5 and 6 indicates the levels of knowledge and the types of understanding and types of attitudes which the History or RE teacher might expect to find in a lower secondary school class when teaching about religious traditions in the context of the cross-curricular themes of Cultural Heritage and EMU. Teachers are more likely to challenge pupil perceptions effectively through classroom discussion if they possess a mental map of the territory being explored and some insight into the thinking of the pupils whom they are guiding.

'Education for *The Choice*' as an educational strategy is a logical development of the work of Boyle and Hadden. It fits well with the objectives of Cultural Heritage and EMU. The main question to ask is: are the resources available for implementing it adequate to the scale and importance of the task?

The most important resources of all are the teachers, particularly the History and Religious Education specialists. Ironically, the *Opposite Religions?* trial had very limited success in its aim of promoting co-operation across the traditional boundaries of the two subjects. Various factors connected with the nature of Education Reform and the internal organisation of schools militated against closer co-operation. These apart, however, the *Opposite Religions?* trial confirmed the hypothesis that teaching about the inter-connection of religion and politics in Northern Ireland is generally poor because RE teachers tend to leave the teaching about the Northern Ireland conflict to History teachers and History teachers tend to neglect the religious dimension of history. For example, the foreword to a recent school textbook on the history of Northern Ireland confidently denies that the conflict is 'primarily religious':

> The terms Protestant and Catholic and unionist and nationalist have been used frequently in the text to describe the main groupings in Northern Ireland but readers should be aware that these terms are open to a range of interpretations. *The labels Protestant and Catholic are particularly misleading because they imply that the dispute is primarily religious, which it is not* (author's italics, Gillespie and Jones 1995, v).

If this state of affairs is to be improved, two main difficulties need to be overcome.

Firstly, History teachers need to take better account of the religious dimension in their teaching generally and in their teaching of the history of the Northern Ireland conflict in particular. Their neglect of it has been understandable since historians and social scientists have not shared an agreed framework of cultural analysis which gives due weight to the religious dimension. Only recently has Irish religious history become established as a respectable sub-discipline with historians studying it on an inter-denominational basis. Now that Irish religious history is on a firm footing and the introduction of Cultural Heritage and EMU has provided teachers with an agreed framework for cultural analysis, the excuse for neglect of the religious dimension in the teaching of History disappears. For example, *Medicine through Time*, which is currently the most popular Study in Development for GCSE History, could be complemented by a new option *Religion through Time* (equally a life and death matter).

Secondly, RE teachers need to take a more 'historically-minded' approach to their teaching by using resources which explore the historical dimension of their subject. Relatively few are also trained History teachers. As a result, RE teachers tend to present pupils with a 'Whig' or 'inevitable' interpretation of church history, which short-circuits historical investigation in explaining the past which has led to the present state of affairs. Many RE teachers found the methodology of the *Opposite Religions?* trial unfamiliar or uncomfortable because it was based on the use of evidence and discussion. With greater use of history-based teaching materials, RE teachers might become more confident about moving into the territory traditionally reserved to their History colleagues. The inter-connection of religion and politics is so complex in Ireland that the task of exploring it cannot be left adequately to one subject alone.

It needs to be recognised, however, that the interpretation of religious traditions in Northern Ireland is still at a very early stage of development. The projects which preceded *Opposite Religions?* (such as *Religion in Ireland* and *Looking at Churches and Worship*) and more recent ones such as *What It Means to be a Roman Catholic, Presbyterian etc*, (a series of videos sponsored jointly by the four main Churches) and *The Power to Choose* (teaching materials produced jointly by the Irish Council of Churches and the Irish Commision for Justice and Peace) have laid good foundations.

What had not been attempted previously was a systematic interpretation of the historical development of the various religious traditions in Ireland, including their inter-relationships with each other and their political connections. The *Opposite Religions?* trial made a start on this. Out of it came revised materials, published in three books to facilitate their use by both RE and History teachers, under the title *Opposite Religions? Protestants and Roman Catholics in Ireland since the Reformation.* This, though, is only a start.

The Churches as museums

It is a paradox that relatively little attention has been given to the interpretation of religious traditions in Northern Ireland precisely because it is still such a 'religious' society. Thriving traditions have no need of museums. The tradition is its own history since its present is continuous with the past. Religious traditions in Northern Ireland are still so much part of the living fabric of social life that it is not yet a common perception that they may need their own museum or interpretation centre.

Museums are usually needed only when things become obsolete but are too valuable to throw out. Traditions generally emphasise continuity with the past rather than change. *A fortiori* this is true of religious traditions as vehicles for 'unchanging truths'. Museums, on the other hand, testify to discontinuity with the past. It is therefore indicative of the relatively healthy state of religious traditions in Northern Ireland that the museum provision made by the four largest Churches is so minimal, as discussed below.

Healthy religious traditions until now have had no need of museums or interpretation centres for themselves. Children are initiated into membership more effectively by participating in the 'actual' performance of the tradition rather than by having 'virtual' performances interpreted to them in a classroom (although, of course, classroom teaching may play a part). Healthy religious traditions for the most part are not transmitted from one generation to the next as a schoolteacher teaches a subject. Children learn the tradition mainly by living it. Often they receive their most telling interpretation or explanation of the tradition in the context of a religious service; as, for example, when a parent makes an explanatory comment to a child *sotto voce* during a church service or when a minister or priest takes a marriage preparation class. Ordinary tradition members (as distinct from the clergy) tend to build up their knowledge and understanding of their tradition fragmentarily on a 'need to know' basis, rather than programmatically as in learning a school subject.

As long as it is the norm for religious traditions to have little to do with one another it is both sufficient and efficient for tradition members to have this kind of self-understanding. If religious traditions are to remain healthy, the next generations of members will still need to be initiated in this way. However, it is predictable that initiation of this kind alone will no longer be sufficient or efficient. One result of increasingly friendly cross-community and inter-church contact is that separate Church traditions come to be seen increasingly as 'old-fashioned'. An indication of how sensitive Church members are to being perceived in this way is the increasingly often-heard protestation that 'we are not a museum people' (Kinahan 1995, 57).

The introduction in schools of Cultural Heritage and EMU since 1990 has transformed a situation which was already changing gradually. At the core of the Cultural Heritage and EMU curriculum initiative is the belief that it is good for children of different traditions to have contact with each other and to learn about each other from each other. The consequent educational strategy is based on the premise that pupils (and their teachers) are able to act as articulate representatives of their own tradition. There are strong reasons for doubting the soundness of this premise.

The *Opposite Religions?* trial did find that pupils generally are more knowledgeable about their own than about the traditions of others but it also found that pupils' knowledge and understanding of their own traditions is weak in certain respects which are vital to fruitful cross-community contact. The conclusion to draw from this is not that pupils are incapable of becoming

180

articulate representatives of their own tradition. Rather, they require greater educational support to become such.

Such support is more urgently required among Protestants than Catholics because of their considerably lower level of church affiliation and practice (Francis and Greer 1992b, 20-1). Several *Opposite Religions?* trial teachers in Protestant schools reported difficulty in working with pupils who had virtually no knowledge of their religious tradition beyond an awareness that they were 'Protestant'; that is, not Catholic. Such negative definition of identity in relation to 'the other side' tends to collapse when sustained friendly contact is made. The conclusion of psychologists is that the conflict is 'based on normal psychological processes operating in an atypical context' (Cairns 1994, 25). In a 'normal' context children may be expected to behave 'normally'.

The fruits of cross-community contact, however, may eventually turn bitter. Individuals may shed their negatively defined identity (I am not a Catholic, therefore I am a Protestant; or vice versa) through contact schemes or integrated schools. However, they may also develop, to a greater or lesser extent, a sense of disconnection from their home community. This may be a good thing for community relations in the short term but it is unlikely to be good for individual self-esteem in the long term if it turns out that they have paid the price of a more or less total rejection of their community's past.

For the theory of Cultural Heritage and EMU to be put into practice effectively, pupils need to be supported in developing critical awareness of the religious tradition (amongst others) of the community in which they are growing up. They need this in order that they may avoid having to throw out the baby with the bathwater.

The assumption, of course, is that there is a baby in the bathwater. Certainly, the Churches believe so. However, it would be unreasonable and inappropriate to expect the Churches alone to give pupils the scale of support required. The critical interpretation of religious traditions is a task for the education service (including schools, universities, and museums) as well as for the Churches. It is especially a task for the museums service. Museums facilitate the process of change. They enable tradition members to dispose of cherished but nonetheless non-essential or obsolete items with a good conscience.

A museum, or interpretation centre, is the type of institution best suited to give the comprehensive over-view of religious traditions and their historical development, which the *Opposite Religions?* trial found to be so lacking in schoolchildren. Is it tolerable that Catholics and Protestants should continue to have such distorted perceptions of themselves and of each other; that they should underestimate the degree of similarity between their traditions; that they should underestimate the degree to which their traditions have changed for the better; or that they should correspondingly over-emphasise the degree of difference between them and the degree of their traditions' continuity with the past?

If, as is argued here, religious traditions in Ireland are presently at a stage of critical transition, this means they are approaching a point of major discontinuity with the past. It is a further paradox that religious traditions best accomplish major change or 'paradigm shift' by emphasising continuity with the past (unlike science which now expects periodic 'revolutions' as a matter of course). The original Reformers claimed lines of tradition running back to primitive Christianity. They sought to make their radical changes more acceptable by emphasising a return to origins. Now, in similar fashion, modern ecumenists claim continuous lines of tradition back to the Reformation and beyond and emphasise a return to origins in order to make the project of Christian unity more acceptable.

As Bruce has pointed out, while the fundamentalists object (quite correctly from their point of view) that the ecumenists are innovating, the ecumenists in response distort history by claiming the mainstream of the tradition for themselves and by representing the fundamentalists as eccentric. Like the reforming ancestors of the fundamentalists before them, ecumenists tend to cope with religious change by minimising it.

They do so largely because ecumenical leaders have invested relatively little in interpreting to their followers the historical development of their tradition. And yet the theology of ecumenism is fundamentally historical. It is based on the idea of development within the tradition, as distinct from innovation. Explaining this to a mass membership, however, is a major and difficult educational task. If religious truths are eternal, tradition members ask, how can religious practices change? A way of avoiding this problem is to pretend that no real change has taken place, rather a restoration of former practice or belief. This course of action is almost irresistible when circumstances are pressing and the educational means to explain change properly are not to hand.

It seems clear that more could be done to ease the pain of shifting from an opposite-communities, opposite-religions picture of Catholic / Protestant relations to the one-community, one-religion picture. People need clearer interpretation of the process of change in order to make sense of living through it and to participate responsibly in it. They need to have articulated the core issue of community choice: separation or sharing? Fundamentalists need to understand why ecumenists perceive ecumenical change to be development rather than innovation (that is, the retention of essentials and the abandonment of non-essentials). Conversely, ecumenists need to understand why fundamentalists perceive ecumenical change to be innovation. Again, it should be emphasised that everyone in Northern Ireland, whether by commitment or default, is either a 'fundamentalist' or 'ecumenist' according to their core choice in favour of separation or sharing, or else a modulator.

The process of changing choice can be painful if it involves abandoning attachment to familiar and often cherished beliefs and practices. It is the pain of seeming to betray one's ancestors. The *Opposite Religions?* trial showed that this process is underway in the school population but that it is making slow progress against the inertia set up by core choice modulation. Curriculum intervention can accelerate the process by clarifying the issue of community choice through 'Education for the Choice', but not, it seems, beyond a certain critical point. When challenged to re-evaluate their preference for the opposite-communities, opposite-religions picture, about 10% of pupils changed their minds to prefer the one-community, one-religion picture. This tipped the overall balance in favour of the one-religion picture but left 38% of catholics and 44% of protestants as firmly committed as before (if not more so) to the opposite-religions picture.

The encouragement from this for educators is that less than 25% of pupils are so 'closed' in their preference for the opposite-communities, opposite-religions picture that they express extreme or bigoted views toward 'the other side'. Correspondingly, the majority are positively 'open': they are either already committed to the one-community, one-religion picture, or they are likely to become committed to it (after being challenged to re-think their position).

The liberating effect of historical interpretation

Even if there is still no general agreement about the role of religion in the Northern Ireland conflict, there is at least a consensus about the need for such a consensus. Historians and social scientists share a belief that the way in which the politico-religious heritage of Ireland is popularly perceived constitutes a mental prison-house from which people need to escape if an unacceptably grim present is not to continue indefinitely. Further, they share a belief that the way of liberation lies through an understanding of the results of professional, scholarly study of that heritage.

Comerford (1988, 225) has summarised the case for the liberating benefit of doing history:

> There is a mystique about history in Ireland and about historians. They are seen as people whose job is to explain how we have arrived where we are. There is an assumption that everything in the past is the story of how the present difficulties, the present conflict, have come about. I think it

would be a very liberating thing for Irish people generally to see the numerous possibilities of the past.

Thus, interpreting the cultural traditions which constitute the past through the study of history is both limited and liberating. It cannot identify for us to the best future possibility that we should choose but it does teach that there is no future which is inevitable. The study of history in this sense is open-ended: conclusions arrived at through historical study do not pre-empt necessarily any options for the future.

In this way it is possible to speak about 'Education for *The Choice*' as choice between separation and sharing. The process of re-assessing and interpreting cultural traditions (including all dimensions of the culture - political, economic, social, artistic, aesthetic and religious) has a liberating effect. Given the central role of religion in the Northern Ireland conflict, this is especially true of religious traditions. McDonagh (1986), for example, looks forward to 'not some radical transformation of the Irish Churches into some great Church but a more profound conversion to one another that will release them from their quasi-political Babylonian captivity'(154). If the members of the Churches are still in a 'quasi-political Bablylonian captivity', then the conditions of their captivity are in some ways less oppressive than they were and in large part this is due to a better understanding of their religious heritage:

> It is only with the advent of the Second Vatican Council and the spirit that preceded it in certain quarters in Ireland that more - although by no means many - Irish Protestants and Roman Catholics began to meet in a religious context and so gradually become more aware of themselves as together forming the one people of God on a pilgrimage of self-discovery and towards liberation from constraints of their different religious, cultural and national identities (Ellis 1992, 98).

Ultimately, it may be this metaphor - the one people (of God) travelling together on a journey (pilgrimage) of self-discovery - which proves more powerful and beneficial. It has the advantage of transcending the weakness of the present dominant metaphor for reconciliation - bridge-building. Like the bridge-building metaphor, it is capable of both secular and religious interpretations which conveniently reinforce each other. What makes it more powerfully transcendent is that its character is nomadic rather than territorial. The idea of battle, betrayal and surrender (going over to 'the other side') is not intrinsic to it, as it is to bridge-building. There is an idea, but no clear picture, of a final destination and no detailed itinerary. The wisdom of sharing, rather than separating, on the journey (pilgrimage) becomes self-evident to fellow-travellers (pilgrims) who are uncertain of the route and are contracted (vowed) to be together still on arrival.

Disentangling religion and politics

An important part of the ongoing controversy about the role of religion in the Northern Ireland conflict is the extent to which the Churches need to be part of any solution. However central (or otherwise) religion may have been to the origins and development of the conflict, there is a strong argument that at least the co-operation of the Churches would be helpful in its resolution. And further, since it is generally agreed that Northern Ireland is still a 'religious' society (Morrow 1991; Cairns 1991, 142-156) there is a good case to be made from Dawson's analysis that the co-operation of the Churches is essential:

> One might go so far as to say that it is only by religion that a religious culture can be changed. The fact that a way of life has been consecrated by tradition and myth renders it singularly resistant to external change, even when change seems obviously advantageous from a practical point of view. But if the impulse to change comes from above, from the organs of the sacred tradition itself or from some other source which claims superhuman authority, the elements in a society which are most sensitive to religious impulses and most resistant to secular influences themselves become the willing agents of change. (Dawson 1948, 214-216).

Murphy has identified a specific task for the Irish situation:

> Even the most obtuse and bigoted are now beginning to see that one of the essential things to be done in Ireland, if we are ever to have a minimum level of peace and reconciliation, is to dissever 'faith from fatherland'. The fatherland has historically been torn between its conflicting faiths and therefore it must cherish on equal terms *people of all religions* and, increasingly, of none. The heart of the matter is that aspects of Irish identity which have been meshed by historical circumstances must now be disentangled (author's italics, 1988, 151).

There is a problem. If the meshing of religion and politics has been so fundamental, it would seem to follow that the very act of disentangling or separating the strands necessarily threatens the integrity of the identities which they in part constitute. The problem, however may be more apparent than real:

The process of separation should not involve the destruction of any part of the Irish heritage, but rather a surer preservation ultimately. For example, dissociating Irish language-culture from the cult of murderous violence is an essential national salvage operation. Desectionalising our identity and finding a wider and more transcendent base for our nationality is a vital task of our time. Separating 'Catholic' from 'Irish', indeed separating 'religion' from 'Irish', does not mean a rejection of the 'religion' aspect of Irish identity (Murphy 1988, 151).

The task of dissociating 'Irish language-culture' from militant Republicanism has already been taken in hand by the Northern Ireland Community Relations Council through the establishment in 1990 of the *Ultach Trust*, which has the aim of widening appreciation of the contribution made by the Irish language to the culture of Northern Ireland and to increase knowledge of the language through all sections of the community. Less progress has been made in the disentangling of religion and politics. The *Opposite Religions?* project was one example from post-primary education. Another example, from adult education, has been the 1987 project of the Irish School of Ecumenics, called *Reconciling Memories*. This project gathered contributions from theologians, political scientists, historians, philosophers, and literary critics precisely in order to find a transcendent base for identity. It made a bolder claim for the liberating effect of the interpretation of cultural traditions than those referred to already:

> Reconciliation involves the recognition of the interdependence of our histories. Reconciliation entails the appropriation of each other's history, through which each empowers the other to be free. Through the reconciliation of memories a new identity is born (Santer 1982).

According to this analysis, the major problem in the Irish situation is that 'one section of the Irish people has an inadequately developed sense of 'belonging', i.e. the 'Protestant' people of Ulster, and it is only if this belonging can be fostered and nurtured that any genuine fusion [of the two traditions] can take place (Ellis 1992, 127). The recent publication of *A Precarious Belonging* (Dunlop 1995) confirms this analysis.

The process of reconciliation of memories offers a way out of the dilemma posed by the divisive character of Irish history. On the one hand, as Wright (1988, 68) has pointed out, however deeply it is studied, honest historians are never going to discover that relations between Catholics and Protestants in the past were substantially more harmonious than is currently thought. On the other hand, it is dangerous to avoid the study of history and forget the past altogether because 'to attempt to erase historical remembrance can result in enslavement to the ephemeral immediacies of the present' (Kearney 1988, 8).

The way out of the dilemma is to recognise the importance of myth. Myth is here defined as a concept such as 'the national territory' or 'national sovereignty' and an associated narrative which is used to justify a political position or action (Comerford 1988, 1-17). Within any given tradition, myth may serve either a negative or a positive function. In the Irish context the negative function is that of the two-communities, two-religions paradigm of the Catholic Nationalist and Protestant Unionist traditions and the positive function is that of the one-community, one-religion paradigm. In other words, every tradition stands in need of being de-mythologized and re-mythologized.

It is the job of the historian to de-mythologize. But de-mythologization is not enough. A subsequent process of re-mythologization is inevitable. Reinterpretation of myth by historians will result in the creation of new myths but, as Comerford points out, these will be 'scarcely anything as misleading as the one that is being challenged' (1988, 14). It is the job of theologians, political theorists, artists and others to re-mythologize. If they do so in dialogue with historians they may ensure that the new myths by which we choose to live are as consonant as possible with our best understanding of the past.

Interpreting myths of separation and sharing

The alternatives of *The Choice* identified by Boyle and Hadden - separation or sharing - are effectively the core concepts of myths by which we may choose to live. Each may be interpreted in either a secular or religious way (or both combined). Boyle and Hadden set out to present the alternatives impartially but indicate their preference for the secular (rather than the religious) version of the 'myth' of sharing. The religious version may be called the new 'ecumenical' myth. Both versions are capable of being formulated in terms which can be shared by each. For example, one leading ecumenist asserts:

> that people, despite their different languages, cultures and religions, can live together, that dogmatic all-or-nothing programmes can never help, that compromise is not surrender, that the only realistic way out entails the effort of mutual understanding, moderation, accommodation and co-operation ... and last, but not least, that the most elementary presupposition for such a solution is to build up trust, one small step at a time (Küng 1986, 50).

Examples of secular expression of the sharing myth are the cross-curricular themes of EMU and Cultural Heritage in the Northern Ireland Curriculum. Examples of religious expression of the sharing myth are the *Reconciling*

Memories project and the core syllabus in Religious Education, promoted jointly by the four largest Churches in Northern Ireland. The convergence of the secular and the religious versions of the sharing myth is evident in the commitment of the Churches to supporting EMU and Cultural Heritage and in the support given by the Department of Education to the Churches for their joint initiative.

A central idea which is common to both the secular and religious versions of the sharing myth is that cultural traditions (including religious and political ones) are not dangerous *per se*: the danger lies in the way in which they are interpreted. There needs to be interpretation which is dynamic rather than static. If traditions are not interpreted in a dynamic way, their more or less static reproduction by successive generations becomes increasingly harmful as the gap widens between the historical horizon (the Reformation, 1690, 1798, 1916 etc) which gave rise to the tradition in the first place and the present horizon. Without re-interpretation, the tradition becomes increasingly ill-equipped to respond to present needs which are new. Interpretation, or more accurately re-interpretation, rather than mere repetition is the one way in which people may develop a full sense of belonging in their historically constituted world. What is required is a 'fusion of horizons' which at the same time affirms the givenness of traditions in their historical contexts but also reinterprets them to meet the needs of the contemporary situation (see Gadamer 1975).

Wright (1988, 83) has argued persuasively that 'the only freedom we have in looking at our past is to choose a different angle of vision, to look in the past for things which we believe have healing power in the present'. The objectives of EMU and Cultural Heritage which focus on similarity and difference, continuity and change, and inter-dependence, define such a new angle of vision in the Northern Ireland Curriculum, especially in History and Religious Education. In so far as the conflict in Northern Ireland is between groups defined by religious identity, this means 'searching for a history of ecumenism before the time when anyone ever thought of using that word'. Liechty (1993), for example, has taken this approach in studying the origins and development of sectarianism in Ireland.

This is not to condone any distortion or abuse of history. It is to do nothing more than affirm that it is within our power to be selective about those people, events and themes in our past from whom we derive inspiration. This power to choose is related to the core choice between separation and sharing. If we do not make a conscious choice ourselves, we will be 'inspired' *faute de mieux* by the traditions which we inherit uncritically from the preceding generation. History does not dictate the choices we make, but the more accurate our understanding of the history which has led to them, the better our choices are likely to be. If confirmation were needed, the *Opposite Religions?* project provides it: our understanding of the history which has led to the core choice in Northern Ireland is generally far from accurate.

The interpretation of cultural traditions to schoolchildren and to the public at large may result in a more accurate historical understanding. Which elements of those traditions we choose to draw inspiration from, however, remains a moral matter. The dynamic (as opposed to static or passive) interpretation of cultural traditions is ultimately a question of individual choice. There is, therefore, a duty for educational institutions to equip individuals to choose. It may even be appropriate for state or church institutions to offer guidance as to which choices they believe most appropriate. So it is that the Catholic and the Protestant Churches, having re-evaluated their past theory and practice of inter-church relations, now exhort their members to better mutual understanding in the spirit of ecumenism. Similarly, the British Government, having re-evaluated its theory and practice of community relations policy, now exhorts its citizens and schoolchildren to better mutual understanding.

Institutions which educate for choice

How can state and church institutions educate in such a way that individuals are equipped to make choices, particularly the core choice between separation and sharing? They need to encourage all individuals to play an active part in the re-interpretation of the traditions which they inherit and to develop in them the knowledge, skills and attitudes which will enable them to do so. Given the importance of understanding the still controversial role of religion in the Northern Ireland conflict, they need to do three things.

First, they need to lead their students or members to a better understanding of the role of religion in society through an historical interpretation which attempts to disentangle or separate religion from politics, thereby making the inter-connections between them more apparent. Second, they need to enable them to arrive at a better understanding of their situation in the present by challenging them with the issue of Boyle and Hadden's *Choice* and interpreting the origins and development of core choice modulation. Third, they need to lead their students and members to a position where they are capable of evaluating critically the traditions which they have inherited and of making choices about how to behave accordingly.

This raises the question of whether current resources which the state and the Churches provide are adequate to in carry out such a large-scale educational project or whether a new institution devoted to the task is required.

As argued in Chapter 4, living church buildings, old church sites and museums (especially those where church buildings are reconstructed and the religious beliefs and practices of their traditions interpreted) are key resources in this regard. Their importance needs to be seen in the wider context of the heritage industry and the metaphor of one people together on pilgrimage. Horne (1984) sees the modern tourist or sightseer as 'pilgrim' and what is looked at as 'relic'. The analogy between tourism and religion is strong:

> The ceremonial agenda can be part of growing up. Children are taken to a museum for instruction in life's mysteries as once they might have been taken to a cathedral to see stories in its stone carvings or stained glass or frescoes or mosaics. Now they learn human and cosmic significance from the 'exhibits'! (1984, 12).

What is important to note here is that in pluralist or multi-cultural societies historic monuments and museums (whether protected or provided by non-state bodies or by the state itself) are normally public. No presumption is made about the identity (gender, ethnic, political, social class, or religious background) of visitors. All, including visitors who are not citizens of the state are welcome. Non-state-provided museums may be semi-private in practice in the sense that they are used primarily by particular groups (for example, the majority of visitors to the Jewish Museum in London are Jewish) but they are open to the public nevertheless.

What public institutions like museums do is interpret cultural traditions by 're-presenting' rather than 'presenting' them. Members of a living tradition unselfconciously 'present' the tradition to each other and to outside observers simply by 'living' the tradition; that is, by behaving as the tradition requires. However, in order both to be passed on to the next generation of members and to be understood by non-members, the tradition needs also to be 're-presented'; that is, interpreted or explained. Re-presentation can be either internal or external to the tradition. Internally, tradition members re-present to other members (faith speaks to faith) or to non-members (faith speaks to unbelieving outsiders). Externally, non-members may re-present to other non-members (or even to members). External re-presentation is usually done by 'secular' scholars, educators or journalists using academic disciplines such as history, anthropology, theology or religious studies.

In the case of a religious tradition, for example, the older generation of members may re-present it (for the purpose of transmission) to the younger generation through Religious Education in a denominational primary or secondary school or Sunday school. To outsiders they may re-present themselves by disseminating information about their tradition through means such as denominational museums or societies such as the *Society for the Promotion of Christian Knowledge* or the *Catholic Truth Society*. At the same time, outsiders may be re-presenting their religious tradition to other non-members; for example, a Jewish teacher teaching about Protestantism or Catholicism in a Jewish school using materials written by a Jewish author.

Re-presentation may be considered formal when it takes place in a setting such as a classroom. It can also take place informally, even during the presentation of the tradition as, for example, when parents make explanatory asides to their children at family prayers or during a church service. Similarly, a tradition may be re-presented informally by outsiders as, for example, when a parent or teacher makes *en passant* a comment (approbatory or otherwise) to the child or pupil about another tradition. Informal re-presentation of this kind is influential in the transmission of benign or malign stereotypes of other traditions. This is why in Northern Ireland church leaders have urged members to avoid careless 'sectarian' remarks.

In short, to analyse the re-presentation (interpretation) of cultural traditions, particularly of religious traditions, two types of distinction need to be made: the external/internal and the formal/informal. Thus, the re-presentation of religious traditions in schools in Northern Ireland needs to be considered in terms of the way Catholic/Protestant teachers interpret or explain Catholic/Protestant traditions to Catholic/Protestant pupils (internal re-presentation, which is usually formal but occasionally informal). When it comes to Catholic/Protestant teachers teaching their pupils about Protestant/Catholic traditions, they may use the more traditional approach where teacher and pupils proceed from a shared commitment to their own tradition (internal re-presentation) or the more recent 'secular' approach where teacher and pupils either do not have, or suspend commitment to, the Catholic/Protestant tradition (external re-presentation). Alternatively, RE teachers may combine the two approaches since they are not necessarily mutually exclusive.

Even though informal re-presentation may only be 'occasional', it is probably more influential than formal re-presentation, especially in transmitting the two-communities, two-religions perception of 'the other side', Catholic or Protestant. Twin examples from schools studied by Murray (1985, 113-114) illustrate the point:

> Protestant schools in the North Eastern Education and Library Board area are required to fly the Union Jack outside daily. Individuals within such schools will obviously see this as a natural proclamation for a state school to make. It did, however, provide a general reaction from staff in St Jude's [a Catholic school].

'They fly the flag down there to show that they are more British than the British themselves. It is also to let us know that they are the lords and masters and we (Catholics) should be continually aware of it.' ... One Protestant teacher said: 'We play St Jude's often in games and visit their school regularly. I never fail to be impressed by the plethora of religious pictures and icons staring at you around every corner. It's hard to escape the view that a special show is being put on for our benefit ... This doesn't apply to St Jude's of course, but they must know that these are the very things that we object to, yet still they are flaunted everywhere.'

Murray, seeing the two-communities picture, concluded that [author's italics]:

These two examples give insight into the gulf which exists between intention and perception in Northern Ireland. *The two dominant cultures* are so mutually antipathetic that any demonstration of one is perceived as an assault on the other.

The transmission and reception of knowledge and attitudes about one's own tradition and about other traditions is all the more powerful for being 'largely an unconscious process'. Again, the point bears repetition: it is not the fact of two traditions (or cultures) that is the problem; it is the fact that they are still perceived as 'opposite', not complementary.

Learning the languages of religion

The process of initiation into a 'cultural tradition' in general, and into a religious tradition in particular, may be compared to language learning (Hall 1995, 177). Contrast, for example, the case of a person who learns Welsh 'naturally' from parents who are native speakers with that of a native English speaker who learns Welsh as a second language. The 'cradle' learner acquires the language mainly through its speaking (presentation) with informal teaching (re-presentation) playing a part, as when a parent *en passant* corrects grammar mistakes. The adult second language learner, acquires the language mainly through formal teaching (re-presentation). Native speakers generally are more fluent than second-language learners. Conversely, second-language learners may be more critically aware of grammar and syntax than native speakers (unless they too have had the language formally re-presented to them in school). So it happens that converts are often more knowledgeable and conscientious about their new tradition than those born into it.

The important point about the analogy between linguistic and religious traditions is that their strength, richness and fluency depends largely on their 'native' members. Learning environments may change, benficially or detrimentally. The tradition may be reduced to isolated pockets, as has happened, for example, to the Irish language; or it may be expanded, as has happened with the spread world-wide of traditional Irish music.

Certainly, the learning environment for religious traditions in Northern Ireland is changing rapidly. This is happening not least through the government's introduction of EMU and Cultural Heritage as compulsory cross-curricular themes in the Northern Ireland Curriculum (which is followed by all children) and government encouragement and support for cross-community contact schemes and for integrated education. Whether this change to the learning environment for religious traditions in particular is perceived as beneficial or detrimental depends largely upon one's core choice preference in favour of either sharing or separation. What is predictable is that if change continues in the same direction, without adjustment of the learning environment accordingly, both Catholic and Protestant religious traditions will be severely weakened.

One of the effects of the conflict in Northern Ireland has been to sustain the attachment of people to the Catholic and Protestant religious traditions. After the conflict, the 'native speakers' of Catholicism and Protestantism will be exposed increasingly to the dominant European 'language' of secularism.

At present they are still largely 'bilingual'. However, the strong temptation will be for them to lapse from their religious language and become monoglot secularists. The *Opposite Religion?* trial showed that many schoolchildren in Northern Ireland find serious difficulty with Christianity because of the way it has been implicated in the conflict. As with the Irish language in the nineteenth century, the Christian tradition (both Catholicism and Protestantism) may come to be seen as a badge of poverty - this time of intellectual rather than economic poverty - which increasingly parents will be disinclined to force upon their children.

Three options

'Religion-loss', therefore, is a predictable outcome of an end to the conflict and the shift from the opposite-communities paradigm of Catholic / Protestant relations to the one-community paradigm which current trends in the education system are encouraging. There are three possible ways of responding.

The first option is to do nothing and regard religion-loss, if not as something beneficial in itself, then as a price worth paying for the healing of community division. The second option is to resist the paradigm shift and protect and strengthen Catholic and Protestant traditions by preserving and promoting their status as 'opposite religions'. The third option is to embrace the paradigm shift to the one-community picture but at the same time prevent religion-loss by promoting the shift from the opposite-religions to the one-religion picture.

The first option may be preferred by secularists or humanists as a matter of principle, but it is probably not prudent. If the analogy between language and religion holds, the price of religion-loss in the long term will be too high. The legacy of language-loss world-wide is a bitter one. A central aim of many nationalist movements has been for the revival of the native language in a separatist state. The Irish experience has not been exceptional in this respect, not only with regard to Irish but also to Ullans, being promoted recently as the native language of the mainly Presbyterian settlers of Ulster.

It may be similar with religion-loss. Many may come to regret it eventually. Having cast off a 'badge of intellectual poverty', they may still feel impoverished spiritually. Again, experience suggests that the fortunes of religious traditions are recovered most effectively through fundamentalist revival movements. The alliance of religious fundamentalism and militant nationalism is a commonly observed phenomenon world-wide. The eventual re-emergence of militant political separatist movements would therefore be a predicatable outcome of failure to prevent religion-loss in Northern Ireland.

The second is the only option likely to be preferred as a matter of principle by those who are firmly committed to the exclusive truth of their religious tradition. In practice this option would mean working to maintain the exisiting mechanisms which are most effective in preserving the tradition intact, namely separate schools and discouragement of marriage outside the group. Even if the trend towards religion-loss proved to be irreversible, integrity would demand that tradition members should hold out, as a 'museum people', until the last.

The third option is the one likely to be preferred by those who are committed religiously to the principle of unity in diversity. This would mean working to ensure that the secular shift from the opposite-communities to the one-community picture is complemented by the shift from the opposite-religions to the one-religion picture. Otherwise the secular shift will most probably generate first religion-loss and then at a later stage fundamentalist revival.

The first two options require no new resources. The third option does. What might these be?

The need for new resources

Outside the family, schools in Northern Ireland are the primary means by which religious traditions are formally re-presented and transmitted to the next generation. The secondary means are of four main types: publishing (books, magazines, newspapers); broadcasting (television, video, radio); church buildings; and museums. Provision of these secondary resources may be internal to the tradition (as in the case of a parish magazine) or external to it (as in the public broadcast of a televised religious service or an item about a tradition on a radio religious current affairs programme). At present, the use which schools make of them is slight. Like most other subject teachers, RE teachers rely heavily, if not exclusively, on standard classroom text-books. A recent survey found that the three most popular resources for the support of text-books were: discussion, the Bible and prayer/meditation. The three least popular resources were: field work, guest speakers and audio tapes/ records (Weafer and Hanley 1991, 62-63).

Up until now, both the Catholic and Protestant communities have relied heavily on the largely unconscious process which takes place in separate schools for the initiation of the next generation into membership of their religious traditions. The more integrated and less separate education becomes, the less effective this unconscious process will be. It was the state of separateness which gave value to the tradition. Increasing cross-community contact, therefore, tends to devalue the tradition. Left to their own devices, Catholic and Protestant schoolchildren mixing together in a non-threatening environment quickly make friends with each other. The similarities between them make a stronger impression than the differences. As the *Opposite Religions?* trial showed, schoolchildren are often hard put to articulate as well as their parents and teachers might like the importance of the undoubted differences between Catholics and Protestants. After the conflict, it will be increasingly likely for children to see no significant difference and associate the separate religious traditions more or less exclusively with the bad old days of conflict. This is the route to religion-loss.

If EMU, Cultural Heritage, cross-community contact schemes and integrated schools are not to lead down this route, there needs to be substantial investment in the kind of education which will enable schoolchildren who are religiously fluent to remain so. In order to remain fluent they will need to become 'bi-lingual' in the languages of both the Catholic and Protestant traditions. Assuming that their parents continue to wish it, Catholic and Protestant children will still need to be educated as full members of their religious tradition, but their religious education is not likely to be effective unless it is organised in such a way that they also grow up understanding the related religious language of their Catholic or Protestant neighbours. They will need to speak both their own religious language as a native and that of the other as a second language. At the same time, all (religious and non-religious) will be speaking together the *lingua franca* of the secular side of modern culture.

For those who are already secularised, or wish to become so, religion-loss is not a problem personally. Nevertheless, they may recognise religion-loss as a problem for the wider or whole community of which they are a part. Even those who are not speakers may see the benefit of enrichment to the whole culture which can be gained by preserving and even promoting the lesser-used 'languages' or traditions of religion.

What is required to prevent religion-loss and ensure the enrichment of the whole culture, rather than the reverse, is an educational project to interpret the process of cultural development. The religious traditions of Protestants and Catholics are still sufficiently different for them to be seen as completely separate religions or 'languages'. While that is so, the languages remain closely related, deriving from a common ancestor as recently as five hundred years ago. Through increasing contact with each other the religious languages are interacting and developing. Ecumenical development may eventually reach a stage, if it has not already, where it will be more accurate to think in terms of Catholic and Protestant 'dialects' of the same language (Christianity) rather than two different languages. Most citizens, whether secular or religious in outlook, may consider that such a future is preferable to Catholicism and Protestantism becoming lesser-used languages (spoken by militant rumps of their formerly separate communities) or to religious language becoming extinct altogether.

If the project of interpreting the process of religious development (and of disentangling religion from politics) is preferable to either simply letting political and social change take its course or to struggling to restore the *status quo ante* of religious separation, the conclusion is clear. The type of institution best suited to resource such an educational project is the museum or interpretive centre. That being so, how adequate to the task would current provision be?

Current museum provision

Generally in western Europe, living religious traditions are not well represented in museums, precisely because they are living. National, metropolitan, county and local museums usually contain some religious artefacts on display. For example, there are religious vestments on display in the Victoria and Albert Museum in London and in the National Museum in Dublin and various items relating to St Patrick in the County Down Museum in Downpatrick. There are also denominational museums.

The most numerous type of denominational museum in Britain and Ireland as a whole are the Treasuries and Museums associated with Anglican cathedrals (Chichester, Durham, Hereford, St Asaph's and Winchester). There are also museums associated with smaller Anglican churches (St Nicholas's Church Museum, Bristol; the Old Rectory Museum, Loughborough; and St Peter Hungate Museum, Norwich). The Methodist Church has John Wesley's House and Museum, the Museum of Methodism in London and the Old Rectory, Epworth. There is a Primitive Methodist Museum at Englesea Brook Chapel, Crewe. There are museums of other non-Conformist denominations at places such as Ashington (Woodhorn Church Museum) and Bedford (John Bunyan Meeting Room and Library). The Roman Catholic Church has the Cistercian Museum at Hailes Abbey and the Bar Convent Museum at York. There is a Moravian Museum in Pudsey and there are Jewish Museums in London and Manchester.

In Northern Ireland, the Presbyterian Historical Society has a small museum in Church House, Belfast and the Wesley Historical Society (Irish Branch) has a library and small museum in Aldersgate House, Belfast. In Ireland as a whole there are no other denominational museums as such which are open regularly to the public, apart from the Irish Jewish Museum in Dublin. There are also various other small-scale collections and displays such as Knock Folk Museum, Co. Mayo, which deals partly with the history of the shrine, Maynooth College Museum, which holds a number of notable ecclesiastical artefacts, and the Masonic Museum in Dublin.

As well as these institutions there are learned societies devoted to the study of Irish religious history. These sustain the journals in which the scholars who work in the universities and museums usually publish their research. The religious divide in Ireland is reflected in the journals which are primarily concerned with Irish religious history. They are denominationally based: for example, *Bulletin of the Presbyterian Historical Society; Bulletin of the Wesley Historical Society (Irish Branch); Irish Baptist Historical Society Journal; Archivium Hibernicum/ Proceedings of the Irish Catholic Historical Committee; Seanchas Ardmhacha - Journal of the Armagh Diocesan Historical Society*).

Ireland still lacks a non-denominational specialist journal devoted to Irish religious history. The founding of the *Irish Religious History Society* in 1984 was a significant development, but it was scarcely active since its secretary resigned in protest at the signing of the Anglo-Irish Agreement in 1985 (see Brooke 1994, 9). In spite of this set-back, there is a growing trend for scholars to co-operate more closely across denominational boundaries. A more broadly-based *Society for the History of Religion in Ireland* was formed in September 1995. New regional studies of Irish religious history go beyond a narrow focus on their own denominations to consider the range of religious traditions and their interactions (Hempton and Hill 1992, xi).

Learned journals and books are not of course forms which are generally accessible to the public and it is mainly through school textbooks and other educational publications, television and radio broadcasting and museum exhibitions that the findings of these scholars are mediated to a wider public. To schoolchildren they are being mediated to a certain extent through the cross-curricular themes of Cultural Heritage and Education for Mutual Understanding. There is a developing historical dimension in youth work (McMaster 1993, 1995). In adult education at various levels, the work of the Irish School of Ecumenics is substantially historical in character. Similarly, both the activities and journal of PACE (Protestant and Catholic Encounter) have a strong focus on the historical development of religious traditions.

The museum, however, is the key interpretative institution because (as defined by the Museums and Galleries Commission) it is 'an institution that collects, documents, preserves, exhibits and interprets material evidence and associated information for the public benefit'. The museum is the type of institution which is pre-eminently concerned with the interpretation of ways of life (cultures) or particular aspects of them. According to Popplewell (1989), there are about 200 museums in Ireland. The specialist museums (as distinct from the national museums which aim to be more or less comprehensive) are spread fairly evenly between the political, economic, social (educational, domestic, leisure) artistic and scientific dimensions of culture with the religious dimension coming a poor sixth (Lambkin 1993, 113-116).

Of all the museums in Ireland, the one which most successfully integrates all the dimensions in its interpretation of culture is probably the Ulster Folk and Transport Museum at Cultra, near Belfast. Its organisational structure of four departments derives from a comprehensive analysis of culture: buildings; transport; material culture (agriculture, textiles and dress, crafts and occupations, and domestic life); and non-material culture (music, dialect, oral narrative and social institutions). The integration of all the dimensions of culture is 'pictured' in the outdoor museum.

'Social institutions' at Cultra include political and religious traditions. These, however, are probably the least well represented aspects of culture in the public display. A reticence in dealing with the traditionally taboo subjects of religion and politics in Northern Ireland is understandable but the reason for religious traditions being under-represented at Cultra has more to do with wider trends in museum development (for an alternative view see Brett, 1993).

Museums are driven by discontinuities in tradition. They preserve what would otherwise pass away because it has become obsolete. Religious traditions have been low priority. Of all the dimensions of culture, the religious dimension has probably registered the least discontinuity in popular

198

perception. For example, the rate of change in religious traditions is generally perceived to be much slower than in farming traditions. Whereas technological tradition tends to pride itself on change, religious tradition tends to pride itself on continuity. A fundamental problem for the Churches, as Lampen has pointed out, is that 'in general [they] have not found a way to represent the views of their communities without appearing to support sectarianism' (1995, 118). A solution to this problem may lie in their joint-cooperation in the development of a museum or interpretive centre for their religious traditions, a Centre for Religion in Ireland.

Up until 1993, the only country in western Europe to have a major museum devoted to religion was the Netherlands. The Museum of Christianity in the Netherlands at Utrecht was opened in 1976. Since then there have been further developments. St Mungo's Museum, Glasgow, opened in 1993. It is the world's first museum devoted to all the world religions together under the same roof (as distinct from Utrecht, which is concerned only with Christianity, and the smaller denominational museums). The Ulster Folk Museum is due to open a new gallery devoted to the religious traditions of Ulster in 1997. Protestant and Catholic Encounter (PACE) has a project in hand for an RE Resource and Interpretive Centre in Belfast.

Perhaps most significantly, in 1994 Armagh District Council announced plans to open a Centre for Religion in Ireland. The site will be that of the old Armagh hospital, recently acquired as an outreach centre by Queen's University, Belfast. It is symbolically located between the Church of Ireland and Roman Catholic Cathedrals in what is generally regarded as the ecclesiastical capital of the island.

The idea of such a centre is not new. In 1976 it was mooted jointly by the Churches in their report *Violence in Ireland* (Worrall 1976, 91). In 1993 the Opsahl Commission lent its support to the idea (Pollack 1993, 121). McLachlan (1994, 26) has argued the need for 'interpreters' of religious traditions which such a centre could meet. However, the importance of interpreting Northern Ireland well after the conflict is great. Rolston, for example, has already warned that 'the troubles as theme park' is not such an unlikely eventuality:

> It is probably only a matter of time before some body, subsidised by the EU or the International Fund for Ireland, establishes a 'troubles museum'. Such an official institution will undoubtedly present a highly sanitised version of 'the troubles', one that attempts to be balanced between 'both cultural traditions' as well as resting on notions of the impartiality and genuine, albeit sometimes bumbling, goodwill of the British state. The likelihood that exhibits will be chosen from a perspective which prioritises human rights, justice and anti-imperialism is slim (1995, 38).

199

The argument of this book has been leading to the conclusion that some centre for interpreting Northern Ireland after the conflict is needed. In order that it should not be of the sanitised type which Rolston fears but rather a truthful, vibrant and constructive one, what can be said about what such a centre should be like? The final chapter turns to this question.

8 Summary and Conclusion: A Centre for Religion in Ireland

The task of interpreting Northern Ireland is so complex that as full and as widely dispersed a range of resources as possible is needed. Resources at local level are needed in different contexts to tell the varied stories of their local communities. No single publication or national or international centre could do justice to the richness of their diversity. But a centre is needed to give some kind of overview and coherence to the epic of which the many local stories are sub-plots. One way of telling the epic is in terms of the story of religion in Ireland from the earliest times to the present. People in Ireland, residents and visitors alike, need a centre, a neutral venue, where they may investigate:

- the distinctive artefacts, practices and beliefs of their own religious tradition,
- the distinctive artefacts, practices and beliefs of all the other religious traditions represented in Ireland,
- the similarities and differences between all the religious traditions,
- continuity and change in the historical development of their own and of all the other religious traditions,
- the inter-connection of religion and politics in Irish history,
- the role of religion in the Northern Ireland conflict,
- the core issue of *The Choice* between separation and sharing and the question: opposite religions still?

Such a centre would be an expression of the principle of unity in diversity. Sensitively designed, managed and developed, it would be a project in which all religious groups could participate. Such a centre would be capable of being used by all without loss of either personal or group integrity.

The interpretation of the story of religion in Ireland requires long-term study, both because the story of the role of religion in society and the relations between religious groups is still in progress and because likely to continue being controversial. Such a centre would play a major role in mediating the fruits of on-going scholarship to a wider public.

Research on religion is a burgeoning field, as is evident from the proceedings of the international conference on 'Religion and Conflict' held in 1994 at Armagh under the auspices of the University of Ulster's Centre for the Study of Conflict and Armagh Together. In January 1995, the University of Cambridge opened CARTS, the Centre for Advanced Religious and Theological Studies, under the directorship of David Thompson, as an international centre for the academic study of world religions. A Centre for Religion in Ireland would both draw on the growing international expertise in the field and contribute significantly to it.

Given that Northern Ireland already has a formidable, international notoriety for the intractability of its conflict and for the implication of religion in it, the potential importance of a Centre for Religion which engages with the issue of interpreting that conflict must be great.

More immediate than the need to develop a positive international reputation, however, is the need for a Centre of Religion to help the people who are growing up in Northern Ireland to interpret their homeland after the conflict. If they can work together in the task of interpretation, the prospects of a lasting settlement will improve. As mutual understanding and trust grows, a more positive international reputation may well follow.

The *Opposite Religions?* project indicated the scale of the educational programme required to achieve two key objectives. The first is that of bringing closer the still elusive consensus on the nature of the Northern Ireland conflict. The second is that of challenging schoolchildren and the public at large to reconsider the core issue of *The Choice* between separation and sharing and the question: opposite religions still?

'Whyte's challenge' was to find an improved paradigm of explanation or interpretation of the Northern Ireland conflict. If the theory of 'choice modulation' advanced in Chapter 3 successfully explains the conflict's intractability, that challenge may be said to have been substantially met. But the challenge of *The Choice*, as formulated by Boyle and Hadden, remains.

The argument advanced here is that a major new institution in the form of an interpretative Centre for Religion is needed to help meet this challenge. The main purpose of the proposed Centre for Religion would be to support and develop 'Education for *The Choice*': choice between the two options of sharing and separation, between a one-community, one-religion future and an opposite-communities, opposite-religions future for Northern Ireland - or, better still perhaps, a third option of more deliberate and judicious modulating between the two.

This is how a political scientist describes the situation:

> In Northern Ireland most people are, in fact, torn in two directions: 'torn', that is, while their political leaders will not recognize that people can, with dignity, face in two directions culturally at once, and refuse to invent political institutions to match (Crick 1988, 10).

Seamus Heaney puts it better: 'the whole population is adept in the mystery of living in two places at one time' (1995). It is a mystery rooted in the ambiguities of 'culture', 'tradition', 'community' and 'religion'. Like most mysteries, it has both beautiful and terrible aspects. Interpreting or unravelling the ambiguities we unravel the mystery. The skill of interpreting Northern Ireland after the conflict will be in disentangling both aspects; unravelling the terrible in order to dispose of it properly, while leaving the beautiful still intact.

The terror of ambiguity lies in the conflict of opposites, its beauty in their creative tension or marriage. Are the opposites of *The Choice* facing Northern Ireland - separation and sharing - to be in creative or destructive tension? This is the challenge of interpreting Northern Ireland after the conflict: to make the nature and historical development of *The Choice* clear. The key way to do so will be by investing in a Centre for Religion in Ireland which will put in context the central and appropriately ambiguous question: opposite communities, opposite religions still?

Bibliography

Akenson, D.H. (1970), *The Irish education experiment: the national system of education in the nineteenth century*, London.

Beeman, J.H. and Mahony, R. (1993), 'The institutional churches and the process of reconciliation in Northern Ireland: recent progress in Presbyterian-Roman Catholic relations' in Keogh, D. and Haltzel, M.H. (eds), *Northern Ireland and the Politics of Reconciliation*, Cambridge University Press.

Ben-Amos, D. (1984), 'The seven strands of tradition: varieties in its meaning in American folklore studies', *Journal of American Folklore*, xxi, 97-131.

Bossy, J. (1982), 'Some elementary forms of Durkheim', *Past and Present*, xcv, 3-18.

Boyd, A. (1969), *Holy War in Belfast*, Anvil Books, Belfast.

Boyd, R. (1988), *Ireland: Christianity discredited or pilgrim's progress?*, Dublin.

Boyle, K. and Hadden, T. (1994), *Northern Ireland: The Choice*, Penguin Books.

Brett, D. (1993), 'The construction of heritage' in O'Connor, B. and Cronin, M. (eds), *Tourism in Ireland: a critical analysis*, Cork University Press, 183-202.

British-Irish Inter-Parliamentary Body (1994), *Report from Committee D on Culture, Education and Environment*, No. 32, December.

Brooke, P. (1994), *Ulster Presbyterianism: the Historical Perspective 1610 - 1970*, 2nd edition, Athol Books, Belfast.

Brown, R.M. (1969), *The Ecumenical Revolution: an interpretation of the Catholic-Protestant Dialogue*, London.

Bruce, S. (1986), *God Save Ulster: the religion and politics of Paisleyism*, Oxford University Press.

Bruce, S. (1992), *The Red Hand: Protestant Paramilitaries in Northern Ireland*, Oxford University Press.

Bruce, S. (1994), *The Edge of the Union: the Ulster Loyalist Political Vision*, Oxford University Press.

Buckley, A. (1988), 'Collecting Ulster's Culture: are there really Two Traditions?' in Gailey, A. (ed.), *The Use of Tradition*, Cultra, 49-60.

Burgess, T.P. (1993), *A Crisis of Conscience: moral ambivalence and education in Northern Ireland*, Avebury, Aldershot.

Cairns, E. (1991), 'Is Northern Ireland a conservative society?' in Stringer, P. and Robinson, G. (eds), *Social Attitudes in Northern Ireland: the Second Report, 1990-91 Edition*, Blackstaff Press, Belfast.

Cairns, E. (1994), *A Welling Up of Deep Unconscious Forces: psychology and the Northern Ireland conflict*, University of Ulster, Coleraine.

Chomsky, N. (1980), *Rules and Representations*, Oxford.

Churches' Religious Education Core Syllabus Drafting Group (1991), *Proposals for a Core Syllabus in Religious Education in Grant-Aided Schools in Northern Ireland*, Belfast.

Comerford, R.V. (1988), 'Political myths in Modern Ireland' in Sandulescu, C.G. (ed.), *Irishness in a Changing Society*, Monaco.

Connolly, S.J. (1983), 'Religion and History', *Irish Economic and Social History*, x, 66-80.

Conway, W. (1950), 'Comment on the 1949 Instruction of the Holy Office on Religious Unity, *Irish Ecclesiastical Record*, 73, 360-365.

Corish, P.J. (1981), *The Catholic Community in the Seventeenth and Eighteenth Centuries*, Dublin.

Corish, P.J. (1985), *The Irish Catholic Experience*, Gill and Macmillan, Dublin.

Cosgrove, A. (1985), (ed.), *Marriage in Ireland*, Dublin.

Crozier, M. (1989), (ed.), *Cultural Traditions in Northern Ireland: Varieties of Irishness*, Institute of Irish Studies, Belfast.

Crozier, M. (1995), 'Tradition and Culture' in *Giving Voices: the work of the Cultural Traditions Group 1990-94*, Community Relations Council, Belfast.

Daly, C.B. (1979), *Peace the Work of Justice: addresses on the Northern Tragedy 1973-79*, Veritas, Dublin.

Daly, C.B. (1991), *The Price of Peace*, Blackstaff Press, Belfast.

Darby, J. (1995), 'Conflict in Northern Ireland: a background essay' in Dunn, S. (ed.) *Facets of the Conflict in Northern Ireland*, Macmillan Press, London.

Dawson, C. (1948), *Religion and Culture*, London.

DENI (Department of Education of Northern Ireland) (1992*), Curriculum (Educational Themes) Order (Northern Ireland)*, Bangor.

Dewar, M.W. (1959), *Why Orangeism?*, Belfast.

Dudley Edwards, R.W. and O'Dowd, M. (1985), *Sources for Early Modern Irish History, 1534-1641*, Cambridge University Press.

Dunlop, J. (1995), *A Precarious Belonging: Presbyterians and the Conflict in Ireland*, Blackstaff Press, Belfast.

Dunn, S. (1986), *Education and the Conflict in Northern Ireland: a guide to the literature*, University of Ulster, Coleraine.

Dunn, S. (1995), 'The conflict as a set of problems' in Dunn, S. (ed.) *Facets of the Conflict in Northern Ireland*, Macmillan Press, London.

Eames, R. (1992), *Chains to be Broken: a personal reflection on Northern Ireland and its people*, Weidenfeld and Nicolson, London.

Ellis, I.M. (1992), *Vision and Reality: a survey of twentieth-century Irish inter-church relations*, Institute of Irish Studies, Belfast.

Empson, W. (1930, reprinted 1995), *Seven Types of Ambiguity*, Penguin, London.

Farren, S. (1985), 'Unionist Protestant reaction to educational reform in Northern Ireland, 1923-30, *History of Education*, 14, 227-236.

Farren, S. (1986), 'Nationalist Catholic reaction to educational reform in Northern Ireland, 1921-1930, *History of Education*, 15, 19-30.

Farren, S. (1989), 'Catholic-Nationalist attitudes to education in Northern Ireland, 1921-1945', *Irish Educational Studies*, 56-73.

Farren, S. (1991), 'Culture, Curriculum and Educational Policy in Northern Ireland', *Language, Culture and Curriculum*, iv, 1, 43-58.

Flannery, A. (1975), (ed.), *Vatican Council II*, Dominican Publications, Dublin.

Frazer, H. and Fitzduff, M. (1986, reprinted 1990), *Improving Community Relations*, Belfast.

Fulton, J. (1991), *The Tragedy of Belief: division, politics and religion in Ireland*, Oxford University Press.

Gadamer, H-G. (1975), *Truth and Method*, London.

Gailey, A. (1988), 'Tradition and Identity' in Gailey, A. (ed.), *The Use of Tradition*, Cultra, 61-67.

Gallagher, A. M. (1995) 'The approach of government: Community Relations and equity' in Dunn, S. (ed.) *Facets of the Conflict in Northern Ireland*, Macmillan Press, London.

Gallagher, E. and Worrall, S. (1982), *Christians in Ulster, 1968-1980*, Oxford University Press.

Gillespie, S. and Jones, G. (1995), *Northern Ireland and its Neighbours since 1920*, Hodder and Stoughton, London.

Greer, J.E. (1981), 'Religious Attitudes and Thinking in Belfast Pupils', *Educational Research*, xxiii, 3, 177-189.

Greer, J.E. and McElhinney, E.P. (1984), 'The Project on Religion in Ireland: an experiment in reconstruction', *Lumen Vitae*, xxxix, 3, 331-342.

Greer, J.E. (1985), 'Viewing "the Other Side" in Northern Ireland: openness and attitudes to religion among Catholic and Protestant adolescents', *Journal for the Scientific Study of Religion*, xxiv, 3, 275-292.

Greer, J.E. and McElhinney, E.P. (1985), *Irish Christianity: a Guide for Teachers*, Gill and Macmillan, Dublin.

Greer, J.E. (1987), 'Bridge-building in Northern Ireland', *The Furrow*, vii, 38.

Greer, J.E. (1988), *Hardest to Accept: a study of the religious difficulties experienced by adolescents in Northern Ireland*, University of Ulster, Coleraine.

Greer, J.E., McElhinney, E.P., Harris, J.E. (1989), 'A study of classroom discussion in Religious Education', *British Journal of Religious Education*, xi, 92-102.

Greer, J.E., Ferguson, E., Wilson, B., Baker, D. (1989), *Three Churches in Ballycastle: an educational trail*, Coleraine.

Greer, J.E. and Long, J. (1990), 'The religious profile of pupils in Northern Ireland: comparative study of pupils attending Catholic and Protestant secondary schools', *Journal of Empirical Theology*, iii, 35-50.

Greer, J.E. and Francis, L. J. (1992a), 'Measuring Christian moral values among Catholic and Protestant adolescents in Northern Ireland', *Journal of Moral Education*, xxi, 59-65.

Greer, J.E. and Francis, L. J. (1992b), 'The teenage voice: the religious profile of pupils attending Catholic and Protestant secondary schools in Northern Ireland' in Hiscock, V. et al. (eds), *Irish Christian Handbook*, London, 20-23.

Gregg, J.A.F. (1943), *The Ne Temere Decree*, revised edition, Dublin.

Gregg, J.A.F. (1950), *Pastoral Letter* (signed jointly with the Archbishop of Dublin on behalf of the House of Bishops), Representative Church Body Library, Dublin.

Hall, S. (1995), 'New Cultures for Old', in Massey, D. and Jess, P. (eds*)*, *A Place in the World? Places, Cultures and Globalization*, Open University/Oxford University Press, 175-215.

Hayes, M. (1991), *Whither Cultural Diversity?*, Community Relations Council, Belfast.

Hayes, M. (1995), *Minority Verdict: experiences of a Catholic civil servant*, Blackstaff Press, Belfast.

Hazlett-Lynch, J.E. (1990), 'Objections to the Ecumenical Movement' in Love, M. (ed.), *Church Reunion - When?*, Social Study Conference and SSC Publications.

Heaney, S. (1995), *The Redress of Poetry: Oxford Lectures*, Faber and Faber, London.

Hempton, D. and Hill, M. (1992), *Evangelical Protestantism in Ulster Society, 1740-1890*, London.

Hewison, R. (1987), *The Heritage Industry: Britain in a climate of decline*, London.

Hickey, J. (1984), *Religion and the Northern Ireland Problem*, Gill and Macmillan, Dublin.

Holmes, R.F.G. (1985), *Our Irish Presbyterian Heritage*, Belfast.

Horne, D. (1984), *The Great Museum: the re-presentation of history*, London.

Inglis, T. (1987), *Moral Monopoly: the Catholic Church in Modern Irish Society*, Gill and Macmillan, Dublin.

Jenkins, D. (1980), with others, *Chocolate Cream Soldiers: a Final Evaluation Report on the 'Schools' Cultural Studies Project'*, University of Ulster, Coleraine.

Jenkins, R. (1986), 'Northern Ireland: in what sense religions in conflict?', in Jenkins, R., Donnan, H. and McFarlane, G. (eds), *The Sectarian Divide in Northern Ireland Today*, Royal Anthropological Institute of Great Britain and Ireland, Occasional Paper No, 41, London, 1-21.

Kearney, R. (1988), *Transitions: Narratives in Modern Irish Culture*, Dublin.

Kuhn, T.S. (1970), *The Structure of Scientific Revolutions*, 2nd ed., University of Chicago Press.

Küng, H. (1986), *Church and Change: the Irish Experience*, Dublin.

Küng, H. (1991), *Global Responsibility: in search of a new world ethic*, SCM, London.

Lambkin, B.K. (1990), *Religion in Ireland: yesterday, today and tomorrow*, Northern Ireland Centre for Learning Resources, Belfast.

Lambkin, B.K. (1992), *Opposite Religions?: Protestants and Roman Catholics in Ireland since the Reformation*,
Book One: Comparing What Protestants and Roman Catholics Do,
Book Two: Comparing Protestant and Roman Catholic Churches,
Book Three: Defining Protestant and Roman Catholic,
Northern Ireland Centre for Learning Resources, Belfast.

Lambkin, B.K. (1993) *The Re-presentation of Religious Traditions in Northern Ireland: a study of the Opposite Religions? Project, 1988-92*, unpublished D.Phil. thesis, University of Ulster, Coleraine.

Lampen, J. (1995), *Building the Peace: good practice in community relations work in Northern Ireland*, Community Relations Council, Belfast.

Lee, J. (1989), *Ireland, 1912-1985: Politics and Society*, Cambridge.

Lee, R.M. (1979), 'Interreligious courtship in Northern Ireland' in Cook M. and Wilson G. (eds), *Love and Attraction: An International Conference*, Oxford.

Lee, S. (1990), (ed.), *Freedom from Fear: Churches Together in Northern Ireland*, Institute of Irish Studies, Belfast.

Lennon, B. (1995), *After the Ceasefires: Catholics and the Future of Northern Ireland*, Columba Press, Dublin.

Liechty, J. (1993), *Roots of Sectarianism in Ireland: Chronology and Reflections*, Belfast.

Liechty, J. (1995), *The Nature of Sectarianism Today*, in Williams and Falconer (eds), 1995.

Liechty, J. (1995), *Historical and Theological Origins of Sectarianism*, in Williams and Falconer (eds), 1995.

Longley, E. (1991), (ed.), *Culture in Ireland - Division or Diversity?*, Belfast.

Lynch, J. (1987), *Prejudice Reduction in the Schools*, London.

Malone, J. (1940), with McCaughey, J.D. and Kay, T., 'A Report based on a month of Camps for Unemployed Boys, Ballymoyer, June - July 1940', unpublished report for the National Council of YMCA, Belfast.

Mawhinney, B. and Wells, R. (1975), *Conflict and Christianity in Northern Ireland*, London.

McElhinney, E.P. (1983), *The Project on Religion in Ireland, 1979-82: a study of theoretical and practical elements in a school-based curriculum development project*, unpublished D.Phil. thesis, New University of Ulster, Coleraine.

McElhinney, E.P., Harris, J.E., and Greer, J.E. (1987), *Classroom Discussion: Final Report of the Project Teaching Religion in Northern Ireland, 1984-86*, University of Ulster, Coleraine.

McGlone, P. (1989), 'The North: two communities or one?', *The Irish News*, Belfast, 7 September.

McGuinness, C. (1995), (ed.), *Paths to a Political Settlement in Ireland: policy papers submitted to the Forum for Peace and Reconciliation*, Blackstaff Press, Belfast.

McLachlan, P. (1994), 'Rainbows and religion: the role of different methods of thought in theology, religion and conflict', *Journal* No 8, Community Relations Council, Belfast, 21-26.

McMaster, J. (1993), *Young People as the Guardians of Sectarian Tradition*, Youthlink, Belfast.

McMaster, J. (1995*)*, *Understanding Irish Churches: Historical and Political Perspectives*, Youthlink, Belfast.

McSweeney, B. (1989), 'The religious dimension of ''The Troubles'' in Northern Ireland' in Badham, P. (ed.), *Religion, State and Society in Modern Britain*, Lampeter, 67-83.

Morrow, D., Birrell, D., Greer, J. and O'Keefe, T. (1991), *The Churches and Inter-Community Relationships*, University of Ulster, Coleraine.

Murphy, J.A. (1988) 'Religion and Irish Identity' in Sandulescu, C.G. (ed.), *Irishness in a Changing Society*, Gerards Cross.

New Ireland Forum, Government of Ireland (1984), *Report*, Dublin.

NICC (Northern Ireland Curriculum Council) (1989a), *Cultural Heritage: a Cross-Curricular Theme. Report of the Cross-Curricular Working Group on Cultural Heritage to the Parliamentary Under Secretary of State for Education*, Belfast.

NICC (1989b), *Education for Mutual Understanding: a Cross-Curricular Theme. Report of the Cross-Curricular Working Group on Education for Mutual Understanding to the Parliamentary Under Secretary of State for Education*, Belfast.

NICC (1989c), *Cross-Curricular Themes: Consultation Report*, Belfast.

Northern Ireland Community Relations Council (NICRC) (1991), *First Report*, Belfast.

NICRC, *Community Relations: magazine of the Northern Ireland Community Relations Council*, Belfast.

O'Connor, F. (1993), *In Search of a State: Catholics in Northern Ireland*, Blackstaff Press, Belfast.

O'Duffy, B. (1993), 'Containment or regulation? The British approach to ethnic conflict in Northern Ireland', in McGarry, J., and O'Leary, B., (eds.), *The Politics of Ethnic Conflict Regulation*, London.

O'Leary, J.S. (1988), 'Religion, Ireland: in Mutation', in Kearney, R. (ed.), *Across Frontiers: Ireland in the 1990s*, Dublin.

Pollock, A. (ed.) (1993), *A Citizens' Inquiry: the Opsahl Report on Northern Ireland*, Lilliput Press, Dublin.

Popplewell, S. (1989), *Exploring Museums: Ireland*, HMSO, London.

Presbyterian Church (1988), *Agreements and Disagreements of Irish Presbyterians and Roman Catholics*, Report to the General Assembly by the Doctrine Committee, Belfast.

Rea, D. (1982), (ed.), *Political Co-operation in Divided Societies*, Gill and Macmillan, Dublin.

Richardson, N.L. (1992), *A Study of Controversial Issues in the Classroom, as seen through the development of a programme of cross-community religious education in Northern Ireland,* unpublished M.A. thesis, Queen's University, Belfast.

Robinson, A. (1981), *The Schools' Cultural Studies Project: a contribution to peace in Northern Ireland,* University of Ulster, Coleraine.

Robinson, A. and Smith, A. (1992*), Education for Mutual Understanding: Perceptions and Policy,* University of Ulster, Coleraine.

Robinson, G. (1992), *Cross-Community Marriage in Northern Ireland,* Queen's University, Belfast.

Robinson-Hammerstein, H. (1994), 'History and Reconciliation' in Hurley, M. (ed.), *Reconciliation in Religion and Society,* Institute of Irish Studies, Belfast, 6-22.

Rolston, B. (1995), 'Selling tourism in a country at war', *Race and Class: A Journal for Black and Third World Liberation,* 37, 23-40.

Santer, M. (1982), 'Reconciling Memories' in Santer, M. (ed.), *Their Lord and Ours,* London.

Irish Inter-Church Meeting (1993), *Sectarianism: a Discussion Document, The Report of the Working Party on Sectarianism,* Belfast.

Skilbeck, M. (1976), 'Education and cultural change', *Compass: Journal of the Irish Association for Curriculum Development,* v, 3-23.

Smyth, G. (1995), *Sectarianism: Theology Gone Wrong?,* in Williams and Falconer (eds.) 1995.

Stevens, D. (1990), 'Obstacles to Reunion - Irish' in Love, M. (ed.), *Church Reunion - When?: papers delivered at the thirty seventh annual Summer School of the Social Study Conference,* Dublin.

Stradling, R., Noctor, M., and Baines, B. (1984), *Teaching Controversial Issues,* London.

Stringer, P. and Robinson, G. (1991), (eds.), *Social Attitudes in Northern Ireland, 1990-91,* Belfast.

Trew, K. (1989), 'Evaluating the impact of contact schemes for Catholic and Protestant children' in Harbison, J. (ed.), *Growing up in Northern Ireland,* Stranmillis College, Belfast, 131-159.

Two Traditions Group (1983), *Northern Ireland and the Two Traditions in Ireland,* Belfast.

Ulster Television (1990), *Whither Northern Ireland?,* Belfast.

Weafer, J.A. and Hanley, A.M. (1991), *Whither Religious Education?: a survey of post-primary teachers in Ireland,* Columba Press, Dublin.

Whyte, J.H. (1980), *Church and State in Modern Ireland, 1923-1979,* 2nd ed., Dublin.

Whyte, J. (1991), *Interpreting Northern Ireland,* Oxford University Press.

Williams, R. (1981), *Culture,* London.

Williams, T. and Falconer, A. (1995), *Sectarianism: papers of the 1994 Corrymeela Ecumenical Conference*, Dominican Publications, Dublin.

Worrall, A.S. (1976), *Violence in Ireland: A Report to the Churches*, Christian Journals Limited, Belfast, Veritas Publications, Dublin.

Wright, F. (1988), 'Reconciling the Histories Protestant and Catholic in Northern Ireland' in Falconer, A. (ed.), *Reconciling Memories*, Belfast.